Muslims, Christians, and the Challenge of Interfaith Dialogue

Muslims, Christians, and the Challenge of Interfaith Dialogue

JANE IDLEMAN SMITH

OXFORD

UNIVERSITY PRESS

2007

Oxford University Press, Inc., publishes works that further
Oxford University's objective of excellence
in research, scholarship, and education.

Oxford   New York
Auckland   Cape Town   Dar es Salaam   Hong Kong   Karachi
Kuala Lumpur   Madrid   Melbourne   Mexico City   Nairobi
New Delhi   Shanghai   Taipei   Toronto

With offices in
Argentina   Austria   Brazil   Chile   Czech Republic   France   Greece
Guatemala   Hungary   Italy   Japan   Poland   Portugal   Singapore
South Korea   Switzerland   Thailand   Turkey   Ukraine   Vietnam

Published by Oxford University Press, Inc.
198 Madison Avenue, New York, New York 10016

www.oup.com

Oxford is a registered trademark of Oxford University Press

Library of Congress Cataloging-in-Publication Data
Smith, Jane I.
Muslims, Christians, and the challenge of interfaith dialogue / Jane Idleman Smith.
    p. cm.
Includes bibliographical references and index.
ISBN 978-0-19-530731-3
1. Islam—United States.   2. Muslims—United States.   3. Islam—Relations—
Christianity.   4. Christianity and other religions—Islam.   5. Religions—Relations.
6. Religious pluralism—United States.   7. United States—Ethnic relations.   I. Title.
BP67.U6S616 2007
261.2'70973—dc22   2007001268

9 8 7 6 5 4 3 2 1

Printed in the United States of America
on acid-free paper

Preface

The following text is the result of many years of engagement in Christian-Muslim dialogue at the local and national levels. On the Christian side, it represents conversations that have taken place in the World Council of Churches, the National Council of Churches, local ecumenical councils, and churches and denominations. On the Muslim side, it is the product of many personal conversations with Muslim students and friends, and of working with Muslim councils and organizations in a number of different venues in the United States. It also reflects the ongoing mission of Hartford Seminary, at which I teach, to study and reflect on dialogue and to bring together Muslims and Christians for conversation and engagement.

Much of the information conveyed here, therefore, is the result of personal experience. Many Muslim and Christian friends and colleagues have talked with me about their participation in the dialogue, and have shared their reflections on its strengths and weaknesses. I have tried to portray these experiences and opinions as accurately as possible, quoting materials that have appeared in written form and making general reference without specific notation to those things that have been said, or written, to me in person.

As dialogue itself is an experience of mutual cooperation and support, so this book would not have been possible without the help of all of the persons whose dedication to the importance of Christian-Muslim engagement is, I hope, evident in the following pages. My own involvement in dialogue has continued over many years. For the past ten years that involvement has been centered at Hartford Seminary, which I believe to be one of the most important institutions in America for teaching about, and modeling in its classes and other programs, interfaith dialogue. I am grateful for all I have learned from colleagues who have been engaged in the dialogue process over many years. So also I owe thanks to the many Muslim and Christian students at Hartford Seminary who in classes and personal conversations have shown how enriching it can be when people of different religious traditions come together to share with one another.

Contents

Introduction

Phones started ringing off the hook. Email messages piled up. Engagement calendars became immediately filled as those who had some knowledge of Islam and Christian-Muslim relations tried to respond to the question on everyone's lips after September 11, 2001: Why did they do it? Tragedy often begets more tragedy, and the direct and indirect results of 9/11 have brought pain and loss, disillusionment and severe financial repercussions to many Americans as well as members of other societies. Adding to Western fears have been subsequent bombings in Madrid, Bali, London and elsewhere—terrorist acts acknowledged to have been perpetrated by Muslims—as well as the repercussions of U.S. military action in the Middle East. What is going on, Americans ask, and why is it that the religion of Islam seems to allow for such grisly deeds to be carried out on seemingly innocent victims?

Hundreds of books, thousands of journal articles, and an untold number of opinions expressed in cyberspace have been dedicated to trying to analyze terrorist movements linked in some way to the religion of Islam. American Muslims, horrified by atrocities perpetrated in the name of their precious faith, have agonized over the situation. They have spent a great deal of time denouncing violence and proclaiming Islam to be a religion of peace, and in more quiet ways, have begun examining the roots of their faith to find out what, if anything, justifies aggression and retribution in the Qur'an and the traditions of Prophet Muhammad. For the most part, American

Muslims have found themselves in a very difficult position. Many disagree strongly with various aspects of American foreign policy, believing that specific actions on the part of the American government such as the bombing and occupation of Iraq or unequivocal support of Israel serve to exacerbate already tense situations. But despite their conviction that it is the right of every American citizen to speak his or her mind publicly, they find it difficult to challenge the government at a time when the political actions they are critiquing are still popular with much of the American public. As Muslims they feel closely watched, fearful in response to government policies related to the "war on terrorism." And they cannot fail to notice when national polls indicate that anti-Muslim feeling in America has not been dissipated by their efforts to explain true Islam, but in fact has continued to rise.

Yet out of the ashes of the shocking acts of devastation has come increasing recognition on the part of many Americans that not only do non-Muslims need to learn more about Islam, but that Muslims need to be able to understand and articulate their own faith better both to themselves and to others. Part of this mutual process has been the furthering of a number of efforts at dialogue between members of the two religious traditions. This volume provides an overview and analysis of the recent history of Christian-Muslim dialogue in the United States, and the ways in which it has been furthered and enriched since September 11, 2001. So much has been happening in different cities and areas around the country, of course, that the specific examples cited can only suggest to the reader the kinds of events that are taking place, as well as the variety of thinking on the part of both Christians and Muslims as to what it means to be in dialogue and to take seriously the other's faith.

Chapter one, "Encountering Each Other," brings the reader straight into the heart of the dialogue process. Three vignettes about possible kinds of dialogue suggest the issues and concerns that face organizers and participants in these conversations as they struggle to get to know each other and to determine what, if anything, will form a future agenda for their talks. These dialogues represent some of the issues that could arise as members of particular groups struggle to decide how to talk with each other. Two of these sets of conversations are hypothetical, though based on the kind of exchange that actually has taken place, and a third represents the experience of a real group. Examples are provided of (a) Christians and Muslims brought together by a local ecumenical council representing a range of ethnic backgrounds; (b) African American Muslims and Christians struggling to determine what they have in common and what are the most important issues they need to address; and (c) Roman Catholic and Muslim women trying to find common ground as women and the possibility of shared experiences in their individual forms of worship and spiritual life.

Chapter two, "The Legacy of Engagement," provides a brief history of Christian-Muslim relations since the beginning of Islam in the 600s CE. It explores the ways in which conflict as well as times of peaceful coexistence shared by these two great religions inevitably had shaped the responses that their members have toward each other. Is it possible to have useful and productive conversations in the relatively neutral context of a pluralistic America, that in theory supports freedom of religion for all, without acknowledging past realities, both painful and helpful? The Crusades of the tenth, eleventh, and twelfth centuries are nearly a millennium past, and yet they are once again vivid in the consciousness of both Muslims and Christians. In the so-called "peaceful period" in medieval Spain, when Muslims, Jews and Christians for the most part lived in mutual support and cooperation, some of the most creative work in the arts and sciences known in the historical record were fostered. Are there lessons from this period that can inform our life together today in the historically and geographically different places in which we now live? Christian views of the Prophet Muhammad and the Qur'an, the holy book of Islam, have rarely been other than uncharitable, sometimes to the extreme of fabricating wild and ludicrous tales. To what extent are these views latent in our modern Western views of the religion of Islam?

Chapter three, "Islam: A Truly American Religion?" returns us to the American context as it explores the history of the rise and growth of Islam in this country. How has American society been changed by the reality that we now have many millions of Muslims living as fellow citizens? Waves of Muslim immigrants, refugees and asylum seekers have brought new citizens from every part of the Muslim world, who have formed a community unique in the history of the world. Added to this already complex picture is the presence of significant numbers of African Americans who have chosen to identify with the religion of Islam. The chapter will consider how all these people live together, acknowledging both their personal ethnic and cultural affiliations and their bond with the Islamic faith. Woven through the narrative of how American Islam has come to grow and be part of American life are the many efforts that members of the American Muslim community have made to participate in, and sometimes even initiate, dialogue and conversation with their Christian (and sometimes Jewish) neighbors.

What have been the various ways in which Muslims and Christians have engaged in conversation with each other? Chapter four, "Models of Christian-Muslim Dialogue in America," will look at Christian-Muslim dialogue in the American context, suggest what have been the most popular models with both

Christians and Muslims, examine why some work better than others, and discuss the importance of setting specific goals so as to allow for the greatest degree of success no matter which type of dialogue is chosen. Some models are obvious, determined by the nature of the group that wishes to talk together. Others depend on the interests of the participants and the particular ends they want to accomplish. A number of Muslims who have taken part in Christian-Muslim conversations for a considerable period of time speak to their convictions about the importance of one form of dialogue over another.

Chapter five, "When Dialogue Goes Wrong," will illustrate how, even under the best of circumstances and with the best of intentions, attempts at Christian-Muslim dialogue may be disrupted or doomed to failure. Here we will look at some of the reasons why efforts to communicate can lead to disappointment, emphasizing that appropriate planning and anticipation can help avoid problems and frustrations. The chapter will look at how strong political convictions may serve to distract conversations to the point where continuing is impossible. In some cases it simply must be admitted that after a first "getting acquainted" session the group has little to say to each other and probably should not be encouraged to continue. Sometimes insufficient forethought has been given to the reality that certain combinations of persons really do not make appropriate dialogue partners. If you, your church or mosque, or any other local group in your community is interested in getting engaged in interfaith dialogue, you may find information here that will help you avoid the "dead ends" and get your group off to as promising a beginning as possible.

With the heightened interest in the fact of religious diversity in the United States, many Muslims and Christians have been turning their attention to what it means to live in a society in which majority status can no longer be taken for granted. Chapter six and chapter seven, which look at "The Pluralist Imperative" first from the Christian and then from the Muslim perspective, review contemporary scriptural and theological understandings of pluralism and what it means for Christians and Muslims to be part of an increasingly diverse America in terms of religion and of racial-ethnic identities. Chaper six will provide a synopsis of recent theological writings of Protestants, Catholics and evangelicals about dialogue, about pluralism, and about their understanding of why (if they do) Christians believe that interfaith conversation can enhance their own theological understanding. The Association of Theological Schools has encouraged reflection on the reality of theological pluralism as an important element in the training of pastors and religious leaders. Many Muslims also are pondering whether and how they can live as members of a minority faith in a land in which their religion is not dominant. Since 9/11 a few Muslims in the West have begun to address the subject of religious pluralism. For the most part these efforts are being made as part of the concern to prove the legitimacy of pluralism within the Islamic understanding, and thus of Islam itself as a credible part of the American religious scene. Chapter seven will offer an analysis of some of these Muslim writings, comparing them with contemporary Western Christian thinking about pluralism in terms of the themes they address and the intent with which they are written.

Chapter eight, "New Directions," considers some of the ways in which interfaith dialogue in America is changing. Among the topics to be discussed are the following: (a) how our respective local and national organizations are beginning to work, often together, to provide both the impetus and the resources for interfaith conversation; (b) what women bring to the dialogue, and why some have become disillusioned with contemporary conversations, turning from talk to support and action; (c) ways to engage the interest of youth in developing relationships between Muslims and Christians and, increasingly, with Jews and members of other religions; and (d) the pros and cons of expanding the conversation from just Christians and Muslims to include Jews in an "Abrahamic" dialogue. Fundamentally, what is it that makes dialogue between Christians and Muslims in the United States of growing importance? Various answers have been given: National and international events make it essential. . . . Dialogue reduces prejudices. . . . We learn more about our own faith when we learn more about another. . . . It just feels good. These and many other responses are offered by those who have experienced religious dialogue.

This book is written for a variety of audiences. Muslims and Christians who have long been involved in dialogue may find echoes of their own experiences in this material. Church, mosque, or community leaders who would like to plan Muslim-Christian dialogue conversations in their own areas might benefit from guidance and perspective in learning how to do that. Academic audiences will be interested in the history of Christian-Muslim relations and how current efforts at engagement in the American context are a natural and legitimate part of those relations. The American public is searching for answers to questions of Islamic extremism and trying to reconcile what they hear on the nightly news with the efforts of members of the American Muslim community to reach out with care and concern to their Christian neighbors. Theologians in both the Christian and Muslim camps, who are rethinking the importance of developing a pluralist perspective, as Muslims and Christians again occupy common space, must find ways in which to accommodate each other at the deepest theological levels.

Muslims, Christians, and the Challenge of Interfaith Dialogue

I

Encountering Each Other

Following are three vignettes about Christian-Muslim dialogue. Each portrays a situation in which people, who have no experience in such engagement, take the first steps to be in conversation with those of the other faith tradition. The first setting portrays a dialogue envisioned by the members of a local ecumenical council, who are well versed in talking together as Christians but have not yet had the experience of engaging with members of the Muslim community. The second scene involves African Americans, Muslims, and Christians, who are struggling to find grounds for commonality that both include and move beyond issues of racial identity. The third describes interaction between Roman Catholic and Muslim women, raising the question of whether the mode of dialogue is different when men are not involved in the conversation. Each of these scenes could be located in any city or town in America. The first two presentations represent somewhat fictional or hypothetical groups. The descriptions only approximate actual attempts at dialogue, but they reflect many of the issues relevant to Christian-Muslim interaction found in the United States today. The third group is real and the particulars represent the experiences of its members.

A Local Ecumenical Council

"Why did I ever let you talk me into going to this thing?" Joe asked his wife. "I don't know anything about religion and I certainly don't know what to say to any Muslims. I've never even met any." "Oh come on, Joe," responded Lucie, who was beginning to have cold feet herself, "You met the parents of Charlie's friend 'Ali at the fourth grade open house a few months ago. They were very nice."

The truth is that Lucie had let herself be persuaded by their pastor, John, to "have a try" at some interfaith conversation, specifically Christian-Muslim. For a long time Pastor John had been a member of a local ecumenical council, which had begun with conversations between Roman Catholics and Protestants, and a few years ago had invited a local Rabbi to join. Now with growing numbers of Muslims in town, the council had followed the path taken by a number of such ecumenical groups around the country to expand its horizons a bit more and engage in conversation with members of the Islamic faith. Pastor John thought that it was unfortunate that the Rabbi was going to be out of town for this first meeting—he might have been a kind of buffer in helping them get past the initial awkwardness of finding some common ground for conversation.

Knowing that the Muslims in their area had only one Imam or religious leader, the ecumenical council thought that it might be a bit overwhelming to try to have a dialogue with several pastors and priests and only a single Muslim leader. So they decided to sponsor a general conversation between Christians and Muslims that would include both clergy and laypeople, men and women, and to whatever extent possible, some young people. Each of the six member churches had invited one or two representatives. Thus Pastor John had encouraged Lucie, who was especially active in their Lutheran congregation, to be part of the group, and Lucie had made good on a long overdue favor owed her by her husband, who grudgingly agreed to attend.

The event was to be this evening. The members of the clergy ecumenical council had spent some time deciding where to hold it and what would be the best format. Although some members felt strongly that it should take place in one of their churches, they finally decided that the Muslims might feel more comfortable in a kind of "neutral space." So they engaged the meeting room of the local library, and then arranged the seats in a circle. As for format, the council thought a simple get-to-know-you was the best plan for this first meeting and then they would see if there would be interest in continuing the conversation. To begin with, they weren't sure if what they intended was the first step of an actual dialogue, or just an initial get-together so that people could begin to know each other. Probably the latter would be best. They hoped that the total number of people participating would not be more than thirty, but it was really hard to tell how many Muslims might be coming and they couldn't get a clear commitment from the Imam.

It was 7:30 PM and all the Christian participants were nervously waiting at the library. No Muslims had arrived. Then about 7:45 several cars pulled up and about ten Muslims got out, the majority of them men and none younger than thirty. The few Christian teens who had been inveigled to attend were disappointed, as no Muslim kids came. The women of the Lutheran church had provided the requisite refreshments—punch and a few cookies. To their surprise and chagrin, the Muslim women came with trays of pastries made out of finely spun dough, nuts, and honey.

The Imam was part of the Muslim contingent, and it was clear that the other Muslims looked to him for direction. Pastor John took him to the side and asked why no Muslim teens had been able to come. The Imam looked slightly embarrassed, and confessed that many people in the Muslim community have strong reservations about having their young people "socialize" with Christians. "Of course they interact with each other in the context of the school," he said, "but we try to make sure that aside from that required time there is little or no interaction among the kids. Frankly, it's for two reasons. First, we think they might feel like their religious beliefs are being challenged when they hear different ideas from Christian kids. Second, and probably more immediate, we are worried that friendships made in social contexts may lead to dating, which we frown on for our boys and don't allow at all for our girls. The biggest fear, of course, is that the process of getting acquainted might ultimately lead to intermarriage. It's just better to keep them separate. We know that when they get to college all bets are off and we no longer have much control." Asked if it might be okay in the future for teenage Christian and Muslim boys, or girls, to meet together without members of the opposite sex present, the Imam said that he had never considered the idea, and that he suspected many people in his mosque would object.

Meanwhile, several forces seemed to be pulling at the group assembled in the library room. Christians, who all knew each other, weren't sure what to say to their guests. The Muslims seemed to huddle in one corner of the room, the women keeping somewhat apart. As it became obvious that "free-flowing" conversation was not going to be a useful strategy, the Christians tried to break the ice with some opening conversational gambits. Adding to the tension, Muslim men and women seemed not to be comfortable talking in mixed gender groups. So Pastor John called the group to order by suggesting that everyone be seated in a circle.

The Muslim women, who formed a tight group, looked as if they would like to slide their chairs backwards out of the circle. "Nothing doing," thought John, and immediately initiated the process of introductions. The clergy had anticipated that this would take the better part of the session, and that each person would not only identify him or herself but would say what brought them to the conversation, what they hoped to get out of it, and other such pertinent information. Unfortunately nervousness prevailed, and even the Christians cut short their introductions and didn't know what to say next. An uncomfortable silence, John knew, would not be good.

"Now," he said in some desperation, "I think it would be very interesting if each of us talked about some time that we remember from our childhood that involved coming into contact with a person who was different from us. What did we do and how did we feel?" The tension began to ease as the participants clearly enjoyed returning in their thoughts to earlier days. The Christians recalled such things as the first time a Jewish child appeared in their classes, or when they first encountered black people either as new community members or as foreign visitors. "In my village in Pakistan," said one of the Muslims, "we were strictly forbidden from playing with Christian children although we knew where they lived. One time when I was caught talking to a group of them my father beat me smartly. Of course that only whetted my interest in making friends with them, which I suppose is one of the reasons why I accepted to come to this gathering tonight." With a shy smile, a middle-aged woman from Lebanon said that when she was growing up it was impossible to avoid being in contact with people who were different. "Lebanese society is made up of large segments of Muslims, Christians, and Druze—you can't avoid interaction with them all the time. Of course there were always political tensions—just look at the terrible things going on in Lebanon today—but I never experienced much religious prejudice until I married this Kuwaiti husband of mine...." She shot a sly look at her husband who was looking uncomfortable.

"I think," said the Imam, "that the question of presuppositions may be a good topic for us to pursue. What do we believe about the other faith and how are our assumptions different from what is really true? It seems to me, for example, that many Christians are rather vague about what they believe and tend to disagree with each other a lot. Maybe I'm wrong. In any case, I think it's different for Muslims. We may represent a variety of cultures, but we all share the same basic belief in God and his Prophet Muhammad, and know what God expects of us in the way of religious practices. At the risk of being rude, which I really do not intend, might I ask whether you Christians have the same kind of clear understanding of your faith?"

"Well all right," thought Joe. "Now we are getting down to something really interesting," and he jumped in by acknowledging that indeed such differences do exist among Christians, and that in his opinion one of the real strengths of Christianity is that it allows for a variety of interpretations and ways of carrying out one's faith. "But honestly," said another Christian woman, "I don't know how to have this discussion without knowing what you Muslims really do believe. What's all this about praying five times every day and not eating for a whole month?" The Imam tried to give the answers, with other Muslims joining in to give personal examples. The conversation continued for quite awhile, focusing mainly on Muslim beliefs and practices. Finally John peeked at his watch and decided it would be good to quit while they were ahead. "Well," he said, "perhaps it's time to break for some of these fabulous refreshments I see on the table. Would it be fair to assume from the way things seem to be going that you all would like to meet again?" The response was a convincing yes.

Members of the ecumenical council knew that many such gatherings had showed promising beginnings, but then foundered for lack of a concrete agenda or simply petered out because everyone was too busy to add another commitment to their calendars. They also knew that once introductions were over, and basic information shared, it was difficult to structure the meetings so that they could achieve some concrete purpose besides information exchange. So they invited the Imam to meet with them, and pondered seriously whether they had the time, the energy, and the commitment to try to create a real Christian-Muslim dialogue group. The ecumenical council members agreed to give it a serious try, realizing that a number of issues would need to be resolved for the group to be successful:

1. How would they avoid having the clergy and the Imam provide the answers to all the discussion topics with the laypeople simply listening out of respect? They knew that in many cases lay Christians, and even Muslims, are vague about many of the details of their faith, and the Imam said that some of the Muslims he knew thought they were better informed about Islam than was really the case. They were also concerned about the fact that the Christian clergy seriously outnumbered the single Imam.

2. Given the fact that the churches involved in this ecumenical council were mainline Protestant and fairly liberal—thus open and flexible in a way that Joe clearly appreciated—would the Muslims, who seem certain about the details of their religious expectations, find the conversation uneven and frustrating?

3. What can be done to encourage Muslim women to continue to attend the meetings, to be willing to speak in the group as a whole, and to engage in conversation to the point of possibly disagreeing with their husbands or, even harder, with the Imam? Is the topic of different gender role expectations appropriate for such conversations? Or, as one of the other clergypersons put it to the Council, "What right do

we have to try to encourage Muslim women to do anything that they might feel uncomfortable about? We can't just assume that because our women talk freely in a mixed-gender that's the way it ought to be!"

4. What is the real goal of such a group? Learning how to live with each other in a society in which there is growing tension between Christians and Muslims? Modeling good interfaith relations for others in our community? Should we stay on the level of agreement and good will, or should we have the courage to disagree with each other in ways that are mutually supportive and understanding rather than critical?

5. Should lines be drawn excluding conversations about politically charged issues such as American involvement in Afghanistan and Iraq, American support for what Muslims perceive as aggressive military action on the part of Israel, or American branding of countries like Syria and Iran as part of an "axis of evil"? Joe, for example, supports the war in Iraq and American aid to Israel, while Pastor John and others are strongly opposed to it. Most Muslims, John knows, are reluctant to voice any concerns they may have about American policy in the Middle East because they are trying to be seen as patriotic American citizens. Should this dilemma be part of a religious dialogue?

6. When the Rabbi comes back, should the dialogue be redefined as Christian-Muslim-Jewish? The conversation would clearly be changed with different issues brought to the table. How can we avoid falling into the trap of political discussions about Israel in which the Jews and the Muslims are very likely to hold quite dramatically different opinions, especially given the recent war between Israel and Hizbullah and continuing struggles between Jews and Palestinians?

7. Should a secular perspective be brought to bear on these conversations or should they be limited to people who consider themselves religiously practicing? The council knows that the Muslim community might actually benefit if a broader base of people than just church attendees could get to know them and understand their perspectives on a range of issues. But what would be lost if the conversation did not focus on religion and the practices of the faith?

This, then, might be the experience of a hypothetical group of Christians and Muslims in many communities in America. Race was not an issue for this group, although some of the Christian participants seemed very interested in issues related to gender. The questions that their religious leaders were raising are sufficiently sophisticated that we can assume that such a dialogue would have a very good chance of continuing and keeping the interest of the group's members.

African Americans Talk with Each Other

"As far as I'm concerned," said the pastor of the large African American[1] Baptist church, "what we as black Christians and Muslims have in common is the fact that we all suffer from the continuing racism of American society. That should be the basis of our conversations."

"Well that may be true, and of course we've all experienced it, but I think that concentrating on racism is going limit the conversation," said the Muslim Imam who was his copartner in leading the African American Christian-Muslim dialogue. "It seems to me that the starting point for whatever dialogue we want to have is the fact that we are all trying to live responsibly as people of faith in the context of a culture that really doesn't support or appreciate that effort." The Imam cleared his throat, warming up to the topic. "It seems like the more we try to be responsive to what we think God wants from us as Muslims, the more we experience everything from snickering to hostility from members of a society that is putting up with grossly immoral behavior at all levels. I'm sure Christians must feel that way too, and maybe we can have a good conversation about just living faithfully."

"I agree with that, Imam," said a man from his mosque, "and think that it is always better to be positive than negative. However, I also think we should acknowledge that Muslims in general in this country, and not just us blacks, are subject to deep American color prejudice. I've heard people ask whether the response of Americans to Islam isn't basically a racist one? Well I'd say that's pretty much true. White people—you know, those descendents from blond, blue-eyed Calvin and Knox stock—have never been keen on dark-skinned folk whether they are from African or Asian heritage. Add to that the fact that they're Muslim, and whammy! You got prejudice."

The planners of this African American Christian-Muslim dialogue held considerable discussion about the appropriate venue, with options including one of the city's two mosques, a large and comfortable home of one of the organizers, or this Baptist church. The church was selected because planners felt that it not only affirmed the religious nature of the discussion, but they also recognized that black Christians would probably be less comfortable—at least at first—meeting in a mosque than the Muslims would be in a church. "After all," said a rather stout woman wearing a black robe and headcovering, "most of us were raised in Christian churches anyway. Hello Jesus! That's just familiar old ground to us."

What had brought this group of folks together in the first place? Oddly, perhaps, the initiative came not from within the black community itself but as a challenge from an ongoing mainly white and South Asian dialogue group in the city. "If you as African Americans don't want to join our conversation, and it seems obvious that you are either uninterested or uncomfortable, why don't you start your own group? Just black on black, so to speak. Then maybe at some time we could all meet together and see where our talks have gone." A few African American leaders of the city's mosques and churches rose to the challenge, and as a result a group of some twenty people were meeting for the first time, looking for common ground, and trying to establish a basis of conversation that could begin from shared racial-ethnic identity. They knew that there were very few models for such a dialog,[2] and that the odds were small that they would actually establish an ongoing group that could make headway against a background of misunderstanding and misperception of the other. Planners on both sides had decided that they would not waste time with small talk but try to discuss the hard issues right from the beginning.

"Let's just get a few cards on the table," said a soft-spoken man whose Sundays throughout his sixty year old life had been spent attending services, social events, and meetings at his church. "You Muslims have to recognize a couple of things that we bring with us, and there's no denying it. First, most of you have chosen to be Muslim after having been raised Christian, and many of us both resent and fear that choice. What's wrong with the Christian faith that you feel you have to find something better? Second, we see you working on the street corners, in youth centers, at shelters and food banks, in prisons and other places where some of the neediest folks of our community tend to be found. We know that along with service, which of course we appreciate, you are also dishing out a good helping of Islamic propaganda. You make Islam sound really appealing, especially when you serve it up as the latest message of rock and rap music, or whatever it's called. Honestly, that scares us silly. We had a terrible time getting a lot of folks to come out here for this discussion tonight because they just want to stick their heads in the sand and pretend that the problem of losing our kids to Islam doesn't exist."

"OK," responded a young woman who chose to wear her Islam by means of a very chic denim shirt, jeans, and a braided denim turban, "here are a few cards of our own to put on the table, as you call it. When it comes right down to it we think that most of you Christians have swallowed the Christianity of our slave masters whole, and have simply sold out to white society as represented by the very racist white church. What's that old question about the most segregated moment in American culture being 11 o'clock on Sunday morning? You know white people don't want you in their churches, and you respond not by challenging the prejudice and injustice of that but by pretending that you are happier celebrating a kind of black Christianity. We Muslims think *all* races and colors are welcome in the religion of Islam."

"Well, just to push things a bit farther," added a young very black man in a jacket and tie, "I also have to say that we haven't heard many of you Christians speak out for our rights as African American Muslims in the face of a rising anti-Muslim prejudice in this country today. White Christians are better at defending us than you are. Frankly, we think you are happier hiding in your black churches and moaning about American racism than in standing up for the rights of people of faith in general, probably especially Muslims. And we also think that the black church has not shouldered its share of the responsibility for helping solve the problems African Americans face living in the city. We are trying, but we need your help. To put it candidly, we miss our sisters and brothers in the black church."

"Well then let me add one more thing," said the wife of the Baptist pastor. "I read just the other day about how Muslims in Pompano Beach, Florida, plan to build a mosque smack dab in the middle of a black Christian neighborhood. I think that is a real shame, especially considering that land was to be used for affordable housing for folks who are financially limited. Why can't you Muslims stay away from land that has always belonged to us Christians? Of course I also read that in the process of protest the pastor of one of those really huge conservative Black churches in Pompano Beach called Islam a dangerous and evil religion that preaches hatred and killing, which I think is a scandalous accusation!"[3]

Despite their intentions, none of the leaders had quite expected these tough issues to rise to the surface so quickly. The room was quiet for awhile, as the men and women present tried to decide if the tensions were so deep-seated that attempts to move forward with dialogue simply wouldn't work, or if this kind of airing was a healthy and essential beginning that would lay the ground for more constructive conversation. Perhaps because the effort of getting people to come together in the same room had been so difficult, after a few silent moments the group decided to plunge ahead.

"Maybe it would be a good idea if we just made a list of the reasons why we are suspicious of each other," said a public school teacher who was used to putting things on a blackboard, "especially since we have a running start on it." They decided that they had already identified the following very important concerns:

1. On the part of Christians: a feeling of rejection because Muslims have found another faith, suspicion of Muslim attempts to convert, and fear that the black church is under attack for not providing the kind of community that would appeal to their youth, especially their young men.

2. On the part of Muslims: accusations that Christians have stayed in their own enclaves, have not done enough to address the social ills of urban blacks, and have failed to come to the defense of their Muslim brothers and sisters in an increasingly hostile American society.

A number of other issues then came to the fore as the discussion stumbled along. At times the women, both Muslims and Christians, got bored with hearing yet more pontification from the males of their respective communities. Uninhibited by some of the constraints that often keep their sisters from talking very much in the presence of males, some of them asserted their right to speak and to voice their own opinions. "Right on, sister!" affirmed one, recognizing that commonalities may often have more to do with gender than with race. Others were still reluctant to challenge the authority of the male pastors and imams, and eyed the kitchen knowing that it would soon be their responsibility to serve the refreshments.

What, then, did the group as a whole identify as the main concerns it needed to address? The school teacher continued writing on the board:

1. The importance of understanding common history. Starting with African Christians harboring Muslims in Abyssinia, the history of Christians and Muslims has been full of examples of cooperation and understanding, especially among blacks. "Unfortunately," said the Imam, "tensions have separated us because of the ways in which our histories have been presented to us."

2. Concern about the Nation of Islam (NOI). While everyone agreed that members of the Nation have done a great deal to fight drugs and other social ills, both Christians and Muslims expressed their concern that many of the relatively small number of followers of Louis Farrakhan's NOI[4] are racially extremist. The Muslims said that they are particularly annoyed because the average American thinks that any Muslim they see who is black must be part of the Nation. Much of the emphasis on conversion of youth, they said, comes from NOI rhetoric and activity. They did agree that fighting community problems such as drugs is an area where churches and mosques could work together much more effectively than they have done in the past.

3. Differing understandings of the Bible. Here the discussion became much more tentative, as many of the Christians simply did not know

what Muslims think about the Bible, nor did they Christians know the first thing about the Qur'an. They did agree that probably African American Muslims are more "flexible" than some of their coreligionists from places in the Middle East in appreciating what the Hebrew Scriptures and New Testament mean to Christians. Some discussion was held about the possibility of studying the Bible and Qur'an together, and the idea was tabled for discussion after they had gotten to know each other better. "Or the way I would put it," said a Christian man, "is that the conversation is tabled until some of us have a better idea what in the world this Qur'an thing is all about!"

4. Commonalities. Whether it is racist oppression or lack of support for faithful living, as the group noted at the beginning of the discussion, participants recognized that many things do bind African Americans together, whatever their religion. The group members identified lack of education, unemployment, weakened family structures, poverty, and a host of other factors as problems often experienced by blacks that need to be addressed. The subject of terrorism was raised and then rejected as a topic of conversation. "It seems to me," observed a middle-aged Christian man, "that terrorism is more important to whites and immigrants than it is to us anyway—they worry either that they will be the victims of Islamic terrorism or that they will be accused of it! All that worry doesn't seem to give them much time to be concerned about poverty or other issues facing our communities."

5. Intermarriage. One of the concerns raised in the dialogue with the local interfaith council above was the possibility that interaction between young people of different religious traditions could possibly lead to intermarriage. For this group of African Americans, the question was put differently: Which is the greater fear, that a child marry someone not of his or her faith, or that color lines be crossed? In the brief discussion that ensued when the topic was raised, most agreed that they would probably be less concerned with an interfaith marriage than one between a white and black of the same faith, although they felt that both entail huge difficulties. Not surprisingly, black-Hispanic relationships seemed more viable, especially if they shared faith in common.

6. Action over talk. "White folks don't want to get their hands dirty. You and me, brother, we're out here working in the trenches. We're doing the serious work of cleaning up this city. The problem is that you got your trench and I got mine, and we don't talk across them." This

idea really caught hold. "What we need are models of folks who are doing good work in the community. We Christians lack exposure to Muslims doing good work. If we talk too much, we climb out of the trench and that helps nobody." The group made tentative plans to meet next in a mosque, with representatives from each religion bringing various individuals to serve as role models for community service, especially for the youth.

The school teacher was running out of space on the blackboard, the smells coming from the kitchen were more and more tempting, and the group members expressed their general feeling that real progress had been made on identifying important issues for future discussion. "Well I've learned a lot from this conversation," confessed the pastor, "and maybe the most important thing is that we have many things to talk about besides racism. And now let's eat!" The group promised each other that they would meet again, particularly to go forward on the role model idea. Unfortunately they never got around to setting a date, and despite a few attempts on the part of the Muslim leaders to have the group meet at a local mosque, a subsequent gathering never happened. Nonetheless, the items they put forward on their agenda remain important ones for consideration by African American Christians and Muslims, whatever their particular context.

Roman Catholic–Muslim Women's Dialogue

The night was rainy and cold, but the spirits of the women who crowded into the meeting room at St. Ignatius Roman Catholic Church were undampened. For the Catholic women the venue was familiar—they had held many meetings there to foster the spirit of outreach characteristic of their parish church. Not all of their activities were welcomed warmly by the church hierarchy, but these women were dedicated to helping move their congregation courageously in new and challenging directions. This time the task was getting to know about the faith of the growing number of Muslims who were coming to live in their area. Thus over a year ago they had invited a group of Muslim women to meet and talk with them, and the gatherings had proven wonderfully successful.

The Muslim women, now familiar with this church, this room, and this particular group of Catholics, were feeling increasing comfortable in what had initially been a strange new context. Some had come boldly, having been frequent participants in interfaith dialogue sponsored by various groups in the city. Others were new to such activities and were unsure of what was expected of them. Many had never before stepped into a Christian church. Yet now all of them—unlike some of their other Muslim sisters—were comfortable being in a place where their husbands were not present and where they were expected to contribute fully to the conversation. Many were professional women representing disciplines such as medicine, business, and education, while others were homemakers and caregivers for their husbands and children. When the portable phone of one of the Muslim women rang, she answered and giggled to her husband, "I'm here in my church!"

The first meetings had been tentative, each side afraid that they might say or do something to offend the other. "I'm really a little nervous," confessed one of the Catholic women, "because I know so little about Islam and am not sure what is appropriate to say." But now they were not only comfortable but enthusiastic, eager to continue the engaging conversations that had taken place over the last year and recognizing that hospitality had grown into genuine friendship. They were beginning to be united by their commitment to helping Christian women learn more about Islam and to furthering Christian-Muslim relations, and also by the simple fact that they were women. Occasionally they would chuckle with the realization that much as they might love their husbands or other men in their families, talking about serious issues with only women present was a privilege they would not want to give up.

"Isn't it amazing," said a Muslim physician originally from Pakistan, "how important these meetings have gotten to be? I wouldn't miss one no matter how busy my schedule is!" The first lesson learned by the Catholics was the fact that the Muslim women were so diverse. "My goodness," said an elderly nun, "we are all white ladies from the U.S. who were raised with the same Roman Catholic upbringing and probably have pretty much the same expectations for our church and for this meeting with you Muslim women. But you are from different cultures and racial-ethnic groups, and represent such a wide range of backgrounds and even ways of dressing." She and the other Christians had yet to learn that the mix of Muslims would have been even more complex if they had been joined by any Shi'ite women. What no one mentioned, or perhaps even thought much about, was that the entire gathering, Muslims and Christians, also would have been even more heterogeneous had any participants been black.

The Catholic women understood that for the most part when they spoke they represented the thinking of the whole group of Catholics. It was a bit surprising for them to learn that despite their regional and cultural differences, the Muslim women also spoke with a pretty common voice, especially when the topic had to do with religious beliefs and practices. As members of the group grew more comfortable with each other a few courageous Roman Catholic souls broke rank slightly, and admitted that one or another belief within their own faith congregation was not something that they held easily or appreciatively. They also began to ask some of the potentially more uncomfortable questions of their colleagues. The issue that was foremost in the minds of many of the Christians, though it was not mentioned until several meetings had taken place and a comfort zone had been established, was the matter of dress. Why, they wondered, did some of the Muslim women always appear with Islamic dresses and headscarves, while others looked "just like we do." The Muslims felt comfortable in sharing different points of view about the Qur'anic verses on veiling.

On a few occasions Protestant women were invited to be part of the conversations, although the group was clear that it wanted to be defined as Catholic-Muslim. The Protestants, who were from mainline "liberal" denominations, felt somewhat differently from their Catholic sisters about a number of doctrinal issues, which proved both enlightening and confusing for the Muslims. These exchanges gave rise to serious discussions about the nature of dialogue and how specifically the participants should be defined. At one point when two Protestants were present, a Muslim woman who had converted earlier in her life from Lutheranism expressed her opinion that Muslims have it the hardest because they have to perform prescribed duties, such as prayer five times a day. The Roman Catholics have fewer such duties, she thought, but still have certain clear expectations placed on them. But the Protestants have the best deal because they can do pretty much what they want without anyone checking up on them. "Ah no, I disagree," insisted one of the Protestants. "I think that Muslims have the easiest path because it is so clearly laid out for them. Catholics are in the middle, but we poor Protestants have to struggle to make our own guidelines. Being a good Christian is very hard for us," she added with a wink. The dialogue group knows that one of its challenges is helping Muslims to understand that Roman Catholics represent (more or less) one position—at least theologically, if not socially—and that many Protestants might see things somewhat differently.

In the beginning the members of the group tried to explain as briefly and clearly as possible the basic elements of their respective faiths, and how they practice their religion on a daily basis. The Muslims found it amusing when some of the Catholic women quickly jumped to the conclusion that "You really believe just like we do!" It was not long before the rush to commonality waned in the face of some real and significant differences in faith and practice that began to emerge. Gradually the group moved from its initial interest in talking about theological issues, or comparing specific religious practices, to more personal and anecdotal exchanges. How one understands living within a certain religious framework, for example, was communicated through stories about raising children or caring for aging parents. The group solidified into a community of support when some of the Pakistani women lobbied at the state capital to oppose violence and the misinterpretation of Islam and were joined by their Roman Catholic sisters in a gesture of solidarity.

On several occasions the women decided to hold more formal programs to which an outside audience, including men, was invited. These occasions, which turned out to be quite well attended, were designed to compare what were seen as more or less parallel observances in the two religious traditions. A model was established for the open meetings with the following elements:

1. Participants and invitees enjoy a brief informal time with refreshments for meeting old friends and getting acquainted with new people.
2. Either a Muslim or a Christian gives an opening prayer or thought, selected to convey an appropriate respect for the faith of all the participants (Christians, for example, are to avoid such references as "In the name of the only Savior, our Lord Jesus Christ").
3. People are seated at tables in mixed groups of Christians and Muslims, with one person designated to serve as host.
4. A speaker from one tradition gives a short (twenty to twenty-five minutes) presentation on a theme that has a general parallel in the other faith.
5. Guests and participants take a break, refill their plates, and return to their tables.
6. In the context of the small groups at the tables people eat and talk together about the presentation (questions prepared ahead of time are distributed to each table in case the conversation needs a bit of assistance).
7. A closing prayer or thought is offered by a member of the opposite tradition from the one at the opening. The event is designed to last an hour and a half to two hours.

One fall, for example, the Muslim women talked publicly about the month of Ramadan and what it means to fast as a requirement of God. Then in the spring the Catholic women, led by an experienced teacher, discussed fasting as an element in the time of Lent. The conversations were revealing not only about similarities but also about some deep differences. It was quite easy for the Christians to understand Ramadan as one of God's specific requirements for men and women, although they were awed by the ability of the Muslims to sustain the discipline for thirty consecutive days. Lent presented some more difficult problems. While the group had agreed to talk just about the act of fasting and not get into Easter itself, it became clear that the practice makes sense to Roman Catholics only as an act of penitence and obedience leading up to remembrance of the death and resurrection of Jesus. Participants walked to the brink of that theological reality—one that has always been a major sticking point for dialogue between Christians and Muslims, since the Qur'an denies Christ's crucifixion—and decided it was not where they wanted to spend their energies. The comparisons of the two fasting experiences were fascinating to them, and to the outside audiences, and the group is now trying to decide what other such practices they might talk about publicly that would reinforce elements of commonality between the two faiths.

In a happy coincidence, Christians were given the opportunity to engage their questions about what Muslim women wear and why they wear it when an exhibition about Islamic dress opened in their city. The presentation featured paintings, photographs, and others representations of young Muslim women who had chosen to wear various forms of dress that would distinguish them as Muslims. The dialogue group decided to take advantage of the opportunity to build on the exhibition and planned another public event with a somewhat different structure. This time a general audience was invited to view the exhibition, to hear several Muslim women speak about their choice of clothing, and then to retire to small tables (bearing the requisite refreshments—it is not unusual for the Catholic women to bring cakes and cookies while the Muslims bring assorted dishes of meat, rice, and pastries) at which Muslims and Christians could talk together about what constitutes religious dress and what motivates the decision to adopt such dress. Because the dialogue group had reached such a level of trust that honest and direct questions could be asked, even those attending the evening session who were new to the conversation could feel comfortable and free to participate. Muslim women understand very well that Christians often have trouble seeing past their scarves or other headgear, and often actually enjoy discussing the reasons why they have made their own decisions about clothing. "Wow," said one visitor, "I never imagined that I would be able to ask such honest questions. What a great conversation we had!" The evening was a notable success.

The group is currently debating what directions it should now take. At another event open to the public, they viewed the documentary "Peace by Peace," chronicling the struggles of women in various parts of the world to bring about peace and justice in their respective societies. As a result a number of participants in the dialogue group feel that more attention should be given to projects of social action, while others are content to continue the sessions of discussion and prayer. In one unusual experiment, members of the group invited the public—Christians and Muslims—to participate in a common worship service based on the Catholic theme of lamentation. While the turnout was small, the service was exceptional to the extent that members of the two faith traditions joined together in prayer and acknowledgement of the many places in the world in which Muslims and Christians are both suffering great tribulations.

The experiment of dialogue between Roman Catholic and Muslim women has proven successful insofar as the women involved have come to like and appreciate each other far more than they had earlier imagined, have learned a great deal about what it means to be women of faith (whether Muslim or Christian) and have made significant progress in overcoming ingrained prejudices. Members understand that it is now time to take advantage of the built-up momentum and move from simply holding informal conversations and planning public events to a more specific agenda. Among the questions they are considering are the following:

1. While the church has worked well as a venue for both group conversations and larger gatherings, symbolically as well as practically it may be important to meet "on Muslim turf." Several Muslims have offered their homes for meetings, and there is also the possibility of gathering at one of several local mosques. Members worry, however, that any such changes may disrupt the strong sense of continuity and solidarity that the group has developed. The question of venue also points out the imbalance in having one congregation, i.e., a single Roman Catholic church, represent the Christian community while the Muslims come from a range of locations with some active in mosques and others not. What, they muse, might we lose if we contemplate moving from place to place for our gatherings? While the Muslims are generally under fifty in age, some of the Catholic women are in their sixties and seventies and might not be ready or able to move to another locale. (The question of age has frequently been discussed in the group, noting that in general the Catholics are somewhat older than the Muslims.) Despite the trust that has been built up, members also recognize that some in the group may still feel slightly uneasy about going to a mosque. Others, however, are ready to make such a move immediately.

2. Would it be a good idea to invite the Muslims to a Catholic worship service? Vice-versa? Probably only a small number would be able to come—does that skew the relationship that seems to work very well? The idea has been shelved for the time being, although the group

is thinking about another special worship service along the lines of the lamentation gathering.

3. "Do we want to expand our efforts to plan programs for the general public, or should we concentrate on deepening the conversation in our own group?" There is not unanimity among the participants as to this question. Experienced church planners know that finding topics that will appeal to the general public is difficult, and that the group could easily spend all of its time planning for such events to the detriment of the personal interaction that has come to be so important. If open programs are planned, what themes might be shared in the same way that fasting during Lent and Ramadan provided the possibility of an experience with some commonality?

4. "What is at risk if we begin seriously to explore our differences rather than emphasize the things we seem to have in common?" Muslims particularly worry that their efforts to be accepted as contributing members of American society, especially after September 11, may be undermined if emphasis is placed on beliefs and practices that set them apart from Christians. "Will the exercise of focusing on our differences lead to deeper understanding of each other or perhaps to a weakening of the bonds that we have worked so hard to establish?" Muslims also know that while they are in agreement about the basics of the faith, practices often differ because they come from a variety of ethnic and cultural circumstances. That, they fear, might be confusing for the Catholics.

These and other issues are on the agenda for discussion and decision in this group of Roman Catholic and Muslim women. What is certain is that they recognize their success in establishing trust in and care for each other. In a culture in which public fear and prejudice in relation to Islam is growing, they know that this is no mean accomplishment. With luck, women in other areas of the country might look to this fortunate interfaith group as a model of female friendship across faiths and cultures.

These three sets of dialogue encounters between Muslims and Christians are intended to introduce the reader to some of the circumstances, experiences and questions faced by those willing and courageous enough to initiate meeting representatives of other faith traditions. The first steps are the hardest— namely figuring out who will be invited to talk, where the conversations should take place, and what will be the initial agenda. I have offered three different kinds of illustrations in the hope that the reader will sense some of the breadth of possibility for bringing Muslims and Christians in the contemporary United

States together for better understanding and the possibility of serious friend-ships. In the following chapters, we will look at the dialogue process in more detail, recognizing that for serious interfaith conversations to occur, all of us need to know more about our neighbor's faith and history, and how we have come to be fellow citizens in this rapidly changing American society. The first step is to look at the history of engagement between our two faiths, a story that has had its glorious as well as its ignoble moments, and which is still being rewritten both on the world scene and here in the United States.

2

The Legacy of Engagement

The existence of Islam was the most far-reaching problem in medieval Christendom. It was a problem at every level of existence.
As a practical problem it called for action and for discrimination
between the competing possibilities of Crusade, conversion, coexistence, and commercial exchange. As a theological problem it
called persistently for some answer to the mystery of its existence:
what was its providential role in history—was it a symptom of
the world's last days or a stage in the Christian development, a
heresy, an obscene parody of Christianity, or a system of thought
that deserved to be treated with respect. It was difficult to decide
among these possibilities.[1]

This dilemma, outlined by historian R. W. Southern in the 1960s as
describing the situation in which medieval Christians found themselves, has haunting relevance for American Christians today. In
practical terms, Crusade continues to suggest the way many Americans think that the United States should respond to militant Islam,
and the term even slipped from the tongue of President Bush shortly
after 9/11. Evangelical Christians are stepping up efforts to try to
convert American Muslims to Islam. Coexistence is now inevitable
in our pluralistic American society, as is commercial exchange, although many struggle with what it means to live as neighbors with
Muslims. Theologically, some who represent the conservative voice of
the church still see Islam as the religion of hell, while others try to

advocate respect, understanding, tolerance, and even deep appreciation. For many Americans, continuing acts of violence on the part of a few Muslim extremists continue to make it difficult to decide among these possibilities.

As Mahmud Ayoub, professor at Temple University, observes, despite the Qur'an's call for respect for Jews and Christians, most Muslims have condemned Christians as polytheists over the ages while Christians have seen Islam as a religion inspired by the devil.[2] A great many things have happened throughout the centuries of Christian-Muslim encounter, of course, that have added to the storehouse of misunderstanding and mistrust. The Crusades of history, prompted among many factors by Western Christianity's desire to recapture the city of Jerusalem, took place primarily in the tenth through the thirteenth centuries CE. Now many years later, they have taken on new meaning for Muslims as they contemplate waves of Western Christian intrusion into Muslim lands. Muslim are extending the concept of "Crusade" to include persistent evangelistic missionary activity, which Muslims perceive as another attempt to destroy the religion of Islam, Western imperialism and colonization of Muslim territories, scholarly depiction of Islam by the West often critiqued as "Orientalism," and most recently the America's response to terrorism by invading Afghanistan and Iraq. Crusade is also equated with the political and moral support of the Zionist presence in the heart of the Muslim Middle East, represented most painfully at this writing by Israeli incursions into Lebanon in the struggle against Hizbullah.

Muslim memory of various forms of Western incursion into their lands is enhanced and encouraged by the rhetoric of revivalist Islam in many countries today. American Muslims often find themselves caught in a very painful position. At the same time that they decry atrocities carried out in the name of Islam, and are pained that their perception of Islam as a religion of peace is used by terrorists for such dire ends, American Muslims recognize that anti-Western feelings in much of the Muslim world are growing, and they fear that unless Americans as a whole understand how America's international activities are perceived by Muslims around the world, the chances of the escalation of violence are great.

For well over fourteen centuries Christians and Muslims have lived in proximity and have interacted with each other. The responses of each community have been guided religiously by their own scriptures and theological positions, and practically by the reality of conquests and the shifting tides of political power, as well as the everyday circumstances of living and interacting with each other as neighbors. Often, at the same time that religious spokespersons for both Christianity and Islam have challenged the nature of the other faith and even its right to exist, the two communities have developed and maintained cultural, commercial, and personal relationships.

Today as changing political, economic and social realities result in growing numbers of Muslims living in the West, several things are happening simultaneously. Muslims, on the one hand, are thinking seriously about what it means to live in lands where Islam is not dominant. In doing so they separate themselves from the common community and culture of Islam. Their new American counterparts, on the other hand, are struggling to understand that the Muslims they are coming to see in their stores, schools, and other public places are somehow different both from the Muslim warriors with whom the West has so long been struggling and from the fanatics and suicide bombers that provide engaging fodder for Western journalism. New attempts are underway in both communities to understand one another and to find ways of living together.

The Early Islamic Movement

When the religion of Islam arose in the seventh century CE, the Christian world was deeply divided. A series of controversies at the Councils of Nicea and Chalcedon over the nature of Jesus' relationship to God had failed to bring all Christians under one umbrella of belief. Apostolic Sees were located in Rome, Antioch, Constantinople, Jerusalem, and Alexandria. East and West were at odds, and each contained within itself serious tensions and disagreements. Most of the West was still un-Christianized and considered to be pagan land. It is little wonder that the new Islamic faith appeared to most Christians as simply another Christian heresy, since heretic was a term they often used to brand each other.[3] As Islam began to spread rapidly after the death of the Prophet, however, they began to express a much greater sense of alarm. The march of Islam across much of the known world for many Christians was both frightening and theologically incomprehensible.

Muslims, for their part, saw Christians primarily from the perspective of the Qur'an, which from the beginning they have believed to be God's divine word. The Prophet Muhammad understood his role to be that of the final prophet of a monotheistic faith to which Jews and Christians were the earlier adherents and the recipients of earlier revealed scriptures, namely the Torah, the Psalms, and the Gospel Jews and Christians in the Qur'an therefore are identified as *ahl al-kitab* [People of the Book], those to whom God's word was initially given. Muslims believe that the scriptures revealed to the Jews and

Christians were corrupted by the communities to which they were sent, and thus they were abrogated by the Qur'an.[4] It was when Muhammad met unexpected resistance from these communities, as well as their refusal to recognize his status as the final prophet of true monotheism, that his community came to understand that the religion of Islam was related to, but in fact different from, the lived religions of the Jews and Christians. Perhaps because of their greater resistance to the presence of the Muslim community in Medina, Jews are treated more harshly in the Qur'an than are Christians, a reality that played itself out in the life of the early band of Muslims. These Qur'anic and historical realities have obvious implications for interfaith dialogue, perhaps with slightly different assumptions if the conversation is extended beyond Muslims and Christians to also include Jews.

Although a number of Christian communities lived in Arabia at the time of the Prophet, Islamic doctrine holds definitively that he did not copy or borrow from their scriptures and writings and that the Qur'an was revealed directly from God. According to tradition Muhammad was illiterate and would have been unable to read the Bible in any case. The Meccan and Medinan societies in which he lived and preached were polytheistic, and, except for the small band of Muhammad's followers, were not initially persuaded either by the message of the Prophet that there is only one God or that there humans will be held accountable for the actions and choices on a final day of judgment. Revelations came to Muhammad piecemeal as he struggled to form his new community. Because of their position as People of the Book, both Christians and Jews were treated as special citizens in the emerging Islamic community in Medina as they were later in the Islamic state. Muslim polemic, however, has always insisted that the Qur'an supercedes the Torah and the Gospel of the Jewish and Christian communities. This rather complicated matter of the relationship of scriptures is an interesting but somewhat difficult one for contemporary Christian-Muslim dialogue groups to consider. Can one say that the New Testament "supercedes" the Hebrew Scriptures? And in turn, are Muslims committed to the position that the Qur'an supercedes both the Torah and the Gospel? Serious study of history and scripture is necessary before helpful conversation on these topics can be pursued.

Muslims have always found it impossible to understand why Christians apparently impugn the oneness of God by calling Jesus the Son of God. The Qur'an specifically denies that possibility, although it holds the person of Jesus in high esteem. Referred to in 93 verses, Jesus is affirmed as having been born of Mary the Virgin. He is considered a righteous prophet who performed miracles. He also will be a sign of the coming of the judgment day. Because the Qur'an attests that Jesus was not crucified the necessity of sacrifice for expiation of sin is eliminated, thus negating the doctrine of salvation through the blood of Jesus. Nonetheless the Qur'an refers to Christians as those nearest in love to Muslim believers, people of compassion and mercy who will be able to enter paradise so long as they do not compromise God's oneness.[5]

As the Prophet Muhammad encountered the refusal of the Jews and Christians to accept his prophetic mission, his community came to understand itself as the bearers of a faith that was related to, but different from, the existing religions of the Jews and Christians. This faith became known as Islam, submission to the one God. With the growth and spread of the Muslim religion, the People of the Book (including, besides Christians and Jews, also Magians, Samaritans, Sabians, and later Zoroastrians) were treated as communities under the protection of Islam (called *dhimmis*). They were considered to be believers in God despite their refusal to accept the prophethood of Muhammad. Adult male Christians were thus not required to convert or serve in the military, although they had to pay a poll tax. Specific requirements were set out for those with Christian *dhimmi* status. While they could keep their own communal laws, they were forbidden to build new churches, beat the wooden clapper used by Christians to call people to prayer, or to recruit new members to the faith.[6] Both Christians and Muslims should consider this history today as they reflect on the treatment of religious minorities in conservative Muslim countries such as Saudi Arabia, Pakistan, and Afghanistan, as well as the requests by Muslims for parity in the American context.

In the early eighth century, Islam moved across North Africa, then occupied Spain, and tried unsuccessfully to establish itself in southern France. The Byzantine state had ruled its eastern subjects in these areas with an authority that was often experienced as ruthless and oppressive. Thus it was that many Oriental Christians welcomed Muslim political authority as a relief from Byzantine oversight and taxation and cooperated with their new Muslim rulers, one of the most important factors in the remarkable ease with which Islam was able to spread across Christian lands. The *dhimmi* status was preferable to Byzantine oppression. Christians remained the majority in much of what was nominally Muslim territory for a number of centuries after the Crusades. Muslim military expeditions were political in nature, and generally not undertaken for the purpose of forcing conversion to Islam as an alternative to the sword. This fact may be difficult for contemporary Christians to understand, and asking Muslims to explain the concept of *jihad*, which often is portrayed in the media to mean conversion by the sword or some other military means, is one of the questions generally high on their agenda for dialogue. Muslims are only too happy to explain that despite the rhetoric of some militant Islamic groups today, the military side of *jihad* is considered by most Muslims to be of less importance than the personal side, where *jihad* implies struggling with the forces of one's inner soul to act in accord with the will of God.

During the time of the Prophet and his immediate successors—specifically the dynasty of the Umayyads, with the exception of the oppressive Caliph 'Umar II—relationships between Muslims and Christians were quite friendly. Christians even occupied high positions in the courts of the Caliphs.[7] As time went by, however, beginning in the second Islamic century, Muslim attitudes toward Christians tended to harden. They were never free from the whims of individual rulers who might choose to enforce strict regulations, or from the caprice of mobs expressing their passions in prejudicial and harmful ways. The laws became more stringent against them, with the result that free practice of the Christian faith often became more difficult and sometimes Christians and others considered opponents of the state were persecuted. Throughout the Middle Ages, Muslim attitudes toward *dhimmis* became increasingly hostile, more for political than for religious reasons.

Islam Consolidated

The rapid spread of the rule of Islam throughout much of the civilized world, even though the majority of its citizens did not immediately convert to Islam, remains unique in the religious history of the world. The final advance of the Muslims into the Christian West came when Muslim armies crossed over the Pyrenees into the south of France in 718. In 732 Muslim troops were met and defeated by Charles Martel near Poitiers, and Islam's advance into western Christendom was finally checked save for a few minor skirmishes. North of Spain the Muslims were never again serious opponents of Christians, who under the reign of the emperor Charlemagne, crowned in 800, consolidated power down to the Pyrenees. Continuously troublesome, however, were the raids of Muslim pirates along the eastern coasts of the Mediterranean. Attacks on monasteries were sometimes devastating, with the result that many monks were forced to abandon them and move inland. Ports and cities in the western Mediterranean were virtually deserted because of the raiding Muslim pirates.

In the meantime, one of the most successful ventures in interfaith relations was taking place in the area just below where France had finally turned the tide of invading Islam. Contemporary Muslims often point to the five-century Muslim rule in Spain as a model of harmonious relations, and wonder why that model cannot be applied today. History reveals that in fact it was really only in the first several centuries of that rule, particularly during the ninth and tenth centuries, that Christians, Muslims, and Jews can be said to have lived in relative peace and harmony. In this period, they did, in fact, succeed in creating a society rich in scientific and cultural achievements as well as cordial interreligious relationships. By the tenth century, the Iberian Peninsula of Spain was pretty well split between the Christian Kingdom of Leon in the north and the considerably larger Muslim al-Andalus in the south.

During the rule of Caliph Abd al-Rahman, beginning in 929, the Spanish Islamic state reached the height of power and fame. It was a time of great opulence and achievement, in which intellectual circles of Muslims, Jews, and Christians contributed to a flourishing of the arts, literature, astronomy, medicine, and other cultural and scientific disciplines. Muslim tolerance of the People of the Book was high, and social intercourse at the upper levels was easy and constant. Many Christians became Arabized, increasingly appreciating and appropriating Arabic music, poetry, and other forms of culture. Some even chose to convert to Islam, although Christians continued to outnumber Muslims in Andalusia until later in the tenth century.

Growing Tensions

Gradually this peaceful situation changed, and the era of good will was supplanted by the tensions, intolerance, prejudice, mutual suspicion, and ill treatment of minorities by both Muslims and Christians that more often have characterized relationships between the two communities. Muslim plundering of churches and other Christian sites began, and pious Muslims refrained from speaking to the infidels except at a distance. Christians were expected to live in houses that were lower than those of Muslims, and the construction of new churches or monasteries was banned. In 1492 monarchs Ferdinand and Isabella, having reconquered Spain for Christianity, in a particularly ungenerous and vicious move in the name of their faith, expelled Muslims from their homes or forced them to convert, bringing to an end any hope of further Muslim-Christian harmony in the Iberian Peninsula.

Whether or not contemporary Muslim and Christian dialogue includes Jews, but definitely if it does, the question of Jerusalem and its rightful "ownership" is never long out of the conversation.[8] Christians have little trouble understanding why this city is of such spiritual importance to both Jews and Christians, but many do not realize its religious value to Muslims. Originally, it was the place toward which the Prophet Muhammad asked his followers to turn in prayer. Although he later changed the prayer direction to Mecca, the city continued to be a site of pilgrimage and prayer. For Christians,

Jerusalem is the place of the death and resurrection of Jesus. While Muslims revere the city as the sometime home of Prophet Jesus, they do not believe in the crucifixion. Jerusalem, however, is particularly venerated as the location from which Muhammad is said to have ascended on his miraculous *mi'raj* or night journey through the heavens.[9] While the Qur'an itself does not mention this journey, it is venerated in Islamic tradition as a time when the Prophet traveled through the layers of heaven and hell, meeting and talking with the prophets of old, and finally emerging into the presence of God. The *mi'raj* is understood to have validated Muhammad's spiritual leadership of the community of Islam.

Initial Muslim conquest of the city of Jerusalem and its changing of hands from Christian to Muslim was actually one of the most peaceful events of its long and painful history. Shortly after its capture, 'Umar, the third caliph or leader of Islam after Prophet Muhammad, is said to have traveled to the city to establish a treaty with the patriarch Sophronius, by which Christians living there were allowed freedom of life, property, and worship in return for paying the poll-tax and helping to fight off Byzantine raiders. 'Umar ordered the Temple Mount to be cleansed of the piles of garbage that had accumulated on it, and he had a temporary mosque built on the site. Christians remained the majority population in Jerusalem for many years, and for more than four centuries they were allowed to practice their religion in relative freedom. In 692 the long-planned Dome of the Rock was built on the site of 'Umar's mosque; it is the oldest Islamic monument still standing. Visitors to Jerusalem are still dazzled by its shining gold dome, and the adjacent mosque of al-Aqsa on the other side of the Temple Mount is the holiest sanctuary in Islam after the great mosques of Mecca and Medina.

Perhaps the most noteworthy example of unhappy engagement between Christians and Muslims over the centuries was the period of the Crusades discussed briefly above. In 1095, Pope Urban II called for a crusade both to recapture the city for Christianity and to respond to the Byzantine call for help against Muslim persecution. Many complex factors went into the appeal for this remarkable and ill-advised movement into Muslim lands. One was the historical reality that in 1076 Jerusalem had been seized by the Seljuk Turks, who were said to have desecrated the holy places of Christianity and treated the Christian population with a brutality that had never before characterized Muslim response to Christians. Pilgrims returning from Jerusalem brought sad news of their fellow Christians there. Popular support began to rise for avenging these wrongs and regaining the holy city for Christianity.

Franks, the name by which Western Christians were then called, had little sense of what was awaiting those who chose to engage in the Crusade, but were

THE LEGACY OF ENGAGEMENT 31

nearly frenzied by their religious zeal for liberation of the Holy Land. Virtually for the first time since the early spread of Islam, Christians were in a position to react offensively and not just defensively to Islam. It was a heady venture, supported by the medieval papacy, the feudal knights, and the commoners. Many of the crusading efforts were grossly misguided and ended in disaster, such as the ill-fated "Children's Crusade" in which large numbers of youth were sold into slave markets. In the beginning, however, at least in the eyes of the West, there were crucial victories.

By 1099, Christian forces were finally able to claim the ultimate prize of Jerusalem. The victory, very unfortunately, was accompanied by a vicious and cruel slaughter of Jews, Muslims, and even Christians in the city, chronicled by both Christian and Muslim writers. Many Muslim historians refer to the arrival of the Christians not as a crusade but as a Frankish invasion, and they describe the carnage as the result of the acts of savage and cruel Western Christian barbarians. American Christians eager to understand something of the history of Christian-Muslim relations before engaging in serious interfaith conversation would do well to read works such as Amin Maalouf's *The Crusades Through Arab Eyes*[10] in order to better understand why the events of the Crusades are of such importance to Muslims today, particularly when it is they who are accused of fostering a religion of violence and atrocity.

Even the prize of Jerusalem was not enough to ensure a successful Christian rule over the city, and initial crusader zeal gave way to territorial squabbling on the part of Christian rulers. The violent attack from the west in the form of the crusading armies took the world of Islam by surprise, and it was more than half a century before Muslims gathered their forces to move against the Christian invaders in a call for *jihad*. By 1187, the Christian hold on the Holy Land was effectively ended. The great Muslim leader Saladin (Salah al-Din) regained Jerusalem for Islam nearly a century after the first Christian invasion. Saladin's treatment of the Christian population was reported to be humane and reasonable, in notable contrast to the way in which Christians had dealt with Muslims and Jews upon their arrival in Jerusalem.

Further crusading attempts, six in all, over the next several centuries failed to regain the revered prize. During these crusading centuries, while armies fought over their lands, indigenous Muslims and Christians continued to find ways to coexist and sometimes even cooperate, although they constituted two separate societies with their own laws and administration. Battles were pitched, but Christians and Muslims continued as always to carry out their commercial activities uninterrupted. Unfortunately, piracy and pillaging continued, with numerous prisoners sold in slave markets and women prisoners in particular victimized. The Crusades remain a serious blot on the history of interfaith relations, and as indicated above, are portrayed by many Muslims today as the beginning of a multifaceted series of Western imperialist invasions of Muslim lands.

The Middle Ages: Images of the Other

The Christian West in the Middle Ages found it very difficult to formulate a coherent vision of Islam, constrained by its own narrow horizons as well as by a lack of sufficient and accurate information. It was primarily in Spain, where the two communities plus Jews were in a close and, for awhile, reasonably pacific relationship that a clearer picture of the religion of Islam as such emerged in the West. Two quite different populations had an interest in presenting a vision of Islam. First, there were descriptions of Muslims that appealed to the common people. These were fostered primarily by the propaganda that led up to and supported the Crusades and fed by the largely inaccurate information from popular literature such as the *Chansons de Geste,* filled with adventure, romance, warfare and chivalry, and by the tales brought back by numerous visitors and pilgrims to the Middle East.[11] Interestingly, in the literature of the Crusades the Saracens (one of the early terms used in the West for Muslims) are often portrayed as brave and noble, worthy enemies of the Christian knights; their primary fault lay in their following such a depraved religion as Islam. There was an understanding that Franks and Arabs shared a world and even a culture in which certain ideals such as chivalry, loyalty, and bravery were reflected. The goal was not the extermination of the enemy, but the conversion of as many as possible. Unfortunately such respect for character and skill, if not for religion, has not found its way into much of the succeeding Christian discourse about the Crusade period.

The scholastics propagated the other vision of Islam, emerging to a great extent in Spain. A few Christian philosophers attempted a serious study of Islam, but often in the form of a dialogical argument between Christians and Muslims in which Muslims never fared well. Both scholastic and popular writings tended to be contemptuous and even abusive of the Prophet, portraying him throughout his life as a prime example of sensuality, immorality, and violence. This analysis was based both on critique of what they thought they knew about the life and teachings of the founder of Islam and on the actual experiences Christians had of Muslims invading their lands and profaning their churches.

From the emergence of Islam and its immediate challenge to the West, Christians never really believed that Islam was any kind of serious alternative to Christian truth. Christians experienced feelings of both revulsion and fascination toward the Prophet and his religion. Muhammad was almost universally thought of as a man of depravity, dishonor, falsehood, and illicit power. In addition, he was portrayed in various texts as a sexual libertine, demonstrated most specifically by the facts of his own multiple marriages and the details of the Qur'anic descriptions of the sexual pleasures of paradise. Islam, these Christian writers felt, was a religion utterly devoid of spirituality. It was to such a text, written by a Byzantine Emperor in the medieval period, that Pope Benedict XVI made an unfortunate reference in September 2006, recalling classic Christian critique of Islam as "evil and inhuman."

Efforts at a better understanding of Islam, unfortunately, were not reflected in the work of the giants of the Protestant Reformation. German reformer Martin Luther, for example, described the Turks as God's rods of chastisement come to punish wayward Christians, specifically the Roman Catholics. The Swiss theologian John Calvin also likened the Turks to his more immediate enemies, the Papists, attributing to them both the evils of gross deception.[12] Luther and Calvin, the bedrocks of Protestant Christianity, portrayed Muhammad as equal to the devil, and called the Qur'an foul and shameful.

Islam continued to be seen technically by the church as a heresy, although popular literature more often referred to Muslims as pagans. In sum, the general response of Christians over the centuries has been that Prophet Muhammad was a warmonger and a libertine, and that his Qur'an was a terrible and satanic parody of scripture. These images have remained strong in Christian consciousness, and continue to present a serious obstacle to the fostering of harmonious Christian-Muslim relations. Even now reflections of these negative responses can be seen in the statements of some evangelical Christian leaders in America, described in greater detail in chapter six.

For the most part, Muslim responses to Christians have been hardly more charitable. Throughout the Middle Ages and beyond, the vast majority of Muslims had little if any knowledge of the western regions of Christendom, as well as little interest in discovering anything about lands they considered bleak and remote, inhabited by peoples they thought to be little more than barbarians. They considered the Europeans' manners and habits to be loathsome, their level of culture exceedingly low, and their religion to have been superceded by Islam. Even Muslim travelers, with a few exceptions such as the geographer al-Masudi, preferred to go east to areas that they believed were more civilized. What few reports are available come from geographers from the far western reaches of the Islamic empire, namely Andalusia and North Africa. The great Muslim historian and philosopher Ibn Khaldun noted that the qualities of those living to the north are akin to what one finds in animals living in savage isolation.

A body of Islamic literature did develop dealing with Christian doctrine, but it was primarily for reasons of polemic and refutation. As was true with Christian polemic against Islam,[13] Muslims sought to support their refutation by looking to their own scripture. The relatively rare times that Christians and Muslims did engage in theological discussion it was characterized by debate grounded in each party's assurance that its own scripture was infallible. Such retreat into their internal assumptions by both parties doomed the dialogue to failure. While some efforts to understand Islam on its own scriptural terms and to present Christian apologetic in ways that are most sympathetic to that understanding can be found in early century Christian apologetics;[14] it has not been until fairly recently in the history of Christian-Muslim relations that either side has engaged in discourse or defense on the basis of serious study of the other's scriptural texts.

This general lack of interest on the part of medieval Muslims in the lands of Western Christianity did not mean, however, that the Christian religion itself was not a matter of concern for many Islamic theologians and scholars. As Christians could not be persuaded by the Qur'an, a scripture they considered to be false, Muslims could not be persuaded by the New Testament, a scripture they believed to be distorted from its original form. The early centuries of Islam saw a number of Muslim efforts to refute the doctrines of Christianity, particularly as they were acquired through Christians living in Arab lands. The terms of the argumentation gradually changed from scripture to philosophy, and as early as the ninth century the Arab philosopher al-Kindi used Aristotelian logic to combat the Christian idea of the trinity. The eleventh century Maliki jurist al-Baqillani used sophisticated philosophical arguments in his refutation of the claims of Jesus' divinity.[15] The most famous of the critics of Christianity of the late Middle Ages was the fourteenth century Muslim theologian Ibn Taymiyya, whose work of over a thousand pages argued vociferously against the possibility of the incarnation of God in Christ. It provides a good example of the way in which challenges between Christianity and Islam were much more often made through the process of textual refutation than through actual face-to-face exchange. Many Muslims today still look to Ibn Taymiyya as having provided the definitive refutation of Christian theology.

On the Christian side, missionary activity, especially on the part of Dominican and Franciscan friars, continued in the hope of converting Muslims to Christianity. This activity had the fortunate consequence of encouraging more serious study of Islam and Arabic on the part of Western scholars. It has long been recognized that one of the most significant and lasting contributions of the medieval Muslim world to Christendom was to provide access for Western scholars to the great classics of Greece and Rome by their translations from Arabic, from which they were rendered into European languages. Contemporary Muslims make much of this important contribution of Islam to Western understanding of the classics, although they seldom mention the fact that the survival of Greek philosophy in the world of Islam came not because Muslims knew Greek, but through the work done by Arab and Assyrian Christians in translating the classics into Syriac, and then to Arabic.

Christian and Muslim interactions in the Middle Ages were marked both by strife and warfare and by occasions of harmonious relations. Official tensions and hostilities at the political level were often balanced by local cooperation and even friendships between members of the two faiths, yet the seeds of mistrust and antipathy sown from the rise of Islam continued to grow. A very important milestone in the history of interfaith relationship came in 1453, when the city of Constantinople fell to the invading Muslim armies. For over eleven centuries Constantinople had been the capital of the Byzantine empire. Its fall to the Turks signaled a dramatic change in the power relationships between Islam and Christendom. Having a base in Anatolia allowed the Ottoman sultans the chance to lay siege on Vienna in 1542, from which position they remained a threat to the heartlands of Europe. By the end of the Middle Ages hostilities between Islam and Western Christendom were once again at a high level, and for several centuries wars continued to break out on a number of fronts.

The Beginnings of Modernity

Nonetheless, the rise of rationalism, a growing fascination on the part of the West with the cultural trappings of the East, and the necessities of international political and economic exchange soon moved the worlds of Islam and Christendom closer. Westerners who traveled to Istanbul for business, politics or pleasure found themselves intrigued by the glories of the court and enchanted by the "mysterious" east. While serious-minded theologically oriented Christians never really believed that Islam could be a viable alternative to their own faith, or even compatible with it, in the eyes of many visitors Turks became the patrons of an engaging culture. The very mystery of Islam, allowing for the existence of secret harems in which exotic women performed their rituals of seduction for the sultan, both shocked and fascinated the Westerners at home and abroad.

Several important things began to happen somewhere around the middle of the eighteenth century that deeply affected relationships between the Muslim East and the Christian West. One was initiated by Muslims themselves, and another by Westerners, most of whom were Christian, even if religion was not necessarily seen as the motivation for action. Muslims since the early days of their existence had created magnificent empires that were at once opulent and worldly, and were sponsors of some of the greatest spiritual developments in human history. Art, poetry, philosophy, mathematics, medicine, and many other disciplines reached new levels of glory and achievement. The Islamic atmosphere in which they developed encouraged an understanding that these arts and sciences were interrelated, as all were related to the oneness and being of God. In the eighteenth century the three great empires of the world—the Moghul, the Persian, and the Ottoman—were all Islamic. But the great days were waning, and both politically and culturally Muslims found themselves falling behind to scientific and other achievements of the West. This decline was also fostered by the intrusion of Western colonialism, which reduced the income of the empires from trade, leading in many cases to economic impoverishment. Thus, the first of the important developments of the modern age was the struggle on the part of Muslims to determine if their future lay in trying to emulate the West or in returning to the religion and culture that had served them so well for so long. In some senses, that struggle still continues.

On the Western front, so to speak, several things began to happen. One was the rise of the Protestant missionary movement and its attempts to bring Christian teaching and thus Western culture into Muslim countries. The second, intrinsically related to the first, was the rise of Western imperialism and a new series of incursions of the West—economically, politically, militarily, and in other ways—into Muslim lands. Another interesting development, discussed in the next chapter, is the beginning of a real breakdown of the categories of East and West themselves as Muslims gradually began to make Western Europe and America their home.

Missions and imperialism are both important elements in the growing feelings of hostility toward the West and America on the part of many Muslims in the world today, feelings that must be acknowledged as important to honest conversation in contemporary dialogues. The establishment of Christian missions to Islamic lands was started by Catholic mendicant orders in the thirteenth century. Catholic orders have been working in the Muslim world ever since. One of the best known among them is the Jesuit order, founded in 1534. Jesuits have been long recognized both for their scholarly work on Islam and for their close personal relationships with Muslims. Protestant missions did not appear with any serious intent until the Pietist movements of the eighteenth century, perhaps most notably with the founding of the Baptist Missionary Society. One of the major pioneers in Christian mission to Muslims was Henry Martyn (d. 1812), whose contributions to a better understanding of Islam through the translation of the Qur'an and other Islamic texts is acknowledged in the continuing interfaith activity of the Henry Martyn Institute in Hyderabad, India.

Protestant missions grew vigorously between the time of the French Revolution and the beginning of World War I, and experienced their heyday in the interwar period in Syria, Palestine, Lebanon, Egypt, Iraq, and Arabia. They continued to be influential until these nations got their independence and banned missionary activity in their lands. The driving force of the mission movement, beyond the important element of service through work, especially in medicine and education, continued to be the hope of bringing Muslims to the faith of Christianity. Not surprisingly, that hope has always been interpreted by Muslims as the desire for the ultimate disappearance of Islam itself. While many Protestant missionaries developed warm personal relations with the Muslims they served, their attitudes toward the faith of Islam and its founder were rooted in the heritage of Christian denigration of Islam. This heritage is still illustrated today, both subtly and blatantly, in the preaching of a number of prominent evangelicals and in the curricula of some theological schools training persons for ministry to, and conversion of, Muslims. This theme will be developed in more detail later. Over the past century Christians have realized relatively few conversions of Muslims to Christianity, despite the efforts of dedicated missionaries and the conviction of many evangelicals that Islam is on the wane.

While Muslims acknowledge the important humanitarian service provided by many missionaries, the negative Christian attitudes toward Islam that they believe to be illustrated both in missionary activity and in much academic scholarship has not served to promote warm relationships between members of the two faiths. It is sometimes amusing for Muslims to observe, more or less correctly, that the actual number of their rank who have adopted Christianity as a result of missionary endeavors has been negligible. Nonetheless, the information gained by missionaries who have worked in Muslim cultures has gone far toward providing a much more accurate understanding of Islam for those who live in the West.

The Twentieth Century and Beyond

Among the harshest realities affecting Christian-Muslim relationships over the past century has been Western imperialism, with which missionary activity often has been associated. After World War I, the Ottoman Empire was dismembered and the League of Nations established Western mandates over most of the Middle East. It is difficult to overestimate the continuing repercussions of

Western colonialism across the Islamic world. Conversations between Muslims and Christians in the West must be based on an informed understanding of the lasting effects of colonialism on Muslims. Christians who want to engage in serious interaction with Muslims must understand that their outlook on life, and on living in the West, is inevitably deeply colored by their experiences with colonialism, whether or not they come from a country that itself was colonized by Western powers.

The fact of Western occupation of most Islamic countries has played a very significant role in the political and theological reflection of Muslims all over the world. The twentieth century saw many agonizing struggles in countries with Muslim majority populations to free themselves from Western rule. Unfortunately, in the eyes of many Muslims, the West, and in the twentieth century the United States, has continued to exert its power and influence in those areas in which its own self-interest is at stake. Most recently the American incursions into Iraq have been viewed almost universally in the Muslim world as another very visible manifestation of U.S. invasion of the land of Islam for its own purposes, this time in the hope of exploiting Iraq's oil. For over half a century, Islamic countries have looked with shock and anger at American Christian political and moral support of the Zionist presence in the heart of the Muslim Middle East, with only lip service paid to the provision for a Palestinian state with integrity.

Relations between Muslims and Christians today are also experiencing difficult times in parts of the world where the two communities have coexisted for many generations, due partly to American foreign policy decisions and partly to circumstances internal to individual nation states. In many regions of Asia, Africa, and the Middle East, political tensions, historical antagonisms, and economic realities create conditions in which religio-political dominance seems to be a preferable alternative to peaceful habitation. Some countries, particularly in Africa, are finding that after centuries of living together without conflict, they are experiencing pressures from both evangelical Christians and revivalist Muslims that serve to polarize the communities in new and unproductive ways.

Efforts are underway in different contexts and venues to bring Christians and Muslims together for conversation and to help them work together to resolve religious conflicts. Centers for dialogue and action have existed for many years in different parts of the world. The establishment of the World Council of Churches (WCC) in Geneva, Switzerland, in 1948, whose members include Protestants and Orthodox but not Roman Catholics, provided the opportunity for other forms of Christian dialogue with Muslims. The first such organized dialogues took place in the late 1960s, and have continued regularly in various parts of the world, with various agendas and different constituencies. The name of the WCC unit concerned with interfaith dialogue has changed several times; most currently it is called "Interreligious Relations and Dialogue (IRRD)." The IRRD provides resources for program planning on interfaith dialogue, and is located within the WCC's office of the General Secretariat. Because of declining financial resources the activities of the IRRD have recently been cut back. As of this writing, the staff position in Christian-Muslim relations is vacant.

For Roman Catholics, the Second Vatican Council from 1962 to 1965 signaled the start of new ways of thinking about and relating to other religions, and its statement that the Church "has a high regard" for Muslims clearly pointed toward a dramatically new orientation in Catholic response to the religion of Islam. The legacy of a painful past was to be put aside in favor of new ways of achieving mutual understanding. The Secretariat for Non-Christians, later called the Pontifical Council for Interreligious Dialogue, has been the vehicle for promoting this new attitude and for formulating new initiatives at dialogue. In the 1960s Catholic guidelines for dialogue between Christians and Muslims were published, and have since been revised several times. Recent signals from the Vatican, however, may suggest that new papal leadership is moving the church in a more conservative direction, with potential implications for interfaith relationships. In the United States, the United States Conference of Catholic Bishops and the National Council of Churches have fostered the work of interfaith relations and sponsored a number of ongoing dialogues.

Muslim reflection on Christianity over the last several decades has taken place primarily through recent, and now growing, attempts to think seriously about the reality of religious pluralism. Many Muslims are struggling to balance what the Qur'an says about Christianity, as well as about religious diversity, with the long history of stormy relationships between the communities. They are also affected by what they see as contemporary Western Christian support of political policies and activities with which they deeply disagree, and by the anti-Western and anti-Christian rhetoric of revivalist Islam. Christian and Muslim efforts to think seriously about theological responses to the other will be examined more closely in succeeding chapters.

Muslims in America and Western Europe find themselves subject to many conflicting pressures. Some adhere to the view that they should take an isolationist stand and eschew involvement in Western public life, including interfaith activities. All Muslims living in the West are keenly aware of the persistent negative stereotyping of Islam on the part of the media, of the prejudice and fear that continues to linger and to be manifested in the general public, and of the deep concerns they themselves have about elements of Western society and the dangers of becoming too deeply involved in its ethos. As recent world events have ratcheted up the level both of Western Christian fear of Islam and interest in knowing more about Islam, many Muslims are responding by sharing information, holding mosque open-houses to which Christians are invited, and accepting invitations to meet and talk with Christians about their faith and practice.

As they think about relating to Muslims, Christians now must deal with the heritage of what they have long seen as Muslim aggression and invasion, as well as their own history of prejudice and misunderstanding. They must also reflect on their own history of repeated acts of aggression against Islam and Muslims. Getting a perspective on this history is complicated by the reality of international instances of terrorist activity perpetrated in the name of Islam. Muslims who are trying to promote better interfaith relations are recognizing that they must come to terms with a past that they see riddled with Christian territorial intrusion and with deep-seeded antipathy toward Islam and its Prophet. Many are also taking responsibility for the fact of Islamic incursions into Christian territories over many centuries. The immediate future seems to hold the promise both of continued alienation between the faiths regionally and globally, and the hope that the urgency of reaching mutual understanding, appreciation, and cooperation will be understood to be vital to the well-being of a large measure of humankind.

3

Islam

A Truly American Religion?

American Muslims comprise the most diverse Islamic community that has ever existed anywhere in the world. They are immigrants and American born, with an estimated thirty to forty percent of their population consisting of African Americans. Most are Sunni, though the number of Shi'ites has grown to nearly twenty percent. Many Muslims prefer not to use the category immigrant but refer rather to those who are American born and those who are foreign born, the latter including students and other sojourners in the United States. Some American Muslims are conservative in their outlook, hoping to keep customs from their country of origin alive in their religious practices, while others are looking for ways to formulate an American Islam that is at home and comfortable in the West. Most of the Muslims whom other Americans are likely to encounter in Christian-Muslim dialogue adhere to an orthodox understanding of Islam, assuming the structure of beliefs and practices generally common to Sunnis and Shi'ites, although America fosters a wide range of heterodox movements that often claim the label Muslim.

"How many Muslims are there in America today? Is it true that Islam is the fastest growing religion?" Religious professionals generally try to avoid such questions, which they get constantly from reporters and others interested in writing and talking about the phenomenon of American Islam, because exact figures are impossible to determine. It is estimated that four decades ago there were fewer than half a million Muslims in the United States, including immigrants and African Americans. Reasonable estimates today range between three million to seven million, often depending on whether the reporter has a vested interest in portraying the Muslim community as quite large or quite small. American Muslims are deeply involved in determining what it means to be part of the "*ummah* [community] in the West," and through the development of Islamic organizations, increasing numbers of local and national meetings and conferences, and rapidly proliferating communications via the Internet, they are in the process of determining the nature and validity of an indigenous American Islam.

Islam Comes to America

Most histories of Islam in America begin with the saga of Middle Easterners who came to seek their fortunes in the latter part of the nineteenth and early twentieth centuries. While the majority of these Arabs were Christian, a small group of Sunni, Shi'ite, 'Alawi, and Druze Muslims hoped to earn enough money as peddlers and small merchants to return to Greater Syria (the current states of Lebanon, Syria, Jordan, Palestine, and Israel, then ruled by the Ottoman Empire). This dream of return was part of the experience of most immigrants throughout the first half of the last century, and in most cases, was not realized. Slowly the number of Muslim immigrants began to increase, and they settled throughout America both in large cities and in rural areas. The story of this early assimilation is important to both Arab Christians and Arab Muslims, and many Americans fail to make a distinction between them. Since 9/11 Christian Arabs frequently have suffered from the prejudice of those Americans who expect all Middle Easterners to be Muslim, just as they often assume that all people with swarthy complexions are Muslim, as Sikhs, and others have learned to their dismay. It is important for Christian participants in interfaith dialogue to be aware of this history as well as of the current circumstances of all Arab Americans and others who may be part of the conversation.

With the end of World War I, the dissolution of the Ottoman Empire, and the beginning of Western colonial rule in Arab lands, another wave of immigration came from the Middle East. This time a higher percentage of the new arrivals was Muslim, many leaving their homeland for political as well as economic reasons. Often they came to live with relatives and friends from home. One of the most popular destinations for both Sunnis and Shi'ites from the Arab world, as well as Arab Christians, is the Detroit area. Many settled in nearby Dearborn, drawn by the possibility of work at the Ford Motor plant. Muslims and Christians together in Dearborn constitute the largest settlement of Middle

Easterners in America. In the early 1920s new U.S. immigration laws imposed quotas on various populations, including Arabs. The numbers of Muslims and Christians coming to this country dropped significantly, especially as immigration was officially limited to the relatives of people already living in the United States, at the rate of one hundred per year. A small number of Southeast Asians were part of what was call the "Hindoo" presence in America in the late 1800s. A few more came in the 1920s and following, primarily from what is now the nation of Pakistan. They were the Ahmadis, and their mission was to translate the Qur'an and preach to would-be converts in the United States. They have not attracted wide numbers of white American converts, although their ranks have grown through the allegiance of African Americans. Ahmadis have played an important role in providing translations of the Qur'an into many different languages, but they are considered heterodox by most Sunni Muslims.[1]

Immediately after World War II, and continuing until about 1960, Muslims arrived in America. Their population began to change significantly, however, as new residents now came from many countries outside of the Middle East such as eastern Europe, mainly Yugoslavia, Albania, and Russia (some Russian Tatars had come after the Russian Revolution of 1917). A few Muslims came to America from the Subcontinent, when India was partitioned and the state of Pakistan was established in 1947, although they were still limited by the Asia Exclusion Act. By this time Muslim immigrants tended to be better educated, more urban, and more westernized than their forebears, and settled primarily in major cities. They came not simply to make a living, but with plans to continue their education and technical training in the institutions of higher education in the United States.

A major wave of immigrants from Muslim countries has made its appearance after 1965, the year in which President Lyndon Johnson repealed the quota system. This important ruling made a tremendous difference in the immigrant population in the United States, as people from a variety of countries were able to come to this country for the first time without regard to their national or ethnic origin. Muslim populations continued to arrive from the Middle East, East, and South Asia, with significant numbers joining them from Africa, Eastern Europe, Turkey, and most other parts of the world. While many Muslims still come to America for purposes of continuing their education, in recent years a large number have also appeared as a result of the political turmoil in many parts of the Muslim world.

Much of that turmoil is the result of earlier nationalist movements struggling for independence from Western colonialist powers. Many Muslims have arrived on American shores in the status of refugees seeking escape and asylum from repression in their homelands. The defeat of the Arab armies at the hands of Israel in 1967, for example, began an exodus of Muslims and Christians to both America and Western Europe, as did the civil war in Lebanon. Refugees have been arriving in Europe and the United States from Bosnia, Kosovo, and Afghanistan in steady streams, as have those from Somalia and other areas of strife-torn Africa.

Immigrants and Their American-Born Descendants

Many Christians looking to establish contacts within the Muslim community in recent years for purposes of dialogue and conversation have found South Asians from Pakistan and India to be particularly amenable. One reason, of course, is that English has been a second, or sometimes even first, language for them since childhood. Another reason is that often South Asians and their descendants—many of whom are skilled professionals such as doctors and engineers—are among the most vocal Muslims in the American context in attempting to formulate an Islamic response to the events of 9/11. While some South Asians do prefer to remain apart from American society and to resist assimilation to whatever extent possible, others play an important role in the development of Muslim political groups in America and in lay leadership of mosque communities. Many of the latter believe that participation in dialogue is an important way to carry out that work. Muzammil Siddiqi, for example, Director of the Islamic Society of Orange Country in California and former President of the Islamic Society of North America (ISNA), has been active in dialogue for many years and has played an important role on the national scene in helping interpret Islam after 9/11. While South Asians made up only a small part of the Muslim population in the United States in the earlier decades of the twentieth century, various kinds of conflicts, as well as the desire for higher education and economic advantage, have brought many from the Subcontinent to America as well as England. In the last several decades, their numbers have reached well over a million in the Unites States.

As much as one sixth of the American Muslim population today is Iranian, and thus Shi'ite.[2] They began to arrive following the success of Imam Khomeini and the Iranian Revolution of 1979, which came after a long and devastating war between Iran and Iraq. Many Iranian intellectuals who had been close to the Shah were forced to flee, including Seyyed Hossein Nasr, now teaching at American University in Washington, D.C., and one of the most sought-after participants in Muslim-Christian dialogue in America. Iranians have settled in many urban areas of the United States, with a large population now found in

California. Iranian Muslims have had to deal with many manifestations of prejudice on the part of U.S. citizens, caught between the accusations of Ayatollahs Khomeini and now Khameni that the United States is the "Great Satan," and George Bush's labeling of Iran as part of the "Axis of Evil." Tensions are heightened again today in light of what most Americans believe to be the attempts of Iran to develop nuclear powers, the refusal of the current administration to talk to Iran, and the intransigence of the present Iranian regime toward the United States.

Among the refugees from troubled Muslim areas of the world seeking a home in America are Kurds, Africans from such states as Somalia and Sudan, and Muslims who have suffered the infamous "ethnic cleansing" in the former Yugoslavia. Attempts at interfaith dialogue in the United States often have foundered because American participants fail to understand the heavy load of political and personal baggage Muslims bring with them. It is difficult for many of them to talk about their religion in the abstract, without grounding their explanations in the real life experiences that have defined their personal identity and their nationalist sensitivities. Life in the West, while it may be physically less challenging for refugees than the circumstances they have fled, can often be psychologically extremely difficult. Americans—who are often not well informed about international affairs—notoriously have had difficulty understanding the diversity that characterizes the Muslim community in America, as well as the range of reasons why they have chosen to come. While Arabs, South and Southeast Asians perhaps have been the most visible Muslims coming from immigrant backgrounds, increasing numbers are arriving from Turkey, Eastern Europe, and numerous countries of Africa.

Muslims from many different countries of the world are assuming important leadership positions in the American Muslim community today, and are also playing prominent roles in Christian and Muslim dialogue. From the African continent Sulayman Nyang, originally from Gambia and now a professor at Howard University in Washington, has been a regular participant in the dialogue, as has South African liberation theologian Farid Esack, who teaches regularly in the United States. Turkish followers of the twentieth century reformer Said Nursi are becoming increasingly active in initiating interfaith dialogue. Both Sunni and Shi'ite Arab Muslims, who make up an important segment of American Islam and are mainly well-educated professionals, are being drawn into conversation with Christians, with Lebanese and Palestinians particularly active. Among the most deeply involved Palestinians in such exchanges several decades ago was the late Ismail al Faruqi of Temple University, who was uniquely prepared for a deep level of discourse because of his level of scholarship in Christian theology and ethics. His seminal work on Abrahamic dialogue[3] has served as a basic text for the consideration of interfaith issues. Today Arabs such as Egyptian Mohamed Fathi Osman and Kuwaiti American Khalid Abu El Fadl are active in articulating an understanding of Qur'anic pluralism as a basis for interfaith understanding. Lebanese scholar Mahmoud Ayoub has dedicated much of his academic career to fostering interfaith relations, and has written extensively on ways in which to interpret the Qur'an so as to make possible better understanding between Christians and Muslims. Pakistani-born Zahid Bukhari, co-director of the "Muslims in the American Public Square" project at Georgetown University,[4] is a frequent participant in Christian-Muslim conversations. The works of Osman, Abu El Fadl, and Ayoub, along with Seyyed Hossein Nasr, will be dealt with at length below.

African American Islam

Adding to the complexity of the contemporary picture of Islam in America is the fact that for many decades significant numbers of African Americans have considered themselves to be Muslim. In actual fact, the earliest presence of Islam in America was that of African slaves seized for plantation work in the South. Recent studies show that many were probably Muslim, forced by slave-masters to convert to Christianity. The earliest recorded African American groups that identified themselves in some way or other with Islam were early twentieth-century black freedom movements looking for an affiliation apart from the America that continued to discriminate against them. The Moorish Science Temple, for example, founded by Noble Drew Ali, developed a vaguely constructed identity with the Moors of Asia. Drew Ali's *Holy Qur'an,* which until recently was considered secret and to be read only by members of the Temple, has little if anything in common with the Holy Qur'an revered by Muslims as the word of God. The Moorish Science Temple has had a rocky history, but still exists as one of the many sectarian movements in America claiming Islamic identity.[5]

The most noteworthy of the black liberation movements that ran under the banner of Islam was the Nation of Islam (NOI). It was initiated by a person of questionable identity named Fard, who is said to have taught the essence of Islam to Elijah Muhammad, a black man from Detroit with little formal education. Under Elijah Muhammad, the Nation grew rapidly in the 1930s, '40s, and '50s, providing important ways for African Americans in this country to find pride in themselves, ethical responsibility, and communal support. The Nation may have had more in common with orthodox Islam than groups like the

Moorish Temple, but its reverence for Fard and Elijah Muhammad seemed to many to impinge on doctrines of God's oneness and the final status of Prophet Muhammad as Messenger of Islam. Perhaps more practically important, the NOI doctrine that whites are devils obviously contravened the Muslim doctrine of the absolute equality of all people. The famous pilgrimage of NOI spokesman Malcolm X to Mecca in 1964[6] led to his rejection of any NOI teachings that did not coordinate with what he understood to be true Islam. He was assassinated soon after.[7]

When Elijah Muhammad died in 1975, leadership of the Nation of Islam fell to Elijah's son Wallace, who later took the name Warith Deen Mohammed. Wallace, who had classical training in Arabic and the Islamic sciences, gradually moved his followers away from the teachings of his father and into the understanding of orthodox Islam. Muslim ministers came to be called Imams, temples changed to mosques, and practices such as fasting and praying were adjusted to meet the requirements of orthodox Islam. Warith Deen's groups have gone through a number of name changes, reflecting where they were on their journey out of the Nation and into Sunni Islam. Often the group is referred to as the American Society of Muslims, adopted in 2002, or simply the Ministry of Warith Deen Muhammad. Even more recently as part of his growing interfaith interests Warith Deen established "The Mosque Cares/W.D.M. Ministry, dedicated to "Compassion, Commitment and Conscience: Foundations for Interfaith Dialogue."[8]

Warith Deen several times has announced his retirement, but as of this writing he continues to be very active and seems to be taking his followers on a more spiritual path than earlier. In 1977, Warith Deen's associate Louis Farrakhan broke away from the group and reestablished the Nation of Islam on the basis of Elijah Muhammad's original teachings. The outspoken Farrakhan recently has resigned as the NOI's leader, acknowledging that he suffers from a very serious illness. Although the Nation is strongly criticized by Sunni Muslims for its beliefs, it nonetheless is admired for the quality of its work with the needy and in ridding neighborhoods of drugs and unwanted substances. Farrakhan has periodically promises his old friend and theological sparring partner Warith Deen that he has seen the light and will renounce Nation ideologies for the truth of Sunni Islam, but thus far he has not made the move.

One of the many significant challenges facing Muslims in America today is finding commonality, both among the many communities that have their roots in societies outside America, and between those of immigrant background and the various African American Muslim groups. African

American Christians and Muslims have had little conversation with each other, as the example in chapter one suggests, and efforts to involve African Americans in other interfaith dialogue have had only limited success. Most often they simply are not included in conversations initiated by either Christians or Muslims, although this situation is changing slightly as African Americans find their voice in the larger Muslim community. When they are asked to participate it is often on a token basis, with one or two African Americans joining a much larger group of other Muslims, both American born and immigrant. This situation can lead to frustration and resentment. As Africans immigrants become more visible on the American scene, and are more often involved in dialogue, the failure of many non-Muslim Americans to distinguish between them and African Americans is troublesome for all parties.

When I asked Muslims both from immigrant families and those of African American heritage who they thought was more open to involvement in interfaith exchange, I found consistency in the responses: Immigrants think that they are more receptive and interested, and African Americans think the same of themselves. It seems reasonable that African American Muslims who either were once Christian, or have Christians in their families, may find it easier to relate to Christians. "We know where we're coming from!" In general African Americans are better at dialogue with Christians than immigrants, Imam Plemon Amin of Atlanta once commented to me, because it is part of their own heritage and they understand Christianity better. Or as Sulayman Nyang put it, "it's like a family affair." Families, however, have their tensions, and as we have seen, so often do black Christians and black Muslims.

Imam Warith Deen Mohammed has strongly encouraged African Americans to rebuild their family ties and to reaffirm their connection with their Christian heritage. His colleague Ayesha Mustafa, editor of *The Muslim Journal*, said that these connections actually encourage Muslims to participate in interfaith conversations. At various times Imam Warith Deen has made it clear that he believes interfaith dialogues will serve to foster a better understanding of Islam, that they will help provide contexts in which common work on social issues can proceed, and that in general they will go far in creating in America an environment more responsive to the presence of Muslims. Some followers of Warith Deen feel that he is not particularly interested in black on black dialogue, believing that most black Christians are primarily interested in identifying white racism as a common bond. He himself does not want to be concerned with that, instead looking for theological dialogue that does not haggle over points of belief but provides opportunities for exchange so as to enhance the mutual understanding of God.

Sketches of American Islam

It is nearly impossible today to find cities, towns and areas of the United States in which Muslims are not living. They represent a wide range of professional choices, while their children attend public schools (a very small number go to alternative Islamic schools) and interact daily with children from many religious traditions. Muslims are our physicians and our shopkeepers, our schoolteachers and our artisans. Many Americans may not know that they are in everyday contact with a Muslim if that person chooses not to wear identifying dress or otherwise practice his or her faith openly.[9]

Muslims who need a common place of worship increasingly have some recognizable facility, whether it is a purpose-built mosque, a renovated house, or even a remodeled storefront. Muslims first organized for prayers in such places as North Dakota, Indiana, where an Islamic Center was begun in 1914, and Cedar Rapids, Iowa, where the oldest mosque in the country is still in use. During the late 1970s and 1980s Saudi Arabia provided money for building mosques in North America, and a number of eye-catching structures arose in various parts of the country. Today most communities who want to have acknowledged places of worship, either renovate buildings (sometimes even former churches) or go through the process of fundraising to build a mosque or Islamic Center. An American mosque may represent a very traditional structure with dome and minaret(s) or may be indistinguishable from any of the other buildings in its area.

It is to the major cities of the country that Muslims have primarily been drawn. For over a century, for example, Muslims have been present in Boston, many of them attracted by work at the shipyards in Quincy. Individuals and families, who made the south shore area of Boston their home in the early years of the twentieth century, gathered for worship and eventually built a mosque in Quincy. That mosque, along with a newer one constructed in Sharon, combine to form an Islamic complex that serves the religious needs of both professionals and blue-collar workers. Boston is home to a great many places of worship for long-time residents representing a variety of racial-ethnic groupings as well as for students at its many universities, and is the location of some of the most visible interfaith efforts in the country. Talal Eid, for many years the Imam and director of religious affairs in Quincy and Sharon, has worked extensively with Christians, Jews, and Muslims in developing dialogues in the greater Boston area. The many universities of Boston contribute to the intellectual appreciation of the interfaith experience, as in the fall 2004 Boson University conference on "The Role of the Arts in Deepening Christian-Muslim Dialogue" in which lectures were interspersed with musical selections from both traditions.

New York City, the largest metropolitan area in America, has had a visible Islamic presence for well over one hundred years, including business people, merchants and tradesmen, seamen, and educators. As the city is an amalgam of cultures, races and ethnic varieties, this range is represented by Muslims who come from virtually everywhere in the world. Mosques have multiplied all over the city, and most recently have been featured in photographic essays in several journals. Many Muslims living in New York and in nearby New Jersey have been active locally and nationally in promoting Christian-Muslim dialogue, including Ghazi Khankan of the Islamic Center of Long Island, Imam Hamad Ahmad Chebli of the Islamic Society of Greater New Jersey, and Khurshid Khan of the Islamic Circle of North America (ICNA) in Jamaica, New York. The greater New York area is a particularly popular place for national Islamic organizations to meet, and the city is home to a large number of Islamic schools.

Dearborn, Michigan, has already been mentioned as the long-time home of Muslims from many places in the world. Dearborn features a number of Sunni and Shi'ite mosques, as well as a great range of stores and businesses selling products for Arabs and Muslims. Some Muslim groups in the Detroit area prefer to stay as tight-knit as possible, choosing not to engage in interfaith activity. Others such as Muhammad Ali Elahi of the Islamic House of Wisdom in Dearborn and Imam Sayed Hassan Qazwini of the Islamic Center of America have been actively involved in Muslim-Christian dialogue for many years. Many Christian churches in the greater Detroit area have been active in reaching out to the Muslim population for conversation and exchange, although sometimes the hope for evangelism is evident. "Dearborn Christians Reach Out to Muslims," ran an online notice in July 2006, telling of the efforts of Dearborn's large Christian Reformed Church to provide help to Muslims in a variety of ways at the same time that they view the Muslim community as a mission field and a venue for preaching the Christian message.

Muslim immigrants found their way to Chicago in the early 1900s, giving it by some estimates the highest percentage of Muslims of any city in America at the time. The Middle East, South, Southeast and Central Asia, the Indian Subcontinent, Eastern Europe, Africa—all are represented in the burgeoning Muslim population of Chicago today. Chicago Muslims have promoted important models of interfaith and intercommunal cooperation, exemplified in the activities of people like Ghulam Hader Asi, formerly of the American Islamic College, and Laleh Bakhtiar of KAZI publications. Some fifty different Muslim groups can be identified in Chicago, which has also been home to the

Ministry of Warith Deen Mohammed as well as to heterodox movements such as the Nation of Islam and the Five Percenters (the Five Percenter movement was founded in 1964 as a spin-off from the Nation of Islam. It is found in a number of large cities in the United States today, spreading a message of black pride especially attractive to African American youth). In April 2006, more than one hundred United Methodist and Muslim leaders in the greater Chicago area created a "Declaration of Relationship" in which they dedicated themselves to mutual love for God, ethical values, continued dialogue, working together for social justice, and watching for instances of anti-Muslim prejudice. They plan to gather annually to affirm the covenant.

It is in Chicago that Harold Vogelaar, emeritus faculty member of the Lutheran School of Theology at Chicago (LSTC), has teamed with his Muslim wife to provide instruction for people thinking about interfaith marriage. It is interesting, he notes, how those for whom religion was never important suddenly find it so when they want to get married.[10] The Lutheran School of Theology has recently received a sizeable grant for the institution of a "Center of Christian-Muslim Engagement for Peace and Justice," whose inaugural conference entitled "Christians and Muslims Together: Owning Our Pasts— Visioning the Future" was held in September 2006. The Center is designed to provide cultural and educational opportunities for Muslims, Christians, and representatives of other faiths to join with each other for mutual enrichment, understanding, healing, and wholeness.

Southern California has attracted large numbers of Muslims, including Iranians among many others. More recent immigrants to this area are often from troubled parts of the world such as Afghanistan, Somalia, and other parts of Africa. One of the largest Muslim organizations in the world is the Islamic Center of Southern California. It has a remarkable physical operation, with a lovely mosque and a great range of other facilities available for Muslims in the area. The Center has a large staff that, among other activities, publishes the widely read journal *The Minaret*. The Islamic Center is one of the major contributors to Christian-Muslim dialogue, particularly under the guidance of brothers Hasan and Maher Hathout, and welcomes people of all faiths to visit its facility and be in conversation with its leaders and members. Californian activists Salam al-Mariati of the Muslim Public Affairs Council and Agha Saeed, founder of the Muslim Political Action Committee, have also been participants in interfaith conversations.

Like many other parts of the United States, Southern California has also found itself the target of a number of efforts by conservative Christians to spread a message of intolerance. At the Islamic Society of Orange County in California, Muslims following the Friday prayers have discovered pamphlets

and flyers strewn around both praising Jesus and promoting hate for Muhammad and Islam. Muslims are discovering that for these Christians, love
and compassion are preached as the Christian way at the same time that the
supposed wrath of Jesus against Muslims is being propagated.[11] Such actions
and comments are being heard and responded to by Muslims around the
world.

Many other cities—including Atlanta, Houston, Dallas, San Francisco,
Denver, Washington, D.C.—are home to significant efforts on the part of Muslims and Christians to help disseminate information about Islam to the American public and to work toward better understanding between Christians and
Muslims. In November 2004, St. John's Episcopal Church in Denver installed
as a member of its staff Imam Ibrahim Kazerooni, a Shi'ite cleric, with the
responsibility for directing the church's Abrahamic Initiative. In Denver, dialogue between the different religious groups is sometimes broadcast live on
local television stations, which Muslims find to be an effective and important
way to explain the beliefs and practices of their faith to the city. Occasionally viewers have the opportunity to call in with questions or comments to
panelists.[12]

Atlanta was the location of the first formal dialogue between African
American Muslim leaders Imam Warith Deen Mohammed and Minister Ava
Muhammad at the Interdenominational Theological Center in 2000, facilitated by Marsha Snulligan Haney of the Interdenominational Theological Center (ITC). Atlanta is also the home of Sisters United in Human Service, Inc.,
an interfaith service organization that networks across faith lines to provide
services in recognition of the oneness of God and of humanity.[13] Dallas hosts
half a dozen or more groups working to promote better dialogue between
Muslims and Christians. In November of 2004 the priest of St. Katharine
Drexel Catholic Church in Fort Lauderdale, Florida, cried when he read about
the bombings of five Catholic churches in Baghdad at the beginning of Ramadan. As a result several South Florida Muslim organizations are pledging to
work with Catholics with the goal of increasing public awareness of religious
persecution, and helping provide the resources for rebuilding the churches.
Acknowledging the history of poor relations between Catholics and Muslims,
the group came together for prayer at Thanksgiving, giving thanks for the opportunity to join together in this work.

A project with interesting potential for other American cities and groups
to try was undertaken in the fall of 2004 in Columbia, South Carolina. The
Rev. H. Lloyd Norris, former pastor at the Martin Luther King Jr. Baptist
Church in town, organized an interfaith event to offer community support to
a mosque, Masjid Noor ul Huda, that had recently opened. Norris contacted

the mosque, and with the participation of some of its members organized a "Community Service of Welcome." Local politicians cooperated by supporting and speaking at the event. "I wasn't really trying to start any kind of continuing dialogue," the Pastor said to me, "I just wanted to structure a model for other communities to emulate." Time will tell whether or not others find the model appealing.

American Attitudes and Muslim Responses

Most Muslims today would say that one of the most difficult aspects of living in America, whether they are American born or immigrant, is the prejudice that Muslims continue to experience, especially in light of the terrorist attacks of 9/11 and subsequent Muslim bombings in various parts of the world. Since 9/11, for example, right-wing rhetoric against Islam has been on the rise, fueled by each instance of international terrorism in which Muslims are implicated. Popular conservative Christian commentators have been prominent in the news for their vitriolic comments. Jerry Falwell has called Muhammad a terrorist; Jerry Vines at a Southern Baptist convention famously referred to the Prophet as a demon-possessed pedophile; Jimmy Swaggart recommended sending every Muslim college student in the nation back to their home country.[14] A conservative Christian radio announcer in Boston on April 23, 2004, said that all Muslims should be killed.[15] Pat Roberson has said that Muhammad was a robber and a brigand, and in 2004 on the Diane Rehm Show denied that Allah could be the same as the Christian God. In response to the violence that erupted in Muslim countries as a result of the Danish cartoon controversy, Robertson said on his "700 Club" news and talk program that Islam is not a religion of peace, and that Muslims are "satanic."

Among the various reasons that Muslims might be interested in interfaith dialogue is the opportunity it affords them to show other Americans that they are "real people" with family values and a clear sense of responsibility as citizens. The existence of prejudice, of course, is nothing new in America. African Americans have long known the pain of exclusion, and Muslims who are black often report that they experience a prejudice in terms of both skin color and religious choice. Immigrants from various cultures have been the victims of anti-Muslim (and in the case of Arabs, anti-Arab) responses, made more complicated for those with darker skin who have often been associated by Americans with "Negroes" or blacks and thus already subject to forms of racial prejudice.

Earlier in the history of Muslims in America, many immigrants responded to these forms of prejudice by trying to hide their identities, both ethnic and religious. They sometimes changed their names to make them sound more American, and tried not to dress or act in ways that would make them stand out as different. That situation gradually changed, as the number of Muslims in America grew. The discussions among immigrant Muslims about identity, assimilation, and acculturation have been complex and varied, and the responses of Muslims both diverse and changing. Today a number of factors have led most Muslims to try to express their multiple identities as Americans, as members of particular ethnic or cultural groups, and as Muslims. In most cases this has meant emphasizing the importance of accepting American citizenship but not accepting all dimensions of its culture. While some choose to remain as closed as possible, and certainly do not wish to participate in any kind of dialogue with other Americans, most have found ways in which to strike a balance between or among the various identities that claim them.

After 9/11 some Muslims seemed to go back to the earlier response of trying to hide their identity. A few women who had worn Islamic dress decided to discard it. On the whole, however, the events of that day and the inevitable aftermath of American outrage about terrorism—and uncertainty about who the American Muslim community really is—caused a different kind of reaction on the part of Muslims living in America. More than half of American Muslims seldom practice Islam publicly. Some observe their faith in private and others are simply not observant at all. Since 9/11, however, there has been a noticeable effort on the part of many American Muslims to affirm their identity with Islam both vocally and visibly. Women who had never before worn any kind of Islamic dress began choosing to be more modest in their clothing and sometimes to adopt the headscarf. Both men and women have been active in opposing actions of the American government toward which they are strongly opposed, but they are doing so as Muslim American citizens exercising their right to free speech and demonstration.

Major concerns face both immigrant and American born Muslims as residents of America, and they are addressing these issues in a wide range of ways. They need to consider issues of education for themselves and their children; appropriate occupations, especially for women; dress and comportment; identity and acculturation; the balance between what is Islamic and what may only be part of a culture with which they feel affiliation; and relationships between different racial and ethnic groups in America. Added to this is the need to decide whether they feel it is appropriate, and necessary, to engage in relationships with other Americans who may know Islam either inadequately or not at all. Many are in the process of deciding that the lack of involvement in American public life that has characterized many immigrant Muslim communities in America should now give way to active association in a range of activities apart from the home and the workplace. Increasing numbers are choosing to vote and to run for public office. As American Muslims try to balance (a) the requirements of their religious tradition with (b) the expectations of their traditional cultures with (c) new demands from the America that they have chosen to adopt as home, the result may well be that a truly American Islam, woven from the fabric of many national racial and ethnic identities, is in the process of emerging.

It is not surprising that the offer to be part of interfaith conversations comes as one more confusing element in an already very complex agenda Muslims are facing. American Muslims have expressed a variety of concerns over involvement in Christian-Muslim dialogue, and some are very critical of their coreligionists who choose to be involved in such activities. In a recent study on mosques in America, however, researcher Ihsan Bagby found that 65 percent of respondents indicated that they have participated in an interfaith dialogue or program, and 37 percent in an interfaith social service project.[16] Those Muslims who do want to dialogue are clear in saying that their fellow Muslims who continue to consider Christians and Jews to be *kafirs* (nonbelievers, or rejecters of faith), despite their status as People of the Book, are wrong and should not to be part of any dialogue anyway. It seems clear that the more Muslims acknowledge their sense of "belonging" in America, and the more they involve themselves in the public square, the more they are going to be drawn into interaction with members of other faith traditions. As Sulayman Nyang, codirector of the Muslims in the American Public Square project, said to me, "Interfaith is an indirect way of indexing American Muslims, i.e., of seeing the degree to which they have been acculturated." Walid Saif, participant in Christian-Muslim dialogue sessions of the World Council of Churches, argues that "the more one is secure in his/her own identity, the more is he able to be more inclusive."[17] Saif's description seems to apply to most of the Muslims who have elected to become involved in Christian-Muslim dialogue in the American context.

American Muslim Women

Until fairly recently, and with a few important exceptions, it has been Muslim men who have participated most actively in dialogue with Christians. Partly because most Muslims, including African Americans, come from societies in which men traditionally interact in the public arena and women generally do not, it is not surprising that men have been the spokespersons for their respective communities. Now that situation is changing. To some extent this may be because non-Muslim Americans are specifically requesting that Muslim women be part of the dialogue. But for the most part it represents part of a fairly recent movement on the part of American Muslim women, often in concert and communication with colleagues overseas, to reclaim their voices and take a more active role in the practice of Islam and in its public advocacy. Especially since 9/11, after which men have been cautious about their public involvement because they do not want to attract the attention of the increasingly vigilant American government, women have stepped up to describe and defend Islam. To some extent, that has meant their increasing presence and active participation in dialogue sessions, both local and national. Some Imams and other religious leaders, including African Americans, have been conservative in their views about women, making open and active participation difficult to achieve. Women increasingly are finding their own voices, and are justifying their public participation by citing examples of the active roles played by women in the life of the Prophet and the earliest Islamic community.

The discourse about women's public participation inevitably is influenced, positively or negatively, by the claims of Western feminism. Pressures are increased for Muslim women when their Christian sisters assume that feminist conclusions appropriate to them in the West must also be appropriate for Muslim women. Fortunately, Muslim women[18] are getting both more sophisticated about the discussion and more knowledgeable about the sources of Islamic thought that can help them formulate their own understanding of feminism. While they may adopt certain of the feminist assumptions about freedom of access and opportunity for women, they reject the view that a Western understanding of equality is necessarily appropriate in the Islamic context. Muslim women currently are deeply entrenched in conversation with each other about which ideas are most consonant with Muslim values as they work to define their identity within their own family and community settings.[19]

A significant number of women who are involved in dialogue are converts to Islam (sometimes called "reverts," as in reverting to their true religion). Conversion to Islam has caught the attention of the American press recently, the usual assumption being that large numbers of Americans are deciding to become Muslim. In fact the numbers are relatively small, and somewhere near three quarters of them are women. For many black women in particular, Islam has provided a way in which to view themselves positively, to be welcomed into a community, and to practice their faith within a reasonable and manageable structure. For those who are from poor economic circumstances and may be accustomed to being on welfare, the hope is that Islam will offer them a better life. Others share a legacy of participation in black power groups, and Islam provides a way of political participation along with spiritual satisfaction. African

American converts to Islam usually affirm their affiliation with the new faith by wearing Islamic dress and adopting Islamic names. Most black women who adopt Islam are convinced that their new faith does provide a response to the racism and sexism of general American culture.

Sometimes being Muslim, however, does not meet the expectations of African American women. They find themselves caught in the triple prejudice that operates in American society: against women, against blacks, and against Islam. Breaking with their families may be extremely difficult, and sometimes that loss is intensified if they are not made to feel welcome by their immigrant Muslim sisters. In the last few years, a number of African Americans are have expressed their frustration that what they see as the ethnocentricity of some immigrant communities means that there is little tolerance for African Americans who are newly come to the faith. This frustration may keep them from wanting to participate actively in dialogue groups, or make them reticent to speak when they do join.

Small numbers of whites, Hispanics, Native Americans, and others are also adopting Islam, some because they want to marry a Muslim but many because they are attracted to what they see as the clear and straightforward structure of Islamic faith and practice. Non-Muslim wives are not required to convert, but many do so to guarantee that their children are not raised in a household in which two religions are observed. American women converts say that among the reasons they are attracted to Islam are the clarity of the Qur'an, the support of a community that they prefer as an alternative to Western individualism, and the fact that the ethical structure of Islam provides a relief from what they see as the increasing immorality of American culture. Hispanic and Native American women claim to see in Islam elements that resonate with their own individual cultures such as respect for family and elders, appreciation of the rhythms of nature, and the integration of religious and spiritual beliefs with the whole of life. Some women are attracted to the practice of Sufism, enjoying participation in dances, chanting, and other spiritual exercises.

Converts also often experience struggle and pain as consequences of choosing a new religion and identity. They may be shocked to discover that they are more marginalized in the Islamic community than they had expected. Less surprising, but nonetheless difficult to deal with, is the misunderstanding and sometimes rejection they experience from their own families and groups. Family tensions grow as new converts adhere to Islamic customs not understood or appreciated by those unfamiliar with the faith. The adoption of Islamic dress may cause stress and embarrassment to family members, and the disinclination to continue to observe Christian or Jewish holidays may make family gatherings difficult or impossible. The choice of Islam on the part of young Muslim women often appears to parents as a rejection of themselves and of the religious or cultural values that they had struggled to inculcate in their children.[20]

According to Islamic law, Muslim men may marry Christians and Jews, but Muslim women may only marry Muslim men. Men naturally take advantage of this alternative more often in the United States and Canada than in societies where Islam is the dominant culture, putting an additional burden on young Muslim women who may find that the pool of available partners is very small. Marriage in Islam is a contract guaranteeing rights to both partners, not a sacrament as Christians might understand it. Remaining single has not been an option for women in most Islamic societies, and the Prophet taught that everyone should marry. For a few Muslim women in America, however, finding a suitable partner is difficult, traditional practices of arranged marriages are unattractive or not possible, and the pursuit of vocation or career may make marriage a choice rather than an expectation.

Some Muslim women are even opting to contravene Islamic law and marry outside the faith. To the alarm of many families, the incidence of interfaith marriage is on the rise, with Muslim women marrying Christians, Jews, Buddhists, Hindus, and others. Interfaith conversation groups often find that the topic of intermarriage is timely and important. For more traditional Muslims in America, however, the idea is so unimaginable that it is considered unworthy of discussion, and even interethnic, international, and interracial Muslim marriages are to be avoided. For these families Christian-Muslim dialogue is generally considered to be an inappropriate activity insofar as it might put marriageable young people of different faiths into contact with each other. Some young American converts are expressing their frustration that potential marriage partners are inaccessible to them because of their families' insistence that their children, especially their daughters, marry "one of their own."

Non-Muslim Americans often harbor suspicions about several matters related to women in Islam, including the matter of multiple wives, why Muslim men (as they imagine or have heard) treat their wives so badly, and why some women are forced to wear restrictive dress. Unclarity about these matters can make open and free conversation between Christians and Muslims difficult to achieve. The Qur'an allows men to take up to four wives on condition that they relate equitably to all. Throughout the history of Islam this permission generally has been interpreted as a sanction for a man to have more than one wife if he could afford it. Current exegesis of this Qur'anic permission, however, stresses both the particular conditions under which such a practice may be observed (e.g., a lack of males in the community due to war or other circumstance) and the recognition that it is extremely difficult to relate with complete fairness to more than one marriage partner. American law also unambiguously stipulates that polygamous marriages are illegal. Muslim counselors make it clear to their clientele that having a second wife is not an option for a man in the United States.

American Muslims in general decry the fact that some of their sisters in other countries do suffer discrimination and ill-treatment by males. They argue that such behavior has no place in Islam and spend much time illustrating how the Qur'an is, with little exception, one of the most egalitarian of the religious texts of the world's major faiths. Abuse of women in American Muslim cultures exists as it does in American society in general, and Muslims are working to empower women to use the civil and religious resources available to them to escape from situations in which they are treated unfairly and, they say, un-Islamically.

Islamic Dress

The issue of "Islamic dress," which in its most common form means covering the hair, may be a major obstacle in interfaith conversations. Some Christians simply cannot see past the fact that Muslim women may choose to cover their heads or other parts of the body. "I refuse to go to a meeting at which the other women are looking at me like I am a fool to be wearing even a scarf over my hair," says one disgruntled former member of a dialogue group. There is no general standard of dress to which all American Muslim women conform. Some are content to continue wearing a version of the dress characteristic of their home cultures, and others adopt Western dress completely. Still others decide to dress more conservatively than they would have done in the societies from which they came. Most Muslim women do cover themselves in one way or another when they attend the mosque, whether or not they dress Islamically at other times. Within the Islamic community itself the issue can be divisive. Those who choose to wear the *hijab* (headcover) are sometimes sharply critical of other Muslims who are not comfortable with it or do not feel that it is appropriate for them. Those who leave their heads uncovered may consider some of their sisters a bit overzealous if they cover themselves completely. On the whole, however, Muslims try to respect the right of a woman to make her own decision about dress, as about other things, and wish that the rest of the American public would do the same.

Women often believe that if they are dressed modestly they are free to enter any profession because there is no danger that the men with whom they work will make unwanted advances. Unfortunately, the very garb that in her own understanding, or that of her family, allows a woman to work may mitigate against her professional advancement or even getting a job in the first place. Many employers look askance at a woman wearing *hijab,* fearing that customers or other employees will think it strange or that it may indicate some kind of religious fanaticism on the part of the wearer. The headscarf is sometimes prohibited in the workplace as part of general rules against clothing that attracts too much attention. Ironically, regulations that may have originated in response to clothing considered too skimpy, such as miniskirts, now may prohibit clothing that serves the opposite purpose.

Women and the Practice of Islam

As clothing styles differ widely within the American Muslim community, so does women's participation in the public practice of religion. While many American Muslim women choose not to participate actively in the mosque or Islamic center, as is also true of men, others attend prayer services regularly. Some immigrant women find that they have the opportunity, and thus the desire for, greater public participation in religious activities than was true in their home cultures. More women are attending Friday prayers, lectures, or functions than used to be the case either in the United States or in their countries of origin. In some of the larger Islamic Centers, classes are held for women in the study of Qur'an and the Arabic language, even providing special instruction for the elderly. Muslim women's home study groups are a growing phenomenon in America. Young Muslim women have begun to engage in exegesis of the Qur'an and to participate in discussions of religious texts that used to be strictly an arena for men. A few lone voices are now being heard on the American scene calling for the institution of women as Imams or prayer leaders, but thus far they are not influential and the function of Imam remains the province of males. A prayer service led in 2005 for a mixed congregation by Amina Wadud, an African American Muslim professor at Virginia Commonwealth University, caused what amounted to an international scandal. As of this writing few others have followed her lead.

Non-Muslims find it easy to question why Muslim women participate in the prayer in a different area from men. Women pray either at the back of the hall behind the men, on one side with the men on the other (often separated by a partition), on a second floor balcony where they can see the men and the Imam below, or occasionally in very conservative mosques in a separate room with the service broadcast over a speaker or through closed-circuit television. Not all women agree on the most appropriate form of separation, and some feel that "separate but equal" is not served by extreme segregation. Virtually all Muslim women, however, say that not having to mix with men during the prayer service helps them as well as the men to concentrate on the ritual rather than on each other.

Muslim women's organizations are proliferating, and more women are getting involved in them. These organizations, some of which have international connections, are often dedicated to bringing about better understanding of rights, responsibilities, and opportunities for women. Among the most prominent are KARAMA: Muslim Women Lawyers for Human Rights; Muslim Women's Services (RAHIMA) that pursues charitable activities for Muslim families, the North American Council for Muslim Women (NACMW) that initiates programs and provides services to women, the Sisterhood is Global Institute that works to improve women's rights, and Sisters in Islam that reinterprets Islamic principles and practices in light of the Qur'an. Cooperation between Muslim and Christian women in such charitable outreach work has yet to be explored, but promises to be a fascinating way in which to promote interfaith understanding.

A piece of history was made late summer of 2006 when the Islamic Society of North America (ISNA), the largest Muslim religious organization in the United States, elected Ingrid Mattson, a Canadian Muslim, its first woman president. Mattson, who is a member of the faculty of Hartford Seminary, like the immediate past ISNA president Nur Abdullah and Executive Director Sayyed M. Syeed, has clearly affirmed that interfaith dialogue is an increasingly important dimension of ISNA programming.

4

Models of Christian-Muslim Dialogue in America

"Oh-oh, what do we do now?" A slight feeling of panic sometimes comes over groups of Muslims and Christians who have gathered to talk for the first time—especially over those who have taken the responsibility of organizing the dialogue. The impetus to come together can be strong, at least for some Americans, but good will does not always go very far in helping groups decide what they want to talk about or, to put it more specifically, what purpose they want their dialogue to serve.

The first meeting or even two may go quite well, as each side generally discovers that their conversation partners are very nice folks and willing to talk as well as to listen. But then what do they do? It is not atypical for would-be groups to wither away simply for lack of direction and guidance as they struggle to discover where they want to go. This may be particularly true if groups are designed in a rather ad hoc way—perhaps a specific group of Christians (members of an Episcopal church), for example, or an ecumenical group in town) plus whatever Muslims they are able to find to come to talk with them. The capacity of the group to continue meeting beyond an initial hello is often related directly to the group's homogeneity. Two roughly similar sets of Christians and Muslims, for example, may find it relatively easy to set the ground rules. More often, however, the impetus to continue comes from having a specific goal towards which the group is committed to work.

Since 9/11 many Christians have been eager to "find out about" the religion of Islam, and Muslims are often very willing to tell them and thus to prove their viability as willing participants in America's new religious pluralism. Right at the beginning, then, comes a potential imbalance. Very often the Christians' goal for the dialogue, the reason that they want to come, is to gain some better understanding of Islam. The goal for Muslims, the reason they are willing to make a considerably greater effort than might be necessary for Christians, is that they have something very important at stake: their reputation. Initially these two purposes may seem compatible, namely conversation about Islam, but they do not always lend themselves to real dialogue because the street is one-way.

Sometimes the participants in these dialogue groups simply let their conversation evolve in one way or another, and find that together they work their way toward a goal that makes sense to them. Others, however, need guidance in thinking through what it is that they want to do and are capable of doing given the nature and resources of their particular group. "Let's have a dialogue" may be a wonderful way to start, but it is only the beginning. Determining where the group wants to go is both helpful and often essential to its ultimate stability, especially as original conversation partners think about expanding the group to include others who may have particular interests or areas of specialization. It is also important, insofar as possible, for local groups to see themselves in the larger contexts of Islam in America and particularly of the events that are happening worldwide. Not everyone is an expert on world events, but few can miss the barrage of press coverage when events occur involving Muslim countries and movements, Christian leadership, and communities. The local is inevitably one element in a larger picture, and dialogue participants will do well to at least acknowledge that reality from the beginning.

If groups should decide that it is good to give some thought to how they want to be constituted, what their immediate purpose is, and what they envision as a longer range goal, I propose the following possible kinds of Christian-Muslim dialogue for consideration. They are models for conversation that I have configured on the basis of my years of involvement in such groups and on conversations with others who have had such experiences, and are intended as suggestions for possible ways in which groups might want to understand themselves.

The Dialogue of Persuasion Model

For most of the history of Christian-Muslim encounter, "persuasion" has taken a hard edge. It has been debate for the purposes of proving the truth of one's own faith and the consequent falsity of the other. Confrontational debate has been a tried and true, and indeed legitimate, way in which Muslims and Christians have squared off against one another since the earliest days of Islam. Religionists on both sides have moved only as far as the understood strictures of their own scriptures and traditions have allowed. To the extent to which they have had debates, these have been, on the whole, for the purpose of disproving the validity of the other's belief system and thus the truth of one's own. Often the debates are the means whereby either a speaker wishes to encourage members of his or her own faith tradition to hold firm, or they are used to hammer home disagreements with members of the other tradition that are long-standing and generally impossible to resolve.

For the most part, confrontational dialogue, or the dialogue of dispute, is an unattractive option. The World Council of Churches has stated clearly that debate of this kind is no longer (if it ever was) an inappropriate way in which to carry on interfaith dialogue. Much of the literature of the WCC's interfaith dialogue office has urged that participants refrain from trying to prove the truths of their own religious traditions and concentrate rather on a dialogue of mutual respect and understanding.

Persuasion in the form of debate, dispute and confrontation, therefore, is seldom a model appropriate for groups aspiring to better understanding. But it is important to remember that recent immigrants from parts of the Islamic world in which tensions between Christians and Muslims are high often have experienced this kind of confrontational dialogue, either in words or in actions. Sometimes they assume that if they engage in conversation with Christians in America this will be the nature of the business, and are surprised that confrontational dialogue generally is no longer considered a viable model. "For most members of the Muslim community," says Liyakat Takim of the University of Denver, "dialogue between people of different faiths in an environment of mutual respect and acceptance is a relatively new phenomenon. Their experience has been of preaching Islam only, and simply refuting the beliefs of the other."

Today most Muslims who have had any experience in dialogue in America, no matter what they might actually think about the truth of Islam in relation to Christianity, are persuaded that confrontation is not appropriate for the promotion of genuine interfaith understanding. They have still seen remnants of such an approach in the teachings of Muslim zealots such as Ahmad Deedat,[1] but on whole they think that especially in the west today it is important to get beyond argumentation that fosters an "I am right and therefore you are wrong" attitude. Ahmad Sakr of the Foundation for Islamic Knowledge tells his readers in *Da'wah Through Dialogue*, ". . . Allah has reminded us to use the best approach when we are talking with People of other Faiths. In this regard Allah says in Surah Al-ʿAkaboot (The Spider): "And dispute not with the people of the Book, except with means better (than mere disputation)...."[2]

The dialogue of persuasion, however, need not actually be confrontational. One of the important talking points among those who are active in thinking about and carrying out Christian-Muslim dialogue on the American scene is whether there is any role at the conversation table for the practice of evangelization on the part of Christians or da ʿwa on the part of Muslims. No, said the World Council of Churches as early as the 1970s, and it has not relaxed its position on that question. Most practitioners have tended to agree, arguing that dialogue is for better understanding, not for proclamation with the implicit understanding that it would mean encouraging the other to accept one's own faith.

But other opinions are beginning to be voiced. Da ʿwa, which literally means calling, is the Islamic term used for bringing someone into the faith. It also has many other dimensions of meaning, including personally calling oneself to become a better Muslim, and most particularly after 9/11 it has come to mean educating others to an understanding of Islam. "I don't know how it is possible for me to talk honestly about Islam," said one Imam with considerable dialogue experience, "without doing da ʿwa. I want to explain my faith, I want to make sure that I am being as good a Muslim as possible, and frankly I am not at all bothered if my Christian colleagues know that I believe Islam to be the one and only true religion. What more wonderful thing could I talk about than that?" And from another, "If I experience something that I think is good, then it is un-Islamic for me not to try to share it.... This is what Islam is. It may be perceived as proselytism, but we must tell you what we believe. God will ask us at the judgment, 'Why didn't you say so-and-so when you had the opportunity to do it?' I believe that the same integrity exists for Christians."

Some Christians are beginning to express similar thoughts. "If evangelism means following the gospel as expressed in Matthew 28," a clergy friend of mine asked, "and going into all the world to tell the good news of Christ, then why can't I do that in my small piece of the world even when I am talking with people of other religions? Wouldn't it help them understand better what Christianity means to me?" I think of an instance in which a Muslim Imam and I were talking about elements of our faith. "It seems to me very possible for Christians to consider Muhammad as a prophet in line with all the prophets of the Hebrew Bible," I said genially. "Honestly," he replied, "I am really less interested in what you think about Muhammad than what you think about Jesus the Christ." The dialogue of persuasion, in its gentler forms of speaking from the heart about what truly motivates one to be a devoted Christian or Muslim, seems to be entering a challenging and interesting new phase. Certainly for some participants it feels like the only way to really get to the heart of the beliefs of the other.[3]

The "Get to Know You" Model

There is little question that this is the most common mode of Christian-Muslim exchange in America. Both before and after 9/11, Christians have wondered about the nature of this religion that seems so threatening in the international arena but is represented by some very nice people in the United States. Some have called this "the safest kind of dialogue," involving no commitment beyond an objective exchange of information about the participants and about their respective religions. As Christians become aware of the reality that Islam is one of the fasting growing religions in America, and that Muslims are increasingly visible in all walks of western life, churches and denominations are recognizing the importance of better understanding their new neighbors. Often Muslims are the recipients of invitations to meet at local churches, or at the homes of Christians, to introduce themselves and talk about the basic beliefs and practices of Islam. Christians, particularly these days, may be more eager than Muslims to ask questions, and often these initial "get to know you" meetings turn into question-and-answer sessions in which one side does all the asking and the other all the responding. Often a single Muslim is featured as an invited "guest" in a predominantly Christian gathering, thus becoming the focus of Christian attention. One convert to Islam reports that she is often asked to participate in such sessions because she can speak the language of Christians as well as explain Islam.

Many people who have been involved in such basic information sessions indicate that they are getting tired of this model's superficiality. "This isn't really dialogue," complained a Christian woman who had been trying for years to get what she called substance into the conversation. "I find it really frustrating that we can't seem to move to more serious discussions." And Muslims are getting tired of answering questions about violence, treatment of women, wearing the veil, and the like which they feel that they have addressed endlessly in conversations, publications, and on-line postings. Much of the literature on interfaith dialogue points to what is called "The Dialogue of Life" as the most important way in which members of other faiths can actually get to know each other. While this phrase may connote particular things to some individuals or groups, in general it means the dialogue that naturally and inevitably arises when people live alongside and necessarily interact with each other. For purposes of this analysis, however, dialogue of life is more a starting point than a goal. It is precisely because of the pluralism of America and the growth of the American Muslim population that people are beginning to notice Muslims in their neighborhoods, in their children's schools, and even in local political groups. That notice is generating questions, which in turn triggers a range of attempts to begin the process of getting to know who our Muslim neighbors really are.

"Getting to know you," then, is inevitably the first step in any kind of dialogue. Unfortunately for many attempts at conversation in the United States, it is also the last. Without a more specific goal or project in mind and the motivation to continue, groups easily tend to fade away or never have a second meeting. Dialogue can be fun and even exciting, but the reality is that to be successful it also requires a serious dose of intentionality.

The Dialogue in the Classroom Model

For many years in America talk about religion in the classroom, certainly through grade school and high school, was either not permitted at all or was allowed only if religion was dealt with from a purely academic perspective. Such has been the strict discipline of the separation of church and state, ensuring that no public classroom was a venue for any person or group trying to promote its own faith perspective.

This situation is changing a bit, as even public schools are recognizing that the classroom may provide an opportunity for students to learn about different cultures and their various components. The realization that many of those cultures are now represented in America has motivated teachers to find responsible ways in which to help students become aware of these realities. Many Muslim mothers report having been invited into the classrooms of their sons and daughters during Ramadan or at the time of one of the two major Muslim 'ieds or festivals (such as the end of Ramadan or the end of the time of pilgrimage) to talk to the children about their holidays and customs at appropriate times in the Islamic ritual cycle. Ensuing conversation, if there is any in terms of questions and answers between students and the Muslim mom (or her children), is dialogue only in the sense of the most basic exchange of information, a different cut on the "getting to know you" model. Muslim children are now enrolled in Catholic parochial schools, and some Christian children even go to Muslim schools, suggesting the possibility of dialogue among students in their early years that may, in the future, obviate the need for the more formal conversations that their parents are trying to initiate.

A somewhat more dramatic change is taking place today in the classrooms of private and public colleges and universities, and to a limited extent in the country's good secondary schools, one that may provide a possible new model of dialogue. Until about a decade ago, the vast majority of college and university professors teaching Islam were non-Muslims. Trained in the history of

religions, anthropology, or some other western disciplinary study which allowed them to be able to teach some dimension of Islam, they faced classrooms of
students who were not Muslims and who in all likelihood knew little or nothing
about any religion other than their own. Suddenly that situation has changed
dramatically. Students in classes about Islam are increasingly Muslim themselves, and if not challenging the information provided by the professor at least
are in a position to offer new interpretations and new information coming from
their own cultural contexts. The other change, of course, is that as institutions
are under increasing pressure to hire actual Muslims to fill open faculty slots,
more Muslims are joining college and university faculties.

So while the picture is different in different parts of the country, of course,
we in America do have an interesting new situation in which Muslims in the
classroom may be taking with other Muslims, a conversation in which non-
Muslim (though not necessarily Christian) students will inevitably begin to
join. Muslim Professor Ali Asani of Harvard University, for example, says that
the serious dialogue in which he has become engaged with his Muslim and
non-Muslim students often has provided a helpful experience for Muslim students who are struggling to find their identity as Muslims. Imam Talal 'Eid,
who has been active in interfaith dialogue in New England since he first came
to this country in the 1980s, confided that by participating in Asani's course he
has learned some of the ways in which it is possible to engage in dialogue with
non-Muslims.

For DePaul University's Aminah McCloud, the classroom is the venue in
which young people really open up. Youth in her experience, if invited to participate in the usual adult dialogues at all, are not asked to speak and not really
heard if they do. Most youth find such a situation intimidating and prefer not to
be involved anyway. In the classroom, however, they can engage with each other
and try to make sense of what is going on in the world. McCloud takes personal
responsibility for helping students unlearn some of the incorrect information
they have learned about Islam in high school, and for helping them understand
how to air their hostilities so as to better be open to the kind of interreligious
dialogue that she sees happening with such vitality in the classroom.[4] Also,
recognizing that the current mosque/church level dialogue is mainly restricted
to the older generation and needs the infusion of younger thinking, Mahmoud
Ayoub worries that the youth are drifting away from an interest in religion in any
form, let alone dialogue. Perhaps a more hopeful venue than the religious institution for instilling such interest, he says, is the college or university classroom
where some students are showing a deep interest in learning about other faiths.

Some teachers are making special efforts to see that dialogue in the classroom is related to the larger context in which Muslim and Christians live and

interact, and that concerns of racism, sexism, and economic status become significant components in students' understanding of each other. In Atlanta, Marsha Snulligan Haney of the International Theological Center promotes dialogue among her students by enlarging the classroom to become an actual urban setting. Taking her students into the city, she shows them how conversation across religious lines must take into account the real circumstances that determine how people view the world, themselves, and each other.[5] Wake Forest's Charles Kimball, a pioneer in efforts at dialogue and Christian-Muslim understanding in America, sends students out in teams of three to talk with Muslims and Christians (and others) to discover how faith is lived out in various communities. Often invited into individual homes, students learn that dialogue can be most meaningful when it is done personally and informally and with genuine hospitality.[6]

College and university campuses are finding opportunities for interfaith exchange in another important and growing movement, namely through chaplains. For many years Roman Catholics, Protestants, and Jews have been present on campuses, but have worked primarily with their own student constituencies. Over the last several years a small but growing number of schools have started also to appoint Muslim chaplains, a few full time but most working in part time capacities. This change is due to a growth in the number of Muslim students, accompanied by the recognition by admissions offices that providing access to a Muslim chaplain is good publicity in recruiting students. The presence of these Muslim chaplains, who are often male Imams but sometimes are women, has contributed significantly to interfaith relations. On a number of campuses, for example, Muslim Student Association (MSA) chapters host an *iftar* [breaking of the fast] to which members of the Christian and other faith communities are invited for food and a get-together. Some Christian students are also requesting that they be allowed to eat in the *kosher-halal* (food prepared in legally permissible ways for Jews and Muslims) dining rooms available on certain campuses so as to be able to join in the conversations taking place across ethnic and religions lines.

The Theological Exchange Model

"Does theology really matter to the dialogue?" I asked my class on Christian-Muslim Relations (incidentally subtitled "The Theological Dimension"), in which the numbers of Muslims and Christians happened to be exactly equal. "Or perhaps more practically," I insisted, "has it made any real difference over the last fourteen plus centuries in which Muslims and Christians have been arguing with each other?" I told them that at least we know there has been no real theological resolve, so if they wanted to they could consider the course a bust from the beginning and go home for the semester. The final several sessions of this Christian seminary course are devoted to a segment called "Does Theology Matter on the Ground?" in which we look at some of the deadly conflicts being carried out in the name of religion in various parts of the world and see what, if any role, doctrine has to play as Christians and Muslims struggle to live with each other. My students decided that theology, in truth, doesn't much matter.

As we have seen, however, theological dispute was the core of most of what could be called "dialogue" between Christians and Muslims for many centuries. On the international scene today, however, a number of ongoing dialogues, both Catholic and Protestant, are making a serious effort to think theologically together. In most cases these conversations are closely attuned to the social and political circumstances of the participants, recognizing that regional and national association necessitates an attempt to formulate corresponding ideological responses. For a number of years certain Christian groups in America have encouraged the kind of dialogue in which deeper conversation is held about elements of faith within the traditions of Christianity and Islam, although these exchanges often have not had the same degree of sophistication that is illustrated in some international theological conversation.

The theological exchange model has been particularly effective in the annual regional meetings of the United States Conference of Catholic Bishops (USCCB). Working in partnership with the Islamic Society of North America (ISNA), the largest organization of Muslim religious entities in the country, the USCCB has set up dialogue groups in the West, the Middle Central states, and the East Coast. Participants in these dialogues, who attend on a regular basis and get to know each other well, exchange perspectives on a number of different theological themes. The Midwest Dialogue of Catholics and Muslims began in 1996 to meet in the Indianapolis area. Two years later the Mid-Atlantic Dialogue of Catholics and Muslims was started in New York City and continues to meet in the greater New York area. The third and final group, the West Coast Dialogue of Catholics and Muslims, started in 2000 in Orange, California, in partnership with the Orange County Shura Advisory Council. These groups have built up a level of acquaintance and trust that has allowed them to pursue a wide range of theological topics as well as themes that deal with family life. They are designed more as spiritual retreats than simply meetings. Time is set aside for prayer for the members of each tradition with others watching if they choose, for mutual examination of scripture, and for discussing spiritual themes.[7] Also contributing to their sense of comfort and ease with each other is the fact that most of the members are men (priests and

Imams), though not all, and virtually all occupy significant leadership positions within their respective communities. Members of these groups work hard in preparation for their meetings, exchanging scholarly papers, and responding so as to seek out similarities and differences in position.

There is no unanimity among either Muslims or Christians in this country as to whether or not the theological exchange model is ultimately either viable or useful. "Insofar as only men are involved," said one female Christian leader, "or even that it is primarily men who feel they have the right to talk, we might as well forget about it. We have been hearing from them for too long." Some Christians express their nervousness that once theological issues are on the table Christians will have to admit to themselves and to their conversation partners that there are so many theological differences between the different Christian denominations that Muslims will simply be more confused than enlightened.

The concern has also been raised that significant theological engagement can really only take place between persons who have had years of training in their own texts and traditions. As Sayyid Hossen Nasr put it to me, "Those who have theological and metaphysical qualifications should certainly attempt theological conversation. But others should simply settle for respect. It does not help the cause of Christian-Muslim dialogue if people participating in theological debates are without the qualifications necessary to do so, as, unfortunately, has taken place often during the last few decades." That, he said, makes the pool of viable participants so small that the whole subject is not of much interest to the general public wanting to know more about the other faith. A number of Muslims have said that they are discouraged precisely because theological encounter has been going on for so long and the results are seemingly so meager. They are persuaded that this model does not work very well for Muslims in any case because theology is not their primary concern and is not always of great interest to them. Several have said frankly that they think theological dialogue is a waste of time.

On the other hand, there are a number of long-term dialogue participants who are deeply persuaded that theological discussion must not be abandoned, arguing that progress need not be measured in terms of agreement on basic theological issues such as the trinity or the crucifixion, which is unlikely to happen. Progress, they say, means coming to a deeper understanding of *why* each tradition holds the theological positions that it does. We just need to understand each other better, they argue, and accept some of the continuing points of contention without getting distressed over them. Former ISNA president Muzammil Siddiqi of The Islamic Society of Orange County, California, for example, believes strongly that the theological exchange model is still a very important mode of Muslim-Christian encounter. Siddiqi is himself an accomplished theological scholar, having done his doctoral work at Harvard on the medieval Hanbali Muslim theologian Ibn Taymiyya. Siddiqi might be forgiven for wanting to pass on more theological discussion, since Ibn Taymiyya's huge work on Christianity resulted in a very negative theological view of its subject. But it is important, he says, to keep the discussion going.

Many Christians continue to encourage theological discussions not because, like their forebears, they want to try to attack or undermine the precepts of Islam, but precisely because they believe that they may grow theologically in their own understanding of their faith by making the effort. Persuaded by the assertions of people like John Cobb, a firmly Christian theologian who insists that if he has not grown and been transformed through dialogue it has not really been a dialogue (see chapter six), they want to be open to such transforming activity in their own lives. Some Muslims are interested in participation in theological dialogue because it can help further interfaith understanding, but not because they expect to learn something helpful to their own spiritual development. "Do Muslims want to 'grow' from the dialogue?" asks Sheikh Ibrahim Negm of the Islamic Center of Valley Stream, New York. "No, they want dialogue for information but not for personal growth." Others argue that while they do not expect to emerge from the conversation with their theology fundamentally altered, they do recognize the possibility that they may experience some fundamental changes in their openness to the process of dialogue itself and even that they may come to understand their own theology better.[8]

What may really be bothering some Muslims as they ponder the usefulness of theological dialogue is the fear that Christians are trying to hide behind the mask of dialogue when their real concern, as it has been for centuries, is the effort at evangelization of Muslims. Such concern is not without legitimate basis, and there is no question that the hope to make converts out of Muslims both abroad and in America is the deeply cherished hope of many Christians. Some Muslims today would even prefer the use of "interreligious" to describe the conversation that takes place between Muslims and Christians, nervous that the more commonly used "interfaith" might suggest a kind of blurring of the edges in which theological compromises might be made or expected. They are also concerned that Muslims, being relatively new at such conversations across religious lines in the context of America, may not be prepared to understand that the underlying agenda really might be evangelism. The enterprise of dialogue has been going on long enough in this country, however, that in fact most Christians as well as most Muslims feel deeply that if theological exchanges are to happen, they should be for enlightenment and enrichment— and, for those with experience and knowledge, even healthy debate—and specifically not be occasions in which judgments are made or persuasion attempted.

The details of theological arguments in relation to pluralism—what American representatives of each faith tradition think about the theological "acceptability" of the other—are to be found in chapters six and seven below.

The Ethical Exchange Model

It has been my experience when I have been invited to speak in local church-women's groups, that the attention of my audience often fades rather quickly if I talk only about Muslim beliefs and practices. I am usually much more successful when I get down to practical matters. On one particular occasion, for example, I said that among the problems Muslims face in American society today is worry that their young people will fall victim to drugs and alcohol, that they are spending hours at their computers doing more than homework assignments, that they experience a kind of psychological burn-out because of the pressures at school to multitask, and that they may end up marrying non-Muslims who will lead them away from their Islamic background. "Well my goodness," said one of my listeners, "those are the same things we worry about. If my kids even make it through to marriage age—which I worry about given all the pressures they face—I'm afraid that they will marry someone like, well, a Jew or a Muslim or a secular person and not care any more for solid Christian values."

Now I had a hook on which to hold their attention. We began to talk about the kinds of values that we as Christian mothers and fathers still do try to instill in our children, and I was able to assure my church ladies that these are much the same as the values Muslim families enforce in their younger children and hope desperately that they will not lose when they become teenagers. The result of this initial foray into child-rearing principles was a second and wonderful conversation at the same church, to which several Muslim women were invited. When the meeting was over both the church women and the Muslims not only had made some new friends, but were delighted to discover that with only few variations they really do share values and think it would be helpful to try to work together to provide a set of role models for their youth.

It was clear from the conversation, of course, that neither Christians nor Muslims wanted to go so far as to put their stamp of approval on interfaith marriage. "Oh my," an elderly woman remarked to me later, "first it was the Catholics that our families had to worry about us marrying, then the Jews, and now it's the Muslims. I wonder what's next. . . ." Concerns about intermarriage notwithstanding, and in general such concerns may be deeper for Muslims than for most Christians in the United States today (many immigrant Muslims do not want their children to marry outside of their own ethnic group, to say nothing of outside the faith itself), the model of talking about ethical concerns faced by families of growing children is a good one and can offer a quick and easy way into conversation that emphasizes commonalities over differences. Both Christians and Muslims are interested to discover that their counterparts in other religions worry very deeply about the society in which we live, and perhaps especially about the forces that seem to be leading young people away from their ethically-based religious moorings.

Some advocates of Muslim-Christian dialogue, therefore, are adamant that the most appropriate arena for discussion between Christians and Muslims is not theology but ethics, or that while ethnics are informed by theology it is the practical that should be stressed over the theoretical. Unfortunately, few Muslims or Christians who have actively engaged in dialogue have studied ethics as a discipline, and even fewer are acquainted with the theological, legal, and philosophical sources of religious ethics. Perhaps a new generation of doctoral students will have the courage to learn the languages and source materials necessary to undertake this daunting task. In the meantime, concerns in the general populace for the decline in morality in American society, long feared by Muslims and often seen as inevitable given the rise of secularism in the West, have put ethics on the agenda as a matter of crucial importance for many.

One snag that groups, who do gather to talk about common ethical concerns, may face is the fact that Muslims believe that if Christians were to observe the ethical injunctions of their own religion more strictly, many of America's social problems might be alleviated. That aside, however, there seem to be several steps that might be involved for those who would like to pursue dialogue in the realm of ethics. First, both Christians and Muslims can do some initial reflection on the ways in which their respective communities look to the resources of their own traditions to provide ethical and moral guidance. Simply put, is it scripture, theology, or law (or a combination of those) that has served to engender the discipline of ethics? This exercise can be very helpful in understanding what is "behind" the thinking of the various participants in the conversation. Then the group might identify the ethical concerns that most trouble them in contemporary American society, whether it be elements of underworld culture intruding into their lives, the unethical behavior of priests and clergy (and also Imams), corporate scandal, failure to address problems such as poverty and racism, or the implications for religious life of new technologies. Whether or not such conversation leads to particular action, that is, working together to address a social problem, a great deal of interfaith understanding can be achieved by sharing these common concerns.

As advancements in medical science, for example in the field of bioethics, raise disturbing questions in both communities, some Christians and Muslims urge a coming together to share resources and perhaps to find common guidance. Groups whose members know each other well and have developed a fairly high level of trust may want to venture into the realm of criticizing the government for actions some members feel are unethical and even immoral, although such accusations tend to be raised very cautiously by Muslims who are concerned that they not appear to hold any opinions that would raise suspicions about their loyalty to America.

Conversation about civil rights, long considered to apply mainly to African American struggles for equity, now have new meaning for Muslims who worry that their own civil rights are being eroded as a result of the government's war on terror. It could make for a fascinating conversation to bring together African Americans, both Christian and Muslim, and others deeply concerned with issues of invasion of privacy, to reflect on the personal experiences of people who continue to struggle to achieve their rights as American citizens, and what actions such a group might contemplate taking in solidarity with each other.

The Dialogue about Ritual Model

Many local groups are extending invitations to members of other faiths to attend ritual occasions so as to observe and learn how different religions look "in practice." Part of the learning experience, however, is the understanding that there may be certain elements of the respective rituals that are not open either to participation or to observation by those who are outside the particular faith.

Some dialogue groups, usually after they have had a chance to get to know each other and to become acquainted with some of their respective ritual practices, are experimenting with learning firsthand what those practices really entail. A first step might mean having a church or a mosque "perform" a ritual service, or part of a service, as a kind of demonstration piece, taking the time to explain each element of what has been performed. "Why do you do it that way?" is the most common question, and concrete and historically substantiated answers should be provided. Thus it may be important for a priest, pastor, or Imam to be part of the discussion. Sometimes these ritual occasions offer the opportunity to demonstrate some of the cultural variations that are involved even in worship, an experience that can be as eye-opening for the participants as it is for the observers.

In some places Christians and Muslims who have come to know something about each other are taking a second step in the worship/ritual experience. Visitors may actually take some part in the other's worship service. Muslim groups who invite Christians to visit a local mosque commonly include as part of the program an opportunity for the Christians to sit at the back of the prayer hall and observe worship at one of the specified prayer times. In very rare instances, however, usually at more "open" African American mosques, visiting men and even women may be given basic instruction in how to perform the prayer positions, and invited to join the ranks of Muslims—men in front and women in the back or in another room—in actually performing the prayer. It is even more unusual to find Muslims willing to join in worship during a Christian service, although mutually designed prayers are often shared.

It is probably fair to say that Christians find participating in Muslim worship easier, more potentially appealing and more likely to provide an experience that they can learn from than Muslims would say of Christian worship. Or to put it another way, those Christians who would have a great deal of trouble worshipping with Muslims at a mosque perhaps would not be participating in a Christian-Muslim dialogue anyway. Muslims, who might be willing to meet for dialogue in the social hall of a church, would probably not feel comfortable worshiping in the sanctuary. Christians eager for experiences of sharing must realize that most Muslims are also not willing to invite their Christian or Jewish guests to stand with them in the worship lines, to utter the words of praise to God and recognition of God's oneness by which they know they are Muslim, and to prostrate themselves in the ultimate act of submission. "You are most welcome to watch," they say, "but it would not be appropriate for you to join us."

A third way in which Christians and Muslims might participate together in ritual and worship is one that is being experimented with in a number of places, but generally with only modest results. Institutions with long experience in interfaith conversation and interaction may determine that the time has come to plan a joint or common worship service, one in which Muslims and Christians together determine how best to worship God in ways that are not offensive to either group and that, in some way, represent the kind of response to God characteristic of each. The service of lamentation held by the Roman Catholic-Muslim women's group described in chapter one is an excellent example of such a service in which participants, including men, shared a common experience of prayer and worship. It must be remembered, however, as we will see in chapter seven, that not all Catholics will agree on the viability of any kind of common prayer.

In the end a joint worship service is going to look much more like a Christian Sunday morning activity than a Friday communal *salat* (the obligatory prayer, said five times each day by observant Muslims and bringing the community together in common worship on Fridays). For Muslims, an interfaith service might function as a time and way of praising God, but it would not substitute for one of the formal prayers. It is important to understand that most Muslims, and most especially those who are recently arrived from other countries, would not find themselves at all comfortable with anything that resembles joint worship.

Even designing a prayer that might be used at the beginning or end of a dialogue meeting can present potential difficulties. *Theologically*, in terms of what one believes about God, there are few statements that a Muslim might want to use in a joint prayer that Christians could not say with comfort. Muslims, however, worry that they may come in an attitude of prayer and suddenly find themselves asked to say or even hear certain things that they feel are theologically compromising. "There I was," said one young convert, "trusting that the prayer being given was for us all, and suddenly I was asked to pray in the name of Jesus Christ 'our' savior. It was very upsetting for me, and certainly guaranteed that I will not participate in any attempt at common prayer again." This problem is real for Christians as well, many of whom may feel that if a prayer is stripped, so to speak, of all of the language that makes it theologically meaningful for them they may feel that they have had to make all the compromises. "How can I pray from my heart without acknowledging the most important fact of my life?" asked a Christian participant. "Prayer without the name of Jesus is merely words." This question has reached the level of the United States government. As of September 2006, a spending bill at the Pentagon has been held up because of a controversy about prayer. The longstanding custom has been for military chaplains to offer nonsectarian (commonly acceptable) prayer at mandatory events. The new provision, if passed, would allow chaplains to pray according to the dictates of their own conscience at any occasion.[9]

So observant prayer, participatory prayer, and common prayer remain as some of the alternative ways in which to understand and share each others' rituals. Some groups who have tried all three (the last is highly unusual) say that the problems are sufficiently sticky that they have decided not to pursue any kind of prayer experience in the context of dialogue. The rituals of their respective traditions are dealt with in study sessions rather than prayer sessions, where no one can feel offended or intruded upon. Still, dialogue about ritual, whether it implies learning or participation, is an interesting and quite new way to at least *look* across, if not actually *go* across, the boundaries between the faiths.

The Dialogue about Spirituality Model

While many members of both faiths worry that emphasis on spirituality might lead to a "blurring of the lines" that make each religion distinctive, others are persuaded that ultimately the most fruitful kind of interfaith conversation is that which leads to identifying elements of spiritual commonality, with a de-emphasis on differences and a re-emphasis on sharing and mutuality. Most Muslims, and indeed many Christians, are quite nervous about this kind of approach, and think it is not only dangerous but represents what they most fear about dialogue. It is extremely important, they argue, that we not try to do anything that might make less clear the distinctions between our two communities. In its worst form, they believe, such conversation may well lead to a kind of syncretism that Christians and Muslims on the whole have both tried hard to avoid.

One way to foster conversation about the spiritual elements and achievements of Islam and Christianity, of course, is to keep it at somewhat of a distance by studying together the lives and insights of the great mystics and spiritual masters of both traditions. Americans are clearly hungry for spiritual insights no matter where they may come from, illustrated by the fact that the best selling religious book after the Bible is the poetry of the Persian Sufi Jalal al-Din Rumi. Few Muslims are not, frankly, delighted when one of the great masters from Islamic mystical tradition is recognized and appreciated for his poetry, his knowledge, and his (or occasionally, as in the case of the great woman mystic Rabia' al-Adawiyya, her) spiritual achievements. It is possible to study first a group of Sufis and then a group of Christian mystics so as to lower the risk of constant comparison. It doesn't take long, however, for serious students of mystical literature to spot the common language of mystical understanding.

The dialogue about spirituality model need not be an academic one or rely on the teachings of the greats. It may also refer to the spiritual growth that can take place when Muslim and Christians together achieve some kind of spiritual insight. While many Muslims might resist carrying the study of comparisons very far, unwilling to compromise what they understand as the uniqueness of the Islamic experience, others express frustration that more efforts at finding spiritual commonalities are not taking place. Washington, D.C., has often been considered one of the most vibrant centers of interfaith dialogue in the United States. Nonetheless, Towson University's Sanaullah Kirmani commented to me on what he has experienced as "the often dry and turgid academic dialogue" that has taken place there, comparing it with what is actually possible when members of different faith traditions allow themselves to work together to help deepen and increase their faith commitments as part of a common endeavor. Other experienced Muslim dialogue partners agree. "We can learn from each other, consciously or unconsciously coming closer to each other," says Irfan Ahmad Khan of the Council of Islamic Organizations in Markham, Illinois. Such sentiments, it seems, are beginning to be acknowledged a bit more easily in the American Muslim community today, although they would not be heard in most of the Islamic world. Imam Warith Deen Mohammed has developed an interesting spiritual dialogue with the Roman Catholic Focalare group, representing an unusual blend of African American and white along with Muslim and Christian.

Another variation on the theme of dialogue for spirituality is represented in the small number of Muslims who are interested in coming together with Christians for the purpose of "moral healing." Represented in the work of Laleh Bakhtiar of KAZI Books in Chicago, for example, moral healing is associated with an examination of modes of traditional psychology. As Bakhtiar, whose own work is with young women in the area of psychology and healing, said to me, "It is developing dialogue in terms of the virtues and vices that we all share." For others it means pressing forward together into a deeper form of spiritual experience, which necessitates that participants be at more or less the same "level" of spiritual interest and understanding. An Imam expressed such a desire during a dialogue of African American Christians and Muslims in Hartford several years ago. "My hope is always that we be prepared to discuss things at a more transcendent rather than a specific [i.e., issue-oriented] level. We need to address issues that touch the soul, heart, and mind. Do we have the spiritual character to have a true openness that is based on what is eternal and transcendent or not?" While such goals may indeed be the interest of some Christians and Muslims, they do make most potential participants in Christian-Muslim dialogue a bit uncomfortable. These goals will perhaps only be realized by those committed souls whose quest for spiritual understanding may exceed their need to stay firmly within the traditionally expressed bounds of their own religious traditions.

The Cooperative Model for Addressing Pragmatic Concerns

The direction suggested by many of the models described above point toward more action and less talk for its own sake. Young people are clearly among those who want to move the conversation along so as to be able to work together to achieve some desired end. Sometimes such activities take the form of community action, cooperating to achieve a goal that will help others. A Muslim women from Stephenstown, N.Y., remarked in conversation with me that "As actions are a form of connected community, perhaps shared community action projects are one of the deepest forms of dialogue." It is not unusual to hear participants in projects such as Habitat for Humanity, in which they come into contact with people of other religious traditions, comment that they know much more about the faith of Muslims or Christians through such activities than could come from many meetings of just talking. The action mode of dialogue is also particularly appealing to those who have spent a long time with a Muslim-Christian dialogue group and have become discouraged at what may feel like "wheel-spinning." "After the initial phase of getting acquainted," said one, "it just didn't feel like we were getting anywhere. We realized that we needed to find something to do together." Sometimes very innovative programs are being developed between and among religious communities, such as a Canadian venture described by Lilakat Takim that brought people in cold weather off the streets to spend one week sheltered in a mosque, another in a church, another in a synagogue. "Such a program fosters a belief in humanity," says Takim. Since the break-up of the Soviet Union refugees have been pouring into a number of major American cities, providing a wonderful opportunity for Muslims and Christians to work together in resettlement efforts. Some have found that while cooperating on particular projects may be more useful than "one more conversation," the struggle is to find a something that can be realistically achieved and to which everyone can feel committed, as well as to find ways to reflect together about what has been done.

One of the most ardent exponents of a kind of social action or pragmatic concern dialogue is Salam al-Mariati, Executive Director of the Muslim Public Affairs Council in Los Angeles. Warning of the dangers of too much talking, al-Mariati suggests that "Dialogue tends to spiral down to the encapsulation of our social fears, contradictions, and biases, on the one hand, or to float in the clouds of platitudinous mutual complements on the other."[10] Al-Mariati, a person whose primary concern is with the applied side of dialogue, gives an eloquent and important warning about the dangers of too much talk, too little action. The theme of action and its appeal to Christian and Muslim young people will be revisited in chapter eight, "New Directions in Dialogue."

Here, then, are a variety of ways in which American Christians and Muslims are learning to come together to talk about, and work for, better interfaith relations. Different things work for different people, of course, and groups considering moving ahead might do well to experiment a bit with several sorts of models. The sooner decisions are made and directions are set, the greater the likelihood that partners to the conversation will find themselves both satisfied and further challenged.

5

When Dialogue Goes Wrong

"It was wonderful! I wouldn't have missed the experience for the world." "I was amazed to discover that Muslims have so much in common with Christians. This dialogue really opened my eyes." "This was the first time I have every talked about my faith with anyone who is not Muslim, and it was difficult. But in the end I think I gained a lot from this dialogue."

With few exceptions, both Muslims and Christians who have had an involvement with dialogue, either as a one-time experience or in an ongoing group, are enthusiastic about the time they have spent together and want to affirm that good things have come out of the encounter. Nonetheless, not all interfaith experiences turn out well. Those who are lengthy experience in dialogue understand that there are traps into which even the most ardent advocates of interfaith exchange may fall, and problems that must be addressed if real progress is to take place in mutual understanding. Some of the potential problems that will be raised here are implicit in the foregoing chapters.

The Local and the Global

The world appears to many Americans to be getting increasingly troublesome, and to Western eyes all too often it seems that the problem spots are connected either directly or indirectly with Muslims.

Christian-Muslim dialogue has been a part of the American scene for quite some time, and yet anti-Islamic prejudice is rising. Many people feel that they are overwhelmed with a sense that they do not understand what it is that makes Muslims "tick" and why they are resorting to the kinds of violence and extremism that jump out from our newspapers and television screens. American Muslims may in turn be perplexed at what they believe to be unduly aggressive actions toward Muslim countries on the part of their government. Recently, one of the vexing problems to have caught the attention of people in many parts of the world has to do with—of all things—cartoons. Should a Danish newspaper be allowed to print derogatory cartoons of the Prophet Muhammad because of the guaranteed freedom of the press? And if they do, are Muslims then justified in taking what they see as the blasphemy of the act as justification for outraged and even violent action? Equally troubling is the recent statement by Pope Benedict XVI (see chapter six) and Muslim responses that in a few cases led to violence against Christians.

Next week's most newsworthy issue may be different—it is difficult to predict exactly what might set of the waves of anti-Western violence that have rocked Europe, the Middle East, East Asia, and other places in the world—but there seems little doubt that new issues will fuel the fires of Islamic extremism. As of this writing the Middle East is literally ablaze again with violent acts of fear and retaliation. Many scholars and public intellectuals who have long decried the thesis of Harvard's Samuel Huntington that the world is moving toward an east-west split are becoming nervous that the prophecy is in fact being fulfilled.[1]

So what do these global realities have to do with local efforts of Muslims and Christians to get to know each other, to talk about theology, ethics, and projects for mutual edification and for community betterment? For one thing, Americans are worried, and increasingly so, as demographic projections foresee rapidly growing Muslim populations in the West. Despite the fact that the numbers of Muslims in America are growing at a slower rate than predicted, right-leaning journals continue to warn of the possibility that neighborhood mosques might harbor violent cells. For another thing, American Muslims whose families have lived in other areas of the world bring with them a legacy of identity and commitment that may not accord with current American foreign policies. As California dialogue expert Fathi Osman notes, "the heavy psychological impact of certain historical memories will have real and certain effects on our conversations." However, he continues, "Bitter memories of the past, and even certain cases of the present, should not overshadow the substantial change in our time, nor restrict us from developing constructively our present...."[2] Osman insists that these remarks, made in an international context, apply strongly to the situation in America. Nonetheless, fears on the part of non-Muslim Americans about the phenomenon of extremist Islam, along with strongly held affiliations and convictions on the part of both Muslims and Christians from overseas, may certainly raise difficulties for dialogue groups and are likely be among the primary reasons why conversations with the best of intentions can reach a dead end. One obvious example, of course, is Jerusalem, an issue over which factions have been divided for many centuries. Conservative Christians, Christians from the Middle East, and Muslims from many parts of the world may all have very different and strongly felt opinions about what should happen to the "holy city."

It is a truism to observe that one of the major problems of dialogue is the tendency to talk about one's own faith in its ideal form, and to assess the faith of another in terms of the way it is seen to be manifested in everyday life, although few persons who have attempted interfaith relations would admit that they had fallen into such a trap. But there is, of course, a very significant gap between the ideal of Christian life as it is held out in the New Testament and the ways in which Christian people live and make decisions. When an American government claims to be guided by Christian principles and then acts in ways perceived by American Muslims to be threatening to their individual rights or to contravene the rights of Muslims living in other parts of the world, such actions become one of the proverbial elephants in the room of Christian-Muslim dialogue. Another troublesome issue is the way Christians are treated in some Muslim countries, about which many Christians here are deeply upset. And when Muslims talk earnestly with Christians about their understanding of Islam as the quintessential religion of peace, the words ring hollow to those who are reading about violent acts committed by Muslims around the world. As a result, the conversation may become so artificial as to seem not worth the effort.

Some ongoing groups have decided that to whatever extent may be possible, it is better to avoid conversation about international events, government actions, and mass responses. Others recognize that "dialogue in depth," unless it stays dedicated to the discussion of theological and ethical similarities and distinctions, or focuses on local projects that can be engaged at an interfaith level, probably will not be satisfactory unless participants talk openly about these difficult political realities. Certainly it is essential for those engaged in dialogue to have reached a reasonable level of trust before raising such issues, and the risk that the conversation will come to an impasse is significant. It is often frustrating for Muslims, says Muzammil Siddiqi, when Christians don't seem to understand how Muslims view things even after they have been told many times. Siddiqi had in mind the issue of Muslim sensitivities concerning what they see as the one-sided American response to the ongoing conflict in Israel/Palestine.

For dialogue groups that decide to try to keep their conversations local, to talk together about issues that can contribute constructively to their common life as citizens of local communities, still other problems should be thoughtfully considered and addressed. Among them are the following.

The Playing Field Is Not Level

With varying degrees of success, Christian denominations in America have been talking together for many years, sometimes in engagement with Jews. Over time they have come to set certain rules and standards about dialogue, or simply generally understood. Muslims who join these conversations, many of which have been transformed from long-standing ecumenical to interfaith dialogues, are relatively new to the game. Sometimes the only kind of dialogue with which they are familiar is that of confrontation, described in chapter four, where the atmosphere is charged and the goal of the exercise is to prove one's own position right and the other's wrong. Even if they don't mean to be confrontational, Muslims coming from such backgrounds may feel it is their responsibility to present their ideas in a traditional manner that American Christians generally find unappealing and nonconstructive, says Marcia Hermansen of Loyola University. Others have noted that Muslims are a bit behind in knowing how to engage in nonconfrontational dialogue, and must be given time to catch up.

"We Muslims have not yet developed a language of dialogue," commented Liyakat Takim of the University of Denver several years ago. "We should lay the foundations of dialogue as a discipline—with rules, regulations, premises, methodology and guidelines—so that emotions don't take over." Ibrahim Negm of St. John's University agrees but says the responsibility goes both ways. "We need more intellectual work from both Muslims and Christians on the *how* of it." Negm, who has been an active participant in the USCCB/ISNA ongoing dialogue sessions, believes that not only should Muslims and Christians work within their own communities to set this kind of agenda, but that it can be an important mutual project for members of both faiths to work on together.

Former Muslim Student Association President Altaf Husein worries that young Muslims will get discouraged with the dialogue because it is often too freewheeling with no rules or guidelines. He urges an agenda of more issue-based conversation focused on specific topics of mutual interest to Muslim and Christian students. Some Muslims have admitted in conversation with me that they have been tentative about participating in formally organized dialogue activities (the specific example given was a dialogue sponsored by the National Conference for Community and Justice, formerly the National Conference of Christians and Jews), precisely because clear rules for participation have not been established and shared.[3]

Muslims who are recently arrived from overseas, most particularly those who may have come to America to escape political or economic oppression, may be experiencing a tremendous sense of displacement and cultural shock. Already established Christian dialogue groups often respond with enthusiasm to the arrival of these Muslims into their communities, and rush to invite them to join their conversations. Many are not willing to make such a commitment. A number of factors may come into play in their reluctance. Among them, as Takim has observed, is the fact that most large mosques and Islamic centers, to which new arrivals may feel themselves drawn, are relatively new and have looked inward to improving their own facilities rather than outward to establishing links with the non-Muslim community.[4] The truth is that the majority of Muslims in America are really not interested in interfaith dialogue, either by inclination or by ideology. Those who identify with what is perceived as a growing Wahhabi or Salafi influence in this country are among the Muslims who would probably decline the dialogue. This is of particular concern to Muslims who fear that such influence will deter a new generation of young people from engaging in what they consider to be a very important activity.[5] Those who do not want to be involved sometimes argue that part of the doctrine of Islam is being loyal strictly to Muslims, and they fear that somehow that loyalty might be compromised were they to engage in real dialogue. Others are convinced that they have no need for such conversations, that there is really nothing to talk about since Islam provides them with all they need to live in Western society.

Those Muslims who do decide to participate may well find that it is very hard to live up to the expectations of their new hosts, who immediately want them to talk about what it means to be Muslim. Finding ways to welcome new immigrants into a community, and to get to know them and their circumstances before inviting them to engage in dialogue, is a major responsibility of Christian individuals and groups. It is very important for new immigrants to become involved gradually in such ongoing groups so that they do not feel overwhelmed by something that is quite new to them. It is also important to let them know what the rules and expectations are for any already established groups. Ongoing dialogue groups, of course, want and need to get a greater cross section of Muslim representation and to hear new voices in the conversation. But the Muslims must be encouraged to talk at their level of experience and not to meet the expectations of their Christian hosts or to feel intimidated by the fact that other Muslims who are experienced at dialogue already understand the understood rules of engagement.

That "the playing field is not level" may feel particularly relevant to many women, both Muslim and Christian, who are drawn into dialogue sessions, especially if they are invited simply to help redress a gender imbalance. In this case, gender rather than religious affiliation can provide the bond of commonality. Some Christian women have been pastors for many years and have no trouble speaking in mixed-gender groups, and a growing number of Muslim women in America, while not serving as Imams, have no difficulty finding their voices no matter who else is in the group. Both Muslim and Christian women, however, often have been trained to defer to the pastor or the Imam, or simply do not feel comfortable voicing their opinions when the men of their respective communities are present. African American women, who are pillars of their churches, are often conditioned into silence in the presence of their pastors. Christians from communities in which women are as vocal as men may find this reticence on the part of both Christian and Muslim women frustrating, with the result that various means are employed to "draw the women out." The first lesson, of course, needs to be greater understanding of the cultural and the religious circumstances that determine the comfort level of women in common conversation. Understanding and appreciation—often difficult to achieve, especially for "liberated" women—can contribute more toward progressing the dialogue than frustration and insistence that all women must speak up.

Who Speaks for Whom?

Muslim participation in interfaith dialogues to date is most evident on the part of immigrants from South Asia. For some others, particularly Arabs and African Americans, this is problematic insofar as they feel that the perspectives of Indians and Pakistanis may not reflect those of other Muslims in America, especially their own particular group. Many Muslims today, on the other hand, are also concerned that the Wahhabi voice is becoming stronger, bringing a conservative interpretation of Islam to the table that many want to distance themselves from. Much of the writing of Muslim intellectuals who have been involved in dialogue is expressly for the purpose of countering Wahhabi perspectives.

Shi'ite Muslims generally worry that their voices are not being adequately represented in dialogues in which Sunnis almost always predominate. For the most part, Shi'ite representation in dialogue sessions is minimal, often with only one participant alongside a number of Sunnis, and does not reflect the size of the growing Shi'ite community in America. Mainline Sunni Muslims often know very little about Shi'ism, and can easily get caught up in interpretations of Islam that have more to do with culture than with religion. To some extent, of course, the lack of Shi'ite representation is due to the reluctance of Shi'ites themselves to enter into conversations because it is not in their tradition to do so. While one might make the case that most dialogue groups fail to provide across-the-board Christian representation even of Protestantism—to say nothing of Roman Catholicism or certainly of Orthodox Christians—it is clear that the stakes are currently much higher for Muslims, particularly in today's climate of the war on terrorism.

African Americans are sometimes upset both because they feel inadequately represented in many dialogue sessions, and because it may seem to them that they are not always taken seriously by other Muslims when they do participate. "The handmaidens of dialogue are angst and introspection," remarks Aminah McCloud, reflecting on the loneliness she has felt as an African American dialogue participant. "My experiences as a woman of color have never been the center of any dialogue to which I was invited."[6] McCloud says she had to learn fast that African Americans are largely invisible in Christian-Muslim dialogues, both because they are so few in number and because they generally are not heard when they speak. The typical Chicago area meetings in which she has been involved are dominated by middle-aged, white mainline Protestants in conversation with South Asian Muslim immigrants. Finally, she notes, the passion and emotion that many African Americans bring to the conversation, particularly when talking about the pain they have been subjected to through slavery and subsequent exclusion, are viewed as inappropriate to a reasoned dialogue conversation, rendering the black participant silent and, in effect, invisible.

It is certainly true that some immigrants feel that while it is crucial to have the participation of all Muslims, it may be frustrating if, as it appears to them, African Americans want to talk about their own issues before people can talk together. Immigrants, says Imam Muhammad Nur Abdullah, himself an immigrant from Sudan, are generally more open to a range of perspectives than their black co-religionists (a view that many would challenge), and are less obviously concerned about racism. Sheikh Ibrahim Nejm notes that when immigrant and African American Muslims participate together in a dialogue sessions it often turns into a debate rather than a dialogue, or more specifically a sub-debate within the overall conversation.

I have had African Americans express to me their concern that the reason local dialogues seldom include both African American and immigrant Muslims is because immigrants, with Christian initiators, generally control the agenda and the list of invitees. This, they feel, is because immigrants want Christians to talk with "authentic" Muslims rather than "newcomers on the scene." The African Americans, of course, tend to feel that they themselves are the truly authentic Muslims in the American context because of their indigenous identity. At a deeper level than these kinds of judgments, however, African American Muslims do recognize that serious problems sometimes impede their own participation in dialogue. Among the problems that I have heard identified are the continuing struggle with identity issues, the lack of much serious intellectual leadership, and the general inexperience of African Americans with what has been called the "diplomacy of dialogue." Many express the frustration of constantly feeling that they need to "prove themselves" in relation to immigrants; bluntly, they feel caught among the triple pressures of American racism, lack of appreciation by immigrant brothers and sisters, and American anti-Muslim attitudes. "I am very concerned that there is a distorted image of Islam in America," says Sheikh 'Abd Allah Latif 'Ali, Chairman of the Imams Council of New York, "meaning an immigrant image that does not understand prejudice against indigenous Muslims here in America."[7]

Many factors, then, come to play as Christians and Muslims try to find partners for the dialogue. A colleague from Dallas confessed that he has been attempting for some time to get Muslims and Christians more broadly engaged, but is finding that it isn't easy. The Muslim community is hardly united, he says, and is quite capable of being seriously divided over issues of precedence and prestige. For all the talk of the unity of the *ummah,* he finds that ethnicity, secularism, and pure individualistic entrepreneurialism make it hard for Muslims to work together. Such problems, he adds, are not so different from those of Christians.

Redressing the Imbalance

As we observed above, most so-called dialogues really never move past the basic "getting to know you" mode. Very little in terms of preparation is required for this kind of conversation, and much is to be gained from the simple exchange of information. Such basic exchange may, on occasion, even lead to the formation of real individual friendships. But for groups who aspire to move past this basic format of getting acquainted, it is necessary to find ways to address the reality that groups are seldom balanced in terms of factors such as representation, numbers, and religious knowledge. It is the knowledge component that often turns out to be one of the major reasons for the failure of a dialogue group.

Among Christians, for example, there may be some who know very little about Christian history and theology, or even about different sects and denominations, while others (usually pastors or religious leaders) may be very well informed. Obviously those who feel that they know less are reluctant to join the conversation or automatically defer to the clergy present. It can also be frustrating and annoying when mainline Christians, who know little or nothing about evangelical movements and even less about orthodox Christianity, do not have the sensitivity to try to explain to their Muslim colleagues that they cannot speak for the whole body of belief. Some Protestants are annoyed when Roman Catholics, who often know relatively little about Protestant groups, speak in such a way that Catholicism seems to be the only Christian way of looking at things, and vice versa.

The imbalance is particularly noticeable if at least some of the Christians who are asked to represent Christianity are members of the clergy, while the Muslims available in many communities are not religious professionals at all but are doctors, engineers, or blue-collar workers. It is often the case that Muslims involved in the dialogue are invited because there are not many in the community from whom to choose, and they may actually not know a great deal about Islam other than what their own family practices. Another kind of unequal relationship sometimes exists when Christians know more about elements of Islamic history and theology than Muslims themselves do. This may be the case if those who have served on the mission field, or been stationed for business purposes in an Islamic country, or may even be teachers of Islamic studies are invited to participate. Often it is these people who hear that such a dialogue is happening and want to come out of their own interests. The reverse is unusual, but on occasion Muslims really do know more about Christianity than do the Christians.

Some Muslims reflecting on the nature of the dialogue in America have been articulate about the necessity of learning more about their faith before trying to engage in interfaith conversation. "What we are doing now in the dialogue is nice stuff, promoting friendly relations, etc.," says Ghulam Hader Asi of what was formerly the American Islamic College in Chicago. "But we will never have effective dialogue until Muslims are better trained in their own tradition." Asi goes even farther, and insists that real dialogue cannot take place until Muslims understand something of the practices of Christianity apart from what they read in the Qur'an. It is essential, he says, for Muslims to know more about those we are dialoguing with, especially how their sects and denominations differ. Other Muslims have reflected that one of the difficulties of the dialogue is that Christians sometimes speak about Islam without adequate knowledge, which Muslims may feel is both irresponsible and somewhat arrogant.

In the best of worlds, perhaps, aspirants to real dialogue should prepare themselves by becoming more thoroughly grounded in their own beliefs and practices, then of others within their respective traditions, and finally of those of the persons with whom they hope to have conversation. This is actually being done by some Christians, particularly with the ready availability of basic information about Islam prepared by both Muslims and Christians since 9/11. In today's climate, most Muslims are probably more concerned with defending Islam than they are with learning more about different Islamic sects or about Christianity. While education is always to be encouraged, usually the best that can be hoped for is an understanding of the complexities of such informational imbalances. Without some perspective on this issue, members of a dialogue group may find themselves frustrated, perplexed, and at times even angry, and little inclined to pursue the project of better mutual understanding.

Lurking Suspicions

Suspicion persists on the part of many Muslims that the hidden agenda of Christians is the intent to proselytize. The largest mosque in the vicinity of Hartford Seminary continues to turn down invitations to participate in the Seminary's Christian-Muslim dialogue programs because it remembers the earlier history of the school as a training ground for missionaries to Muslim countries. Much of the nervousness of Muslims about being the targets of proselytization, of course, is a continuing response to various forms of Western colonialism, including the strong missionary efforts of the nineteenth and twentieth centuries. Naturally they are also aware that many more conservative Christians still are engaged in serious efforts at evangelizing Muslims, both abroad and in the United States

In general, Muslims, who have had experience in Christian-Muslim dialogue, are no longer worried about such hidden agendas, either seeing for themselves that such intent is not the case or having acquired the degree of sophistication to be able to respond appropriately if they do encounter it. "To educated Muslims there are no dangers but to ignorant conservatives there are many," said Shahid Athar. "They see the interfaith process as compromising on faith. . . . creating doubts in the minds of young Muslims." Other Muslims who are less concerned about attempts at conversion on the part of Christians worry that young people are sufficiently impressionable that engaging in conversation with Christians may encourage them to see the commonalities to the point of making the differences insignificant, resulting in a kind of blending of the faiths.

Interestingly, it is in the post 9/11 period that Christians are becoming more sensitive to the reality that Muslims may in fact be presenting a kind of "conversion" challenge of their own. Muslims who speak and write about dialogue are very clear that *da'wa* must be interpreted as the propagation of correct information about Islam rather than calling others to become Muslim. Yet it is also obvious that *da'wa* with the intent to convert does go on. Most African American Muslims come from Christian backgrounds, and they know how to deal with it if anyone tries to turn them back to Christianity. African American Christians, however, are very worried about the attraction of Islam to their youth through programs of rap music and messages appealing especially to young men. They also recognize that a growing portion of the prison population, the majority of which is black, is finding that Islam as explained by the chaplain Imams offers an appeal and a plan for life that Christian chaplains do not seem able to propose.

Experienced practitioners of dialogue are so eager to insist that urging others to convert is *not* part of the agenda of dialogue that they set rules for engagement that may seem to preclude participants from speaking from the heart about their religious beliefs. Yet repeated Muslim attempts to describe Islam as the true religion, the natural and inherent religion *(din al-fitra)*, and the only religion acceptable to God may feel slightly coercive to Christians. Here, of course, is the neuralgic point in Christian-Muslim dialogue. Groups that have moved beyond initial encounter and want to have more depth in their conversations may discover that honesty of theological conviction can easily lead to proclamation on both sides. This can be a wonderful thing, and for experienced dialogue partners can be exciting and challenging. But participants who are not able to deal with it in a thoughtful way and to learn from it may find that the dialogue has moved onto ground that is uncomfortable and personally unrewarding.

Whose Ideology and Why? Or, Who Sets the Table?

The question of who initiates dialogue sessions, whether they are single-shot events or planned as continuing conversations, is beginning to be taken seriously by those who have experience in such interactions. The fact that Christians have traditionally assumed the responsibility has engendered different responses within the Muslim community. Some feel that it is still appropriate for Christians to make the first move. Zahid Bukhari, codirector of a major project locating Muslims in the American public square, told me several years ago that he thinks many Muslims still consider themselves to be guests in

America, and that they are therefore in a "response" rather than an "initiation" mode. Harvard's Leila Ahmad agrees. Of course it is up to Christians to invite Muslims into the conversation, she says, because Muslims still remain a tiny minority.

Increasingly, however, Muslims are discovering that there are clear disadvantages to having Christians act as hosts. "Generally it is a Christian table set with some Muslim guests who are trying to figure out why they have been invited to dinner," Amina McCloud commented shortly after 9/11. McCloud went farther, accusing some of the Christians who initiate dialogue of being "conflict avoiders" because they set the agenda with items that are likely to engender conflict and then try themselves to avoid it. The problem is further complicated when the theological discussion is formulated in what are basically Christian categories such as salvation and redemption. When this is the case, said Riffat Hassan of the University of Louisville, the Muslim is forced to dialogue in terms that may be alien to his or her religious ethos, or to which he or she may even be hostile.[8]

Many Muslims feel that until they become organized and determine who will be invited, what the agenda will be and on whose terms, there will always be an imbalance in the conversation. Imam Sayed Hassan Qazwini of the Islamic Center of America urges Muslims to initiate dialogue with others precisely because it is implicit in the message of the Qur'an to do so. Qazwini, a Shi'ite who is keenly aware of the differences between certain communities of Muslims in America, told me that very often it is harder for Muslims to get together with other Muslims to talk about beliefs and practices than it is to initiate dialogue with non-Muslims. The same, of course, can be said for Christians.

Some serious initiatives are beginning from the Muslim side, although many Muslims and Christians feel that it will be a long time before Muslims are really active in inviting Christians to dialogue. Soon after 9/11, the Council on Islamic Relations (CAIR) began a project of mosque open houses, urging as many mosques in America as possible to invite Christians and others to visit, see their facilities, and learn first hand about Muslim beliefs and practices. They even published a list of things that mosque members should make sure that they do or avoid doing so as to make their non-Muslim guests feel comfortable. Few mosques had such open houses before 9/11, though the majority reports to have had them since. Moves like this to improve the imbalance in initiating the dialogue, including shifting the venue to mosques and Islamic institutions, will go far in helping conversations be more successful.

One interesting and relatively new development is that Muslims are now inviting Christians to observe, and even participate in, national Muslim conventions of groups such as the Islamic Society of North America, the Islamic Circle of North America, and the Ministry of Warith Deen Mohammed. Such invitations may be interpreted as one more way in which Muslims since 9/11 have tried to stress the open nature of Islam, but in any case they appear to represent a serious new trend in interfaith relations. The Muslim Public Affairs Council (MPAC) has been a leader in organizing interfaith exchanges. MPAC has invited members of the National Council of Churches, the National Conference of Catholic Bishops and local and national Jewish organizations to engage in dialogue efforts.[9] Changes are clearly underway in some quarters, although the it is still uncertain as to how much active initiative the American Muslim community will decide to take.

Meanwhile, and in contrast to the guidelines set out by CAIR for Muslim open houses, Christians often have not been sensitive to ways in which Muslims who are invited into Christian space can be made more comfortable. Many Muslims prefer not to enter a church sanctuary and will not attend conversations where that is an expectation. Wherever the dialogue is held, if it is initiated by Christians, someone from the host congregation should meet and welcome Muslims at the door. When women as well as men are invited it is important to make sure that two people, a man and a woman, be designated as official hosts. Christians should be sensitive to the possibility that Muslim women might prefer to be seated in some way that separates them from male participants. Such seemingly small things can go far in assuring that Muslims are comfortable and perhaps willing to come back.

Dialogue participants have long observed that it may be easier for social and theological conservatives and liberals to talk with their counterparts across religious lines than to try to bridge such divisions within our individual traditions. When Christian liberals and Muslims whose ethical positions mirror those of Christian conservatives try to talk with each other, particularly if they are not aware of the various elements involved, the situation can become frustrating and challenging for continuing the group. Take, for example, the always contentious issue of sexual preference. Several years ago, a group of Christian and Muslim women of which I was a part had spent several days together, enjoying each other's company greatly and delighting in all the things we found we had in common. On the last day, with the group sitting in a large conversation circle, one Muslim woman said that she would like the meeting to conclude with a joint statement condemning homosexuality. "That which is most important for us to take a stand on," she said, "is our disapproval of and opposition to the evils of homosexuality." What she did not know, and many others in the group did, was that sitting next to the conference's organizer was her female partner. After that very discomfiting moment, the group was not able to reclaim its former level of ease and trust and concluded with people feeling embarrassed rather than satisfied.

Muslims often find themselves more comfortable when they are talking about such ethical issues with Roman Catholics or evangelicals than they do with mainline or liberal Protestants, sharing a common perspective on the importance of theological certainty, on a definition of right and wrong in relation to a number of ethical concerns, and even on the understanding that only males can occupy positions of senior religious leadership. Newly emerging talks between Muslims and evangelical Christians may find the same kind of common ground.

When Windows Are Mirrors

A 1989 article by A. K. Ramanujan, "Where Mirrors are Windows: Toward an Anthology of Reflections," suggests an image of mirrors and windows that I find helpful in illustrating one of the subtler difficulties of interfaith dialogue.[10] Conversation and exchange with members of other traditions has many wonderful benefits, but it can also lead to pitfalls that may be both unanticipated and unwelcome, particularly if participants make assumptions that are not mutual. When windows are opened between religious traditions, it allows us to reach through toward mutual sharing. But reversing Ramanujan's simile, we need to recognize that sometimes what we think are windows are really only mirrors, reflecting back only our own assumptions and beliefs. They may serve to provide only frustrating glimpses of beliefs and practices of one tradition in which the dialogue partners representing the other tradition can never hope to participate. In terms of Muslim-Christian encounter, a mirror may reflect for us what Muslims hold dear but really do not wish for Christians to actually experience. Some things cannot be shared.

When engaging in interfaith conversation, how can we be sensitive enough to know when we can not, or should not, cross boundaries, either the boundaries set by our Muslim colleagues or those that in some way serve to distinguish, and perhaps protect, our own faith? We also may need to ask when too much emphasis on those things we genuinely have in common as people of faith runs the danger of scaring off potential dialogue partners for fear that they might be pushed toward a kind of relativity. As we have seen, many Muslims today worry that the terms "interfaith" or "interreligious" relations suggest the possibility of syncretism, preferring instead what they see as the more neutral terms "multifaith" or "multireligious" which they believe better preserve the integrity of each tradition.

Christians may be particularly guilty of mistaking mirrors for windows. "Let's discover what we really have in common," they enthuse. "We know that we aren't going to agree on everything, so let's stop talking about theological differences and try to find our common ground." So long as common ground means sharing the effort to act righteously, work for peace and the like, the dialogue is usually placid. But when Christians make untested assumptions of commonality, problems can easily arise. It is in this potentially more creative alternative to the conversational dialogue that the dangers of being too extreme may lie.

Two experiences that I have had with interfaith dialogue groups may help illustrate how ready assumptions can lead to discomfort and pain on the part of all the participants. Each happens to have been in the context of an interfaith group involving members of other religious traditions beyond just Christians and Muslims.

In the early days of the rise of feminism some friends and I formed a women's dialogue group composed of Christians, Jews, Hindus, Buddhists, and Muslims. We were women, and we all considered ourselves (or, we thought that we did) to be feminist in some definition of that term which was just coming to be so popular. Our window on each other, we assumed, was that we were ready to scrap the traditions (though not necessarily the scriptures) of our particular faiths that seem discriminatory towards women. But as the conversation played out, we discovered that the Muslim women were becoming increasingly silent. In fact they were deeply offended. "You want to say that the rules have been made by men for women to follow," accused one. "But you don't understand that Muslim women believe these to be divine rules. By liberating us from these 'man-made' regulations you are trying to liberate us from our own religion." What we had thought was the window of common frustration about the dominance of males in our traditions turned out for the Muslim women to be a mirror reflecting a faith position that many in the group could not share or even appreciate.

Fortunately, self-proclaimed feminists of various religious traditions have become considerably more sophisticated and thoughtful since those early days, and understand that neither false assumptions of commonalities nor retreat behind perceived differences need bring an end to the conversation. Still, Western Christian women need to be very careful not to assume that their aspirations toward liberating their texts and their positions within the faith will necessarily be appreciated or shared by Muslim women. "I am willing to adopt the label feminist," some Muslims will say (which represents a great deal of reflection and interpretation since the anger expressed by many Muslim women during the early days of Western feminist proclamations), "but you have to understand that it is feminist in Islamic, not Western, terms."

Another example of overstepping boundaries, of mistaking mirrors for windows, goes in the opposite direction. Rather than expecting too much of my Muslim colleagues in terms of sharing, I attempted to bring them into a part of my own church life in a way that I realized, after the fact, was not appropriate. The experience came in the context of a Christian-Muslim-Jewish women's group that I had established. We met for several years and began to share with each other on a number of levels. Symbolic windows began to open. Finally we decided that it would be fun to participate in each other's religious rituals. We had a Hanukkah luncheon at one member's home, and even exchanged small gifts. In preparation for an *iftar* dinner during Ramadan at the home of another all the members of the group fasted for the day. My task then was to find a Christian observance of some kind in which we could all participate. Unwisely I chose the Maundy Thursday service at my own church. We sat, four Christians, four Jews and four Muslims, at a special reserved table. As the service came to its conclusion—the candles were extinguished, the readings became more somber and the clanging sound representing the nails being driven into Jesus echoed outside the worship hall—I looked at the faces of my colleagues and realized that I had made a big mistake. The Jews, as I discovered later, believed that they were being held to account for the death of Jesus, and the Muslims felt they were intruders in a ritual that was deeply Christian and affirmed basic theological claims denied in the Qur'an. Because the church requested absolute silence after the service our group never had a chance to unpack the experience until much later. Here the error was not in crossing someone else's boundary, but in my having failed to set a boundary for my own religious tradition. I had tried to open a window through which my colleagues were uncomfortable looking.

We Must Be Honest

Ultimately, I am quite sure, all our dialogue is doomed to failure if the participants are not ready, sooner or later, to be honest. The stakes are simply too high today for anything less, although new participants usually express their concern that they might inadvertently insult or hurt the feelings of others. We in the United States have long enjoyed the luxury of a cushion of distance from the kinds of historical rivalries that have existed in many other parts of the world. Recurrent skirmishes, and sometimes more serious wars, have made interfaith dialogue difficult to imagine at best and often out of the question. Several points are relevant:

1. We in America long been distanced, until recently perhaps, from the circumstances that make dialogue extremely difficult in many areas of the world. What we hear on the news may not be sufficient to help us know what it is that new Muslim immigrants are bringing to the table. This distance makes it hard for us to understand what their lives have been like, and what lies heavy on their hearts when they think of having conversations with members of the Christian religious tradition.

2. The Western world has changed with the reality of 9/11 and the constant reminder from the American government that our country is in a war against terrorism. Although until now most Americans have been personally inconvenienced only by increased security measures at the airport and the rising cost of gasoline, new threats such as the plot foiled in London in August 2006 seem destined to change that reality dramatically. Americans can ill afford to continue to believe that there is a degree of separation between the United States and the rest of the world.

3. Slowly we are coming to be aware that many of the indigenous Christians and Muslims we invite to the dialogue, persons we in our political correctness insist must be part of the conversation, may not want to come precisely because like their overseas counterparts they have been involved in painful struggles. The difference is that their experiences have been here in America. And many of us white, upper-middle class enthusiasts for getting to know our Muslim neighbors may, in fact, be quite oblivious of the struggles of the African Americans, Hispanics, or Native Americans whose participation we think we want. We know little of the kind of pain they may describe if they do come, pain often inflicted by us in ways we do not recognize. Thus we may be uncomfortable when that pain is expressed.

Loyola University's Marcia Hermansen has written an interesting article entitled "Muslims in the Performative Mode: A Reflection on Muslim-Christian Dialogue."[11] Hermansen, herself Muslim, points out that we often look at our partner in dialogue as an "essential" Muslim or Christian, as if one person could somehow represent all of those who share the same religious affiliation. Hermansen's observation serves to remind us how important it is that we try to discover the real nature of our dialogue partne. It also says that each of us who agrees to join in such a conversation must take on the responsibility of being as honest as possible about our own identity. We need to prepare ourselves to hear what others have to say and not be insulted, hurt, or disbelieving when we hear something painful from our coreligionists as well as our dialogue partners.

Nonetheless, the complex circumstances of dialogue, the factors that may make honest talk difficult, can sometimes be mitigated when participants enter into a kind of role-playing mode. This seems to have proved particularly useful for Muslims. Hermansen discusses what she calls "Dialogue in the Performative Mode," a way of acting on the part of many Muslim students, for example, during events such as Islam Awareness weeks on local campuses. "In a performance," she says, "one creates and transforms an imaginary space, and therefore nonverbal elements such as costume and gesture function as much to persuade as do actual verbal utterances."[12] Hermansen sees performative dialogue as a way for an oppressed minority to claim their space and authority.

Performance may also serve an important function in helping explain elements of ritual to newcomers. In the spring of 2006, at my institution several young Turkish women were explaining the positions of prayer to a group of non-Muslim female college students. The space they created was magical for these young women, especially as they demonstrated that by turning your head from right to left and saying "salamu 'alaykum [peace be upon you]," you are greeting not only your fellow worshippers but the angels who sit on each shoulder recording your deeds and thoughts for the day of judgment. The students understood something about Islam through this performance, and the dialogue that followed, that took them beyond classroom learning.

Performative dialogue can have many useful purposes, and should be used more often as an engaging way of moving beyond the limits of merely talking. When, however, particular forms of identity behavior mask who we really are as individuals as well as representatives of our respective faiths, the performance ceases to be useful and can serve as a severe impediment to the honest conversation that is essential for dialogue to succeed.

6

The Pluralistic Imperative

Christian Perspectives

Among the major challenges confronting American Muslims today, as we have seen, are the following: What binds together a community that is comprised of so many different branches and interpretations as Islam? What does it mean to be Muslim, both personally and communally, in a society in which Islam is not the majority faith? In the next chapter, we will consider a third task that is being assumed by at least a few American Muslims, which is to figure out whether Islam itself values other religions. Is Islam, in other words, a pluralistic or an exclusivist faith?

Christians also face several challenges in light of the growing presence of Muslims. One is to try to come to terms with the sheer fact of rapidly increasing religious plurality in American society (to say nothing of the hotly-contested issues related to immigration), of which Muslims are a single, albeit highly significant, element. In this sense, plurality is to be understood as a descriptive term; we *are* a nation of many different constituent elements. For members of Christian churches, as well as for their leaders and theologians, another challenge is to reflect theologically on the meaning of encounter with Islam. Christian theologians may put the question this way: Is there room in the understanding of Christianity for belief that truth can be found in other religions, specifically in Islam? Is Christianity, in other words, a pluralistic or an exclusivist faith?

The struggle of America, given the reality of its multicultural diversity, is to find a way in which to formulate some kind of common good. America, the land of immigrants, contains major segments of its population who fear, distrust and in general have little use for those coming from abroad, particularly from the two-thirds world. Those fears, of course, have been heightened in relation to Muslims especially since 9/11. Muslims, meanwhile, struggle not only with trying to persuade their American neighbors that Islam is at heart a religion of peace, but also that Islam has a legitimate role to play in American plurality. Those who wish to engage in conversation with Muslims need to take serious note of these tensions, and to understand the struggle of Muslims to find their role and identity in American culture. Thus both Christians and Muslims are dealing with pluralism as a descriptive term for a multiplicity of religions and cultures in one place, namely America.

But it is with the other kind of pluralism—the theological response of each faith to the presence of other religions, and most specifically to each other—that this and the next chapter attempt to deal. First we will look at how some American Christian thinkers have thought about issues of pluralism and the encounter with Islam.

Rethinking the Need for Inclusion

Much has been written about the importance of Christians and Muslims finding some grounds for conversation that beg the theological questions that have encumbered their dialogue for centuries. It is also true, however, that many Christians are struggling for greater clarity about their own faith as they contemplate engaging in conversation with Muslims. Many Christians, who might not have not considered Islam to be a "true" religion alongside Christianity, are finding that they need to rethink the question after personal involvement with Muslims.

Many American Christians are beginning to realize that they need help in thinking about how to balance wanting to be open to the possibility of truth in another religion on the one hand and confession of faith in Christianity (or Christ) on the other. United Methodist theologian John Cobb talks about the Scylla and Charybdis of contemporary Christianity, by which he means revering some historicized form of Christianity almost to the point of idolatry on the one side, and on the other a feeling of lukewarmness toward Christianity such that it is seen then as only one faith among many.[1] The situation becomes more complicated when liberal Christians, eager to be open to the ideas and perceptions of others (and it is often those very Christians who are most enthusiastic about interfaith exchange and dialogue), are either reluctant to talk about or express their own faith convictions or are unsure of what those convictions really are. Meanwhile, our Muslim partners in the dialogue are looking to Christians to be clearer about their faith.

While the literature of Christian theological reflection specifically about Islam is not abundant, there have nonetheless been continuing contributions for a number of decades. Some have been designed specifically to help Christians consider the difficulty of coming to come to terms with a religion that arose after the New Testament and denies some of its most basic affirmations such as the crucifixion and resurrection of Christ, and Jesus as the Son of God. Attempts by mainline Protestant and Catholic theologians to help Christians to think theologically about Islam are often brief, embedded in larger discussions of pluralism or other theological discussions. This situation seems to be changing, although American theologians are significantly behind their British and Continental colleagues in this task.

American evangelicals have written a lot about Islam, but most of it deals with the importance of mission and witness for the specific purpose of converting Muslims to Christianity. Although some of this literature does address the reality of Muslims in America, most of it tends to perpetuate the notion that Islam is still "over there," a foreign field for missionary activity. The question for these writers is less how Christians can make theological sense of Islam than why Christian missionaries have had such a lean "harvest" among Muslims themselves.

Mission and Dialogue: A Necessary Tension?

The primary task of mission from the earliest days of Christianity's encounter with Islam, of course, has been witnessing to Christ, as Matthew 28 directs. This imperative has framed the American missionary movement since its inception at the end of the eighteenth century, and remains the motivating force for the mission movement today. High on the list of those targeted for conversion to Christianity, of course, have been Muslims, especially because of their claim that Islam is a continuation of the faith of the prophets of Judaism and Christianity. Early American missionaries to the Middle East, Africa, Indonesia, and other parts of the world in which Islam is dominant wasted little time reflecting on how to think theologically about Islam. Their challenge, as it remains for many conservative Christians today, was to go into the world and preach the message of Christ's saving grace.

The position of theological exclusivism is held by a majority of the world's Christians, although it has a few more challengers among American Christians today. Theological exclusivism holds that salvation occurs only through God's grace, specifically as revealed in Jesus Christ. Muslims, from this perspective, who revere Jesus as a Prophet but do not believe in him as savior, are in desperate need of hearing the good news of the Christian gospel. For the most part, theologians of the nineteenth century believed the adherents of non-Christian religions in general, and Islam in particular, to be outside the possibility of salvation. In many cases they found it difficult to move past the ancient Christian repertoire of accusations that the Prophet Muhammad was a charlatan, a knave, and an agent of the devil. Early twentieth century missiological writing was gentler in tone, stressing such themes as the Prophet's questionable morality, the faith's overly aggressive characteristics, and the inevitability of Islam's decline.

One of the early twentieth century missionaries deserving of particular notice because of his prolific writing on Islam was Samuel Marinus Zwemer, professor of Christian Missions at Princeton Theological Seminary. He represented the general Christian conviction that the goal of Christian missions should be conversion, and to the extent to which in his time abroad he could be said to have engaged in dialogue, it was to further that end. Zwemer's theological perspective on the relationship of Christianity and Islam is well reflected in the titles of some of his many writings: *Islam: A Challenge to Faith* (1907); *Into All the World: The Great Commission. A Vindication and an Interpretation* (1943); and *The Cross Above the Crescent: The Validity, Necessity and Urgency of Missions to Muslims* (1943).[2] Islam was a baffling problem for Zwemer, who came to greatly appreciate Muhammad as one of the greatest creative spirits that humans have even known and the religion of Islam itself as the truest of the non-Christian religions in its basic affirmations. But he could never have viewed Muhammad as a legitimate prophet because Islam came after Christianity and thus in no way could be considered a preparation for the life and deeds of Christ. Zwemer was convinced that Christ's great commission to preach salvation throughout the world meant that Islam was destined to die out as all Muslims became Christian. Zwemer's conclusion about the fate of Islam position continues to be held by a number of evangelicals today.

Over the succeeding decades of the twentieth century, missionaries came to study Islam much more deeply, both to be able to better understand the nature of the problem and to avoid offending those with whom they were sent to work. Still the theological conundrum that has faced Christians from the earliest days of Islam—how to reconcile it theologically with Christian proclamation—has remained. By mid-century many Christians began to challenge the right of the church to exercise its missionary mandate in the traditional way. This was accompanied by the serious beginnings of a number of attempts to find some kind of reconciliation between Islam and Christianity, either through the emphasis on a common monotheism or in finding similar ethical imperatives. The years of the mid-60s were characterized by increased openness to Islam as a true faith whose adherents are genuine seekers after God and, for many, the impetus toward dialogue as an essential means of communication.

The formation of the World Council of Churches in 1948 signaled the beginning of what has become a continuing debate about the relationship between mission and dialogue. Evangelicals were and continue to be concerned about movements that seem to them to downplay the uniqueness of Christ in the attempt to reach out to people of other faiths. Throughout the succeeding years of this century, the WCC has continued to pursue the agenda of dialogue with Islam as with other faiths, encouraged also by the new mood of openness engendered by Vatican II. Many Christian theologians have continued to justify dialogue as a necessary part of the mission enterprise. "The spirit of dialogue has great value in preparing the way for the apologetic message and must pervade all forms of encounter in mission," says former Methodist missionary Marston Speight.[3]

Contemporary Evangelicals and Islam

Contemporary evangelicals,[4] however, generally do not see the WCC's spirit of dialogue as a virtue. Since its inception they have been deeply concerned about movements to downplay the uniqueness of Christ in the attempt to reach out to people of other faiths, fearing that the emphasis is somehow a betrayal of mission and a tempering of the belief that salvation is through Jesus Christ alone. Following the WCC General Assembly in Porto Alegre, Brazil, in February of 2006, for example, Russell D. Moore of Louisville's Southern Baptist Theological Seminary announced that "The World Council of Churches has long been a boutique of paganism in Christian garb," and that "Regenerate believers across the world, whatever their denomination or communion, recognize the spirit of the World Council for what it is: the spirit of antichrist."[5] For an organization that for the last half century has worked for reconciliation of all groups and persons calling themselves Christian such an accusation may seem excessive, although its roots are found in traditional Christian eschatology. It reflects, however, the tensions that have existed in relation to the World Council of Churches from the beginning between the proponents of dialogue and those who have feared for a loss of evangelistic zeal.

In the last several decades, the amount of evangelical mission literature dealing with Islam has grown significantly, not unrelated to the rise of Islam as an increasingly important world force and more recently in its more militant forms. Many missiologists again have struggled to reconsider their approach to Islam. Evangelical organizations have frequently asked why their efforts to propagate Christ's message have resulted in so few Muslim converts. Urging a redoubling of effort, some have suggested that evangelization of Muslims is the special challenge for the beginning of the twenty-first century. Conservative organizations such as the United States Center for World Mission and the Samuel Zwemer Institute keep the church aware of the ongoing problem of Islam for Christians.

Some of the evangelicals who have been serving the mission field in recent years, unlike their pioneer forebears, have spent considerable time reflecting on the relationship of Christianity and Islam, and particularly about what it means to engage in interfaith dialogue. Especially after returning from overseas duty, they have ended up teaching in theological schools or seminaries and have devoted themselves to imparting what they have learned about Islam to students preparing for a career in missionary work, and to helping think about strategies for communicating the truths of Christianity that are less confrontational than those adopted by Zwemer and others.

Since the early 1970s, one of the major themes of conservative American Protestant writing about missions to Islamic lands has been that of "contextualization," the idea that the church needs to become more indigenous, taking root in social cultures. Contextualization has become a kind of watchword of evangelical Christian strategy, designed to support those Muslims who have already adopted Christianity and to make the faith more appealing to others. The goal is still conversion of Muslims to Christianity, but the tactics are based on the understanding that the church needs to become indigenous so that a convert to Islam while changing faith need not give up his or her culture.

Presbyterian Dudley Woodbury, former Director of the School of World Mission at Fuller Theological Seminary, for example, writes about the ways in which the pillars of Islam can be used effectively to help Muslims who have converted "to bear the weight of their new faith in Christ."[6] Each pillar can become adapted from its traditional Muslim context to now express an aspect of the performance of Christian ritual. American Mennonite missionary Mike Brislen, among a number of others, writes about the importance of developing a Muslim-culture church. In his vision, the "Isa [Jesus] muezzin [one who gives the call to prayer]" ascends the minaret and gives a call to prayer that tries to emulate the Muslim call but actually sounds like this: "I bear witness that [Jesus] is the Word of God who sends forth the Spirit proceeding from the command of my Lord . . . ."[7] Muslims, obviously, can easily be offended by such tactics, and even some Christians might not wonder if they come a bit close to syncretism.

One of the most articulate proponents of a theology of contextualization is Presbyterian missionary (and former Merrill Fellow at Harvard Divinity School) Phil Parshall. Deeply influenced by his friendships with Muslims in Sri Lanka and other Muslim countries, including a particularly close relationship with a Muslim physician, Parshall wants to build bridges by finding commonalities between the faiths of Christianity and Islam.[8] Another advocate of contextualization, he proposes that missionaries live simply, dress as much like Muslim religious men as possible, worship as Muslims do by removing their shoes, sitting on the floor of the worship hall without chairs, and prostrating fully. Parshall even suggests that Christians fast in Muslim style.[9] Despite the many ways in which he is clearly appreciative of certain elements of Islam, however, he remains deeply dedicated to the conversion of Muslims from a faith that he finds "rigid and unyielding," an "erroneous system" that is characterized by "cold, dead orthodoxy."[10]

These strategies for converting Muslims to Islam are important in our discussion of dialogue for several reasons. First, they are now being applied to the growing numbers of Muslims in America, which provides a new field for Christian missionary activity. Christian women, in particular, are being trained to reach out to new immigrant women who may be lonely in their new setting. Developing friendships, they say, can lead to opportunities to pass on the "good news" of the gospel. Second, such literature constitutes the primary reading on Islam in many Christian seminaries and theological schools, training the pastors who may be tomorrow's participants in Christian-Muslim dialogue as well as those who are preparing for the mission field. To the extent to which Christian-Muslim relations is a topic treated in Protestant schools of theology or seminaries in the United States, it is often in the context of a mission-training program such as that at Fuller.[11] Third, many of the former missionaries who are writing, or have written, about Islam have spent long years in the company of Muslims and bring a depth and knowledge of Islam and its adherents that far exceeds that of most Christians who want to be in conversation with Muslims in America. They have often formed deep friendships with Muslims, and like Woodberry, Parshall, and Brislen struggle to reconcile their personal appreciation of Islam with their often-conservative Christian theological convictions.

A few evangelicals who are not specifically dedicated to the mission work of the church are beginning to write extensively and thoughtfully about Islam. One of those is Wesleyan pastor Tony Richie, who describes himself as coming from a Pentecostal-Charismatic faith family. Looking to his roots for guidance in understanding Islam, Richie carefully examined the writings of John Wesley whom, he discovered, himself had a good deal to say about Muhammad and the religion he founded.[12] Richie discovered that while Wesley quite naturally believed Jesus Christ to be God's supreme revelation, he felt it was important to acknowledge that Christians really could not lay claim to more ethically pure lives than Muslims. "Surely Mahometanism was let loose to reform the Christians!" he observed.[13] In these reflections on Islam, John Wesley expanded on what he described as three theological circles: (a) the outer circle of divine providence, in which Muslims, Jews, and heathens reside, (b) the interior circle of the visible Church, meaning Christians in general, and (c) the innermost circle in which all true Christians are to be found, the invisible church. He is clear that those in the first two circles are not "anonymous" Christians, saved by Christ although they do not know it, which as we will see below is a position held by some Roman Catholics. Wesley exhibits the missionary spirit in his intense hope for the conversion of Muslims to Christianity, but trusts that if it happens it will be because Muslims have observed true piety and morality among their Christian brethren. Christians, in turn, are called upon to recognize piety in Muslims when they see it, providing a balance between full acceptance of Islam and consigning Muslims to hell. "If we really believe that divine providence extends to all creation," Richie finds Wesley saying, "we ought to acknowledge his inclusive embrace of every human being, especially those who faithfully walk in the light of their existing knowledge of God."[14] Richie suggests that this represents an "inclusive" view to the extent to which it includes all that God has created under the umbrella of divine providence.

In a 2006 article entitled "Neither Naïve nor Narrow: A Balanced Pentecostal Approach to Christian Theology of Religions"[15] Richie elaborates on this "inclusivist" position. He reaffirms Wesley's assurance that Pentecostal theology should both address differences between religions and acknowledge when truth or piety is to be found in them. Tolerance, he says, rather than diatribe should be the watchword, inviting the possibility of a universal experiential encounter with the Holy Spirit even among non-Christians. Arguing that simple fairness would insist on a kind of theological openness, Richie says that if one believes in the fairness of God it is necessary to recognize the possibility of divine presence and power among all peoples. Always trying to keep a middle position, Richie insists that "Overly simplistic schemas calling for either dialogue or evangelism, effectively forcing a frightening choice between interfaith relations or Christian evangelism, are set aside in favor of integrating both listening and speaking in love, that is, sincere dialogue and sensitive witness."[16]

Increasingly, evangelicals like Richie are calling for an end to the unfortunate diatribe of some evangelical preachers who denounce Islam as demonic and the Prophet as a charlatan, adventurer, and pedophile. In the process they are mounting new efforts to reach out to Muslims, and have held several national meetings to discuss how to moderate their rhetoric and to partner with Muslims in establishing peaceful forms of dialogue. One of their goals is to break down stereotypes and hostile images of the other. "We have stereotypes of Muslims, and they certainly do of conservative Christians," said Richard Cizik, vice-president for Government Affairs at the Washington-based National Association of Evangelicals. "They are both caricatures we need to dispense with."[17]

In March 2006 a Consultation on Evangelical Christian-Muslim Relations was held in Washington D.C., sponsored by the Institute on Religion and Democracy (IRD) and the National Association of Evangelicals. Spokesperson Cizek again lamented the strident anti-Muslim tone of many of the younger evangelicals who are prominent in American political life, suggesting that Islam in their rhetoric seems to have replaced the former Soviet Union as the enemy.[18] The sixty or so participants said that they agreed to the importance of dialogue. A national survey of evangelical leaders, to which 350 responded, however, suggests that over three-fourths look unfavorably on Islam and feel that it opposes freedom and democracy. Cizek does stress the importance of making a clear distinction between dialogue, which the Bible says is necessary for evangelism, and interfaith activities of the kind engaged in by mainline Protestants. We need to have interfaith organizations as means of dialogue and limited cooperation, he says, but they should not suggest that there is theological unity between Christians and Muslims when none exists.[19]

A federally funded multiyear conflict transformation project of Fuller Theological Seminary and the Salaam Peace and Justice Institute of American University in Washington, D.C., entitled "Creating Collaboration and Reducing Conflict in Muslim-Christian Relationships," brought together Muslims and evangelical Christians to develop models for interfaith dialogue. Fuller is one of the largest nondenominational evangelical seminaries in the world, and the Salam Institute is a Muslim center for research and practice in mediation and peacemaking. The Islamic Society of North America (ISNA) and the Graduate School of Islamic Social Sciences (GSISS) facilitated the project. An interfaith steering committee planned the project for several years, starting by interviewing fifty Muslim and Christian leaders as to their views about their own faith and that of the other, and moving through a series of five local training sessions designed to give leaders the skills for deepening communication and developing joint action projects between Christian and Muslim groups. The project, the first of its kind featuring this kind of interfaith collaboration between Muslims and evangelicals, was completed in the summer of 2006. One of the products is a small book entitled *Interfaith Dialogue: A Guide For Muslims,* currently being written by Muhammad Shafiq of the Center for Interfaith Studies and Dialogue (CISD) and Mohammed Abu-Nimr of the Salam Peace and Justice Institute.[20] This project is generally understood to have been the catalyst for a new initiative in Christian-Muslim dialogue under the aegis of the National Association of Evangelicals.

A number of evangelicals have taken to the Internet to work specifically for the spread of Christianity to Muslims. Some sites are clearly designed to denigrate Islam, while others, such as www.answering-islam.org, try to give accurate information about Islam at the same time that it hopes that Muslims will come to the truth of the Gospel. This particular site is run by a team of volunteers who make it clear (a) that they believe the Bible to be the word of God, and (b) that Islam provides a different message that is not compatible with the Bible. The validity of its claim to be a forum for Christian-Muslim dialogue seems to be that it provides opportunity for anyone to give feedback and critique in response to their message.

Many evangelical Web sites are mounted as forums for the direct criticism of Islam. John Piper's personal site, for example, featured an entry on February 9, 2006 entitled "Being Mocked: The Essence of Christ's Work, Not Muhammad's." Piper used the occasion of the so-called "cartoon controversy," to post his message comparing Muhammad to Jesus, suggesting that it was only Jesus who suffered mockery and derision and not Muhammad. He noted that when the Danish newspaper *Jyllands-Posten* featured the unflattering cartoons, Muslims in some areas of the world resorted to violence. "What does this mean?" asked Piper. "It means that this religion [Islam] is destined to bear the impossible load of upholding the honor of one [Muhammad] who did not die and rise again to make that possible." Jesus Christ, he concluded, is the only hope for peace with God and man.

Another site called "Truth for Muslims," centered in Texas, is said to bring a biblical response to Islam in America. Its literature, which is mailed to more than fifty thousand households, deals with such issues as training Christians to know how to counter Islamic objections to Christianity, passing the message of the Gospel on to Muslims, and speaking out about Islam in America. Director John Marion, a former missionary to Afghanistan, founded the organization as a project of Spear Ministries in 2004. Marion insists that the best way to educate Muslims is by emphasizing the positive nature of Christianity rather than by criticizing Islam. It is unclear whether this home-grown missionary project is successful in reaching any Muslims, Hindus, Pagans, or other non-Christian groups to whom it is directed, but the positive response from evangelical Christians to the site has been strong.

Mainline Protestants and Islam

Mainline Protestant theological thinkers also represent a wide range of perspectives on issues of religious pluralism and how Christians might think theologically about the fact that Christianity is only one among many different religious traditions. In actual fact, relatively little has been written to help Christians to engage seriously in theological reflection specifically about Islam distinct from the missionary literature that discusses tactics and techniques. There is, however, a small body of literature illustrating Protestant theological reflection on Islam. Some of this material, too, is written by former missionaries to Muslim countries who now teach in American theological schools. They are struggling to find a way to affirm Islam as a possible way of salvation at the same time that they try not to compromise their strong Christian beliefs.

These Protestant theologians make a particularly important contribution to the conversation about Christianity in relation to Islam precisely because they speak with a kind of immediacy of personal knowledge that often is not the case for Western scholars and theologians. While they hold a position of deep Christian commitment, their direct experience has persuaded them that Islam is more than a misguided faith and they seek sincerely to find some common theological ground between the two religions. The best-known Protestant to have addressed this theme, and he has done so throughout the many decades of his life, is Anglican Bishop Kenneth Cragg. Because Cragg is British, his work by rights does not quite fit in a volume on dialogue in America. He did, however, teach at Hartford Seminary in the 1950s, and there is no question of the import of his work for anyone seeking to understand the theological significance for Christians of the person of Muhammad and of the Holy Qur'an. The reader who wishes to read serious attempts to reconcile seemingly contradictory revelations in the Bible and Qur'an is advised to turn to the intricate arguments developed in Cragg's many works on Islam and Christian theology.[21]

While few students of Islam seem to have struggled with issues of truth in the faiths of Christianity and Islam as personally as Kenneth Cragg has, feelings of frustration at not being able to resolve theological tensions seem almost unavoidable for those who take the two faiths seriously. Paul Varo Martinson, former professor of missiology at Luther Seminary in St. Paul, Minnesota, is a good example of a former American missionary who has tried to find common theological ground between Christianity and Islam. Martinson's *Islam: An Introduction for Christians* concludes with a section entitled "Islam—A Christian

Appreciation," containing sections on the witness of faith and his own Christian evaluation of Islam.[22] He states as a starting point his personal conviction that Islam *is* an authentic faith insofar as it shapes the Muslim's attitude toward life. He discusses Christian and Muslim commonalities, and with seeming reluctance he concludes that while Christians may acknowledge Muhammad's status as a prophetic preacher, they need not see him as bearer of the final revelation. Martinson poses the crucial question whether Islam is as legitimate a way of salvation as Christianity. While not saying a direct no, he makes it clear that for him there can be no salvation outside of the love of God in Christ.

Similar in tone is the interpretation of Richard H. Drummond, former Presbyterian missionary and professor at Dubuque Theological Seminary. In an article entitled "Toward Theological Understanding of Islam" in Leonard Swidler's volume Muslims in Dialogue,[23] Drummond provides a thoughtful introduction for Christians who are serious about preparing themselves for theological engagement with Muslims. He asks, ". . . by what standard may Christians properly evaluate Muhammad and the Islamic movement?" Following a pattern accepted by a number of mainline theologians, he determines that just as the Old Testament prophets are to be considered authentic although not infallible in every detail, so we should judge Muhammad.[24] Drummond hedges slightly the old question of whether Muslims can be saved by asking whether Islam has any significance in the history of salvation. He decides that the answer must be yes, specifically because of Islam's doctrine of the one God, for which he professes himself to be profoundly grateful. He says that understanding Jesus as solely authoritative or normative does not have to mean that God could have no other revelation, and that as the Spirit is at work throughout human history so God's salvation must always be present to those who believe in him (i.e., also to Muslims). Drummond concludes that the practical consequences of such an understanding are enormous, inviting an interpretation of mission to Muslims that can lead to the kind of deep levels of sharing that provide the greatest compliment one person can give to another.

Mark W. Thomsen, writing from the Lutheran missiological perspective, shares much with Drummond and Martinson.[25] He asks the hard question whether the purpose of Christian mission to Muslims is a dialogue for mutual enrichment or is necessarily grounded in the hope of the eventual conversion of Muslims to Christianity. His conclusion is that it must be both. Affirming that God's saving power is available to the whole human community, he struggles to find commonalities between Islam and Christianity but never at the cost of sacrificing the uniqueness of what he calls "the Cosmic Crucified." Drawing a distinction between making disciples for Christ and forcing them to be members of Lutheran churches, Thomsen observes that "It could be that Jesus might be received as Savior and Lord within the Muslim community in ways unknown and unexpected by us."[26] It seems clear that several of these writers adopt a kind of moderate position that might even be described as inclusivist, though each differs slightly from the other in what that means and not all would want to be described in that way.

I have yet to find a former missionary who would consider himself (or possibly herself) to be what one would call a pluralist, but there are some Protestant theologians who do adopt such a position. Consider, for example the work of philosopher and theologian John Hick. Hick has attracted a good deal of attention on the American scene, and much of his written work and his lectures have been done in the context of his tenure at the Claremont Graduate School in California. Hick argues that we cannot continue to claim that the Christian revelation of salvation through Christ is definitive for all persons. He calls for a paradigm shift so serious that he calls it a "Copernican revolution" in relation to traditional Christian responses to other faiths.[27] Islam, according to his definition, is not a rival faith at all but simply a different way of expressing the experience of divine reality. He confirms the suspicions and perhaps the fears of many Christians, at least on the American scene, that there is a kind of "accidentalness" to religion, in the sense that the faith one espouses is usually a simple accident of time and geography. One who is born in a Muslim society will have his or her religious landscape shaped by the reality of Islam. Hick is perhaps most troublesome to conservative Christians when he calls the dominant theological affirmations of all faith traditions "identifying mythologies." Specifically in relation to Islam, he says this: "That the Koran was dictated by God to Mohammed and constitutes a direct verbal revelation of God to man, divinely inspired down to the last syllable, is an identifying myth whose function is to evoke an attitude of reverent obedience to the holy book...."[28] That does not mean that the myth of the Qur'an does not have its own truth, he insists, as is also the case with the myths of the incarnation and the trinity in the Christian tradition. While doubting that there will ever be a single world faith, Hick predicts a growing interpenetration of traditions such that in time there will be no separate religions that can be identified as Christianity or Islam.[29]

Hick has little company among American Christian theologians who are considering interfaith matters. He is, however, widely quoted and even referred to by Muslim thinkers who, though they may find such "openness" beyond their own theological possibility, are attracted by Hick's theism and his denial of the incarnation. The late Wilfred Cantwell Smith, former director of Harvard's Center for the Study of World Religions, does share some sympathies with Hick's decrying of Christian exclusivism. Smith, while primarily an historian, has written a number of works that must be considered theological.[30]

He himself insists that insofar as history and theology cannot be separated, so the historian and the theologian are the same. Smith also argues against Christian uniqueness on both intellectual and moral grounds, identifying what he calls "the fallacy of relentless exclusivism."[31] His pluralist vision of truth extends well beyond the claims of either Christianity or Islam. Deeply committed to the unity of knowledge as well as of humankind, Smith believes that Christians and Muslims are mutual participants in an ongoing process of history, the locus of God's activity, and that it is not possible to talk about "our religious life" or "our knowing" apart from that of the other. We are fast approaching a time, he says, when Islamic history and Christian history must be understood as subthemes in the history of theism. The differences between our two traditions are no greater than the differences within each. He carries this to the conclusion that throughout history Christians have been *muslim* as submitters to God, while Muslims have been Christian to the extent to which they have revered Jesus the Messiah.[32]

One of Smith's early writings, designed specifically for Christian reflection, is entitled "Is the Qur'an the Word of God?" He concludes that not only is it the case that a Christian who reads the Qur'an may indeed find truth in it, but that in the end the only answer to the question must be one that is satisfactory to both Muslims and non-Muslims. "I cannot see how in principle any answer to our question can be truly adequate for a Christian unless it were also and simultaneously truly adequate for a Muslim; and yet if that were true, how profoundly novel the religious history of both our groups has become!"[33] We may recall this insistence when we come to the thought of Isma'il al Faruqi in chapter seven.

Another figure familiar to Christians engaged in theological reflection about interfaith relations—though one who would not, like Hick and Smith, call himself a pluralist—is John Cobb. While focusing his own activities in the Christian-Buddhist dialogue, Cobb has made some compelling theological statements about Christian interaction with Islam. Cobb identifies himself as a theological liberal,[34] although some actually find him to be rather evangelical, and argues for what he calls a "transformationist" position. We really hear and understand the truths of another faith tradition, he says, only when we are transformed by those truths. "Once we have heard the truth of Islam our Christian witness cannot remain what it was. And in our day only those Christians who have really heard that truth can deserve a serious hearing from Muslims."[35] In another writing, he argues that if we are truly open to the spirit of Islam we Christians will see that Muhammad is our prophet as well as the prophet of Islam.[36]

Cobb, like Hick, is both a contributor to and a product of the liberal intellectual environment of Claremont, California. Also a participant in the

Claremont conversation has been Marjorie Hewitt Suchocki, the first professor emerita at Claremont School of Theology. In a recent work entitled *Divinity &* *Diversity. A Christian Affirmation of Religious Pluralism,* Suchocki suggests what she calls the "friendship" model for interfaith, and specifically Christian-Muslim, relations. In effect blending some of the models suggested in chapter four above, she emphasizes the importance of speaking personally as a Christian with Muslim colleagues, telling and listening to personal stories. We must be courageous enough to ask each other such hard questions, Suchocki says, such as whether warfare is really a pillar of the Islamic faith, or if in the Eucharist Christians really think that they are consuming a human body. Friendship goes from sharing personally over a meal, to discussing honestly, to sharing mutual concerns about such issues as discrimination, violence, and poverty. Suchocki, who like Cobb is a Methodist, does not reveal herself as a pluralist in this text. The farthest she seems willing to go theologically is to admit the possibility of seeing the grace of God at work among Muslims. She suggests a common goal, but beyond openness to the other does not specify what that goal is.

These, then, are some of the voices that are being heard in American Protestant theological schools, and somewhat derivatively, in the churches. Heavily missiological in terms of volume, the literature over the last three or four decades has included perspectives that have raised interesting and challenging questions for those who are looking for new ways in which to think about Islam, indeed in some cases new ways to think about Christianity as a result of the encounter. Conservatives may be relieved, and progressives concerned, that with the retirement of veteran theologians like Hick, Cobb and Suchocki, and the death of Smith, few voices are now heard speaking out for the kind of theological openness to Islam that they espoused. It is not immediately evident what will be the nature of the commitment of the next generation of mainline Protestant scholars.

Roman Catholics and Islam

Perhaps the most serious and constructive discussion that has taken place in the American Christian-Muslim dialogue scene is that under the aegis of Roman Catholic leadership. All of us concerned about interfaith relations owe a debt of gratitude to the Catholics for initiating and helping determine the content of a serious ongoing dialogical conversation about theological matters.

The Second Vatican Council from 1962 to 1965, subject to great scrutiny in its interpretation, signaled the start of new ways of thinking about relating to other religions. It culminated in the 1965 *Declaration on the Relation of the Church to Non-Christian Religions (Nostra Aetate)*. John Borelli, for several decades Associate Director of the Secretariat for Ecumenical and Interreligious Affairs of the United States Conference of Catholic Bishops (USCCB), notes that this dramatic change in the Church's position toward non-Christians was nothing short of a revolution in the Christian approach to relations with Muslims.[37] Borelli sees the visit of John Paul II to Syria thirty-six years later as a clear sign of the fruits of Vatican II. "For all the times that Muslims and Christians have offended one another," said John Paul, "we need to seek forgiveness from the Almighty and offer each other forgiveness."[38] The legacy of a painful past was to be put aside in favor of new ways of achieving mutual understanding.[39]

"If Vatican II is a watershed in Christian attitudes toward other religions," says Catholic theologian Paul Knitter, "Karl Rahner is its chief engineer."[40] Rahner is widely credited for helping usher in a new era in interfaith relations. He argues that if one starts from the affirmation that God desires salvation for all people, it follows that God is actively working in every religion and that grace must be available to all.[41] It is through the religions of the world that God acts. Non-Christian religions such as Islam, therefore, can be the means whereby people (in this case Muslims) are included in God's plan of salvation. The means of this salvation is the saving grace of Jesus Christ. Thus the term "anonymous Christian" has come into use to refer to the conviction that Muslims or others can be saved through Christ's action even though they are not aware of it.[42] It is fair to say that Rahner's interpretation has been deeply influential in Catholic thinking over the past forty years, although more recently it has fallen somewhat out of favor.

Another of the first modern Roman Catholics to push the boundaries in terms of theological openness is Swiss theologian Hans Kung. His questioning of papal infallibility in the 1970s led to the formal revocation of his teaching license, though he remains a priest. In terms of Christian attitudes toward Islam, as early as 1986, Kung was asking if this religion can in fact be a way of salvation. Noting that the World Council of Churches has been ambiguous because its member churches are divided on the issue, he questions what kind of dialogue is possible if one believes that the dialogue partners are headed for hell![43] Kung feels that after Vatican II Muslims are no longer subject to everlasting fire prepared for the Devil, but are able to attain eternal salvation. Thus Islam is a way of salvation, though not the "ordinary" but rather an "extraordinary" way. Carrying the argument farther, he suggests that Muhammad should no longer be considered "a false, laying pseudoprophet, a fortune-teller, magician, faker, or at best just another Arabian poet" as Christians have long claimed. In fact, perhaps he should be considered a genuine, even a true pro-phet.[44] After all, he says, the Old Testament and the Qur'an seem to be have a great deal in common, the people of Arabia clearly saw him as a prophet pure and simple, and the New Testament itself suggests that there were authentic prophets who came after Jesus. Kung acknowledges, of course, that "the simple recognition of Muhammad's title of 'prophet' would have momentous conse-quences. . . ."[45]

Belgian Jesuit Jacques Dupuis has been raising some of the same issues. His groundbreaking 1997 *Toward a Christian Theology of Religious Pluralism* is said to have made the guardians of orthodoxy nervous because it contains certain "ambiguities." Some have even charged that Dupuis was the primary target of the September 2001 papal document *Dominus Iesus* (The Lord Jesus) which asserts that other religions are gravely deficient in relation to Chris-tianity. Dupuis argues that the theological problem remains the primary issue in dialogue, and like his Roman Catholic colleague Paul Knitter he believes that a paradigm shift from Christocentrism to theocentrism is essential. In dialogue one must combine commitment to one's own faith and openness to the other, he says, and it is in dialogue that Christians and others walk together on the path towards truth. In a 2002 volume,[46] he turned specifically to Islam, saying that it is possible for God to speak, albeit differently, in the Old Testament, the New Testament, *and* the Qur'an. Unlike many of his Catholic theological col-leagues, he interprets the document of the Vatican's Secretariat for Non-Christians entitled *Guidelines for a Dialogue between Christians and Muslims* (2nd edition 1988) to leave open the possibility of common prayer between Chris-tians and Muslims.

Whether or not Vatican II (*Nostre Aetate*) supports the notion that non-Christian religions really can be vehicles of salvation, then, seems to be a ques-tion about which not all Roman Catholic theologians are in full agreement. The issue, of course, is particularity. Can it be said, contrary to classical church doctrine, that there is salvation outside the church? Roman Catholic theology, to a great extent like its Protestant counterpart, is under great pressure to come to some resolve on this issue. How can one affirm the crucial importance of particularity at the same time that one expresses the degree of openness nec-essary to foster a healthy dialogue? Gavin D'Costa, for one, argues that the text of Vatican II really is silent about that question, though it commends Islam for its theism, belief in one God, veneration of Jesus as a prophet, and belief in the day of judgment. But that, says d'Costa, does not necessarily mean to that Is-lam itself is a salvific faith.[47] Nonetheless it seems clear that while it is open to varying interpretations, Vatican II did represent a major step toward the acknowledgement of other religions and so, as Boston College's Muslim theologian Qamar-ul Huda insists, "opened the doors to unprecedented dia-logical possibilities between Muslims and Christians."[48]

Since Vatican II, however, the Roman Catholic Church seems to have moved away from pluralism, particularly with the publication of *Dominus Iesus*. Pope Benedict XVI, the former Cardinal Joseph Ratzinger, has made it clear that it is extraordinarily difficult to reconcile a pluralist position with Catholic orthodoxy. As of this writing the Catholic Church and the Muslim world are still struggling to understand the import of Benedict's citation of, in September 2006, an obscure Byzantine text referring to Islam as a religion of the sword. Negatively, the Pope's reference has incurred the ire of many Muslims inter-nationally and led to church burnings and even several deaths. It has raised serious issues about his dedication to the cause of better interfaith relations, despite his public statement of regret for any pain caused. Positively, particu-larly in the United States, the incident has led to renewed efforts between Cath-olics and Muslims to reaffirm their bonds of friendship and to pledge future cooperation between the two communities.

For an interesting and thorough coverage of the ways that Roman Catholics have viewed other religions both theologically and in terms of the goals of di-alogue, I suggest the recent collaborative volume written by John Borelli and Michael L. Fitzgerald entitled *Interfaith Dialogue: A Catholic View*.[49] While Bo-relli's position has given him access to dialogue with a number of different religious groups, Fitzgerald's particular expertise is in the conversation with Islam. Archbishop Fitzgerald, who was Secretary of the Pontifical Council in 2002 until he was demoted by then Cardinal Ratzinger, has had lengthy and personal experience working in Muslim countries as well as with the Muslim community in America.

Fitzgerald and Borelli make it absolutely clear that in their opinion, while Vatican II helps Catholics to understand that there are true and holy elements in other religions, "it never puts them on a par with the One, Holy, Catholic and Apostolic Church."[50] This is the position articulated several years ago by Car-dinal Walter Kasper, President of the Pontifical Council for Promoting Chris-tian Unity. While ecumenical and interreligious dialogue are connected and have some overlap, said Kasper, they are not the same and should never be confused. The difference is because ecumenical dialogue is "rooted in the common faith in Jesus Christ and the reciprocal recognition of baptism."[51] His conclusion from this clear theological distinction, unlike that of Dupuis, is that while Christians and those of other religions (in our case, Muslims) can pray, they cannot pray together. Nonetheless, he says, dialogue must continue out of respect for God, the sharing of many moral values, and the promotion of peace and freedom. Archbishop Alexander J. Brunett, addressing the West Coast

Dialogue of Catholics and Muslims in 2001, agreed, adding that while the two faiths have their own difficult histories it is the obligation of Americans to show to Catholics around the world that there can be cordial and meaningful dialogue.[52]

Meanwhile, regardless of precise theological positions, dialogue continues to be promoted as a crucial task of the Roman Catholic Church. However, it must be done in the context of affirming the message of Jesus Christ as Savior. As Fitzgerald and Borelli confirm, dialogue is not a substitute for proclamation. Both must carry on together, and it is up to Catholic participants to join the conversation in an attitude of discernment.[53] The process of conversation together should carry with it opportunities for all participants to witness to the truths of their own faiths. Fitzgerald and Borelli insist that the dialogue should encourage the sharing of beliefs, and the deepening of understanding both of one's own beliefs and those of the other in the common search for truth. It should, in short, be an environment that promotes holiness. It seems a good note on which to conclude.

7

The Pluralist Imperative

Muslim Perspectives

"Does Islam accept pluralism?" or "Do Muslims think that other religions can be true?" or perhaps simply "Does the Muslim who lives down the street think that I'm going to hell because I'm not a Muslim?" In recent years as a teacher of Islam and Christian-Muslim relations I have been asked variations on this basic question many times, and my Muslim colleagues trying to explain Islam to Americans assure me that the same is true for them. The answer, alas, is not always easy to give. I recall my participation in a Christian-Muslim dialogue conference in Islamabad, Pakistan a few years ago when a Muslim colleague to my left was doodling on his list of conference attendees. To my shock I realized that he was writing "kafir" (unbeliever, rejecter of the truth) next to the names of all of the Christians. I knew that such was not the attitude of all of the Pakistanis present at the conference, and certainly not true of its organizer. But just as many conservative Christians regretfully conclude that all those who don't know the truth of Christ will fare poorly in the end days, so many Muslims reach the same conclusion but from the perspective of Islam.

"If you believe your religion to be true," commented a Muslim cleric at a Fulbright seminar in 2002, "and you believe it is your duty to share this truth with others, then why would you think that religious pluralism is a good thing?" These remarks seem to express the attitude of many Muslims toward questions of truth in other religions. Sociologist Patricia Chang, reflecting on this response,

realized that the tolerance that some Americans show toward religious pluralism is actually quite perplexing to many people who hold a clear position in
relation to their faith, no matter what particular culture or tradition they may
identify with. In the article she wrote in response to the conversations at the
Fulbright meeting, aptly titled "Puzzled by Pluralism," Chang notes that tolerance can easily be understood as a lack of religious conviction or, worse, hy-
pocrisy.[1] It seems appropriate to begin our consideration of the question of
religious pluralism in Islam by trying to understand this point of view.

Puzzlement may characterize Chang's response, or even the response of
Muslims in general as they try to see why one would find pluralism more appealing than simple affirmation of the complete and final truth of Islam. But
the fact is that some Muslims—not large numbers but enough to take note of—
are starting to take up the challenge posed to them by some Christians, and by
their own assessment of their place in American society, especially since 9/11.
Muslims have been saying for some time that it is no longer appropriate to describe American society according to the tripartite division proposed in the 1950s
by Will Herberg in which the United States is characterized as Protestant,
Catholic, and Jew.[2] Now, they say, is the time to recognize that in light of the fact
that there are approximately as many Muslims in America as Jews (many would
argue that there are more), we should perhaps used the descriptor Christian-
Jewish-Muslim (or perhaps even Christian-Muslim-Jewish). If Muslims are to
be part of this religiously diverse country, and much of their rhetoric sets out to
prove both to their fellow Muslims and to their fellow Americans that they indeed
are and deserve to be a part, how is this participation to be understood?[3]

It would be incorrect to assume that there has been a great deal of talking
and writing by Muslims about the religious dimensions of Islam in relation to
American pluralism. What we do find is rhetoric insisting that Islam is not an
exclusionary religion, with particular and frequent citing of such verses as
Qur'an 11:118–19 saying that had God willed it, he would made humankind into
one nation [implication: God did not, therefore God accepts many different
kinds of peoples]; 2:256 asserting that there should be no compulsion in religion [implication: no one should be forced to belong to one religion over an-
other]; and 2:148, "Each one has a goal toward which he turns, so vie with one
another in doing good works . . ." [implication: the best way to get along is for
each person to do to the best of his or her ability the good deeds that faith
encourages]. One hears far less often in public discourse references to such
verses as 3:85 which says, "Whosoever desires a religion other than Islam[4] it
shall not be accepted. . . ."

In defense of pluralism, many Muslims have pointed to the "descriptively"
pluralistic nature of Islam in a range of contexts: at the time of the Prophet and

the revelation of the Qur'an, throughout the history of Islam in its relations with other communities of faith, within Islam in the contemporary world, and within the culture of the United States. Only a few writers have tried to distinguish in their arguments between pluralism as a description of multiplicity and pluralism as an attitude—an approach to the world, an affirmation that multiplicity is God's choice. Some have discussed the concept of tolerance that Chang described as the general attitude of Americans toward the nation's many faith traditions, and have advocated it as an essentially Islamic stance without indicating what that might really mean theologically. Others have worried that tolerance as a response is tepid, almost insulting, and not representative of the insistence of the Qur'an on a truly positive attitude toward pluralism.

We will consider here three ways in which the question of Islam and pluralism has been addressed by contemporary American Muslims: first, as it applies to current political realities, second, to ethical concerns within the body of Islam, and, third, to the relationship of Islam to other religious traditions. An understanding of each of these modes of interpretation is essential for anyone who is interested in moving from introductory to deeper levels of discourse between Muslims and Christians.

Pluralism and a "Modernized" Islam

A few American Muslims have insisted that pluralism is essential to a "modernized" Islam. They are not talking about a Qur'anically inspired response of openness to other religious traditions, but about the necessity of Muslims and non-Muslims finding common ground and shared political space. Some address these issues in the context of rebutting the aforementioned popular "clash of civilizations" theory first put forth by Harvard's Samuel Huntington, which has been much applauded by American neoconservatives. Muslims recognize that the rise of militant Islam in many parts of the world serves to prove the validity of Huntington's theory in the eyes of many Americans. Husain Kasim of the University of Central Florida, for example, in the context of trying to counter Huntington's arguments, insists that it is ethical discourse rather than political expediency that should provide the meeting ground for living together in a pluralist society. Such discourse between Muslims and other Americans can lead to what he calls "the universalization of norms," an argument that might well engage the interest of those who are interested in what was described in chapter four as "the ethical exchange" kind of dialogue. Kasim's readers, however, may find it hard to see in his argument how universalization means anything other than what he ultimately identifies as "Islamic ethical discourse."[5]

Some Muslim writers espouse a kind of Islamic political pluralism in their attempts to prove that Islam is compatible with liberal democracy. How, they ask, can we demonstrate that Islamic values really do promote democracy, human rights, and pluralism? Perhaps as part of their attempt to make Islam more palatable in the eyes of the American public, most insist that the goal—as the current United States administration would like to see happen—is the adoption of open political systems and the establishing of democratic governments throughout the Islamic world.[6]

Sulayman Nyang of Howard University gave an innovative presentation on Islam and pluralism in Hartford in the late 1990s entitled "Seeing the Religious Roots of Pluralism in the United State of America: An American Muslim Perspective." Nyang looked first at ways in which American Muslims, including secular humanists, social isolationists, and moderates sensitive to the realities of pluralism within the Muslim community itself, view American pluralism. (In this and others of his writings he characterizes these groups, respectively, as grasshoppers, oysters, and owls.) Acknowledging that American Muslims need to leave triumphalism behind and remember the Qur'anic insistence that there is no compulsion in religion, he suggested that a number of the characteristics of American culture, including excessive materialism, individualism, consumerism and libertarianism, make it difficult for Muslims to appreciate pluralism. If Muslims can promote dialogue about both their own inner pluralism and the outer pluralism of Western society, he concluded, they can help create conditions and opportunities for developing public policies that are not "devoid of moral and spiritual content."[7]

One of the most frequently heard voices in the post 9/11 defense of Islam as a legitimate component of American culture is Adrien College's Muqtedar Khan. Khan also sees pluralism primarily as a political issue, although his concern is less with how Muslims deal with it than with the irony of America's own advocacy of pluralism as an ideology.[8] Because interaction between Islam and the West has generally taken place in what he calls "relations of power" rather than of genuine dialogue, Muslims have learned from the West under conditions of domination. Today, propaganda overrides truth, and because of the globalization of Western values such as democracy, individualism, secularism, and economic liberalism, it is impossible for the United States to tolerate any kind of real international pluralism, by which he means difference in political and economic philosophy. Acknowledging that a similar charge could be levied against Islamic countries and cultures, Khan's main argument is that the West prefers intimidation to dialogue. From this perspective, pluralism itself is held captive to the reality of the power equation.

In the beginning days of Muslim-Christian dialogue in America the most prominent Muslim activist was Isma'il al Faruqi, referred to above. Faruqi spoke up frequently in favor of what he might have understood as a kind of modernized pluralism (which, ultimately, perhaps was not pluralism at all). He was also one of the very few Muslims who engaged in a thorough study of Christian theology and ethics. As the title of al Faruqi's pioneering work *Trialogue of the Abrahamic Faiths*[9] indicates, he was one of the first to advocate the three-way conversation among Muslim, Christians, and Jews. His untimely death in 1986 has been deeply regretted by his many Christian friends as well as the American Muslim community as a whole. One of his long-standing projects was to discover the real Christianity unburdened by the influence of Greek thought and other aberrations, as well as to defend the truth of Islam against the distortions and prejudices through which Christians have always tended to view his faith. Rapprochement between the religions, he insisted, is possible despite these historical aberrations.

Anyone who heard al Faruqi speak, or read his writings, would recognize that his essential aim was to promote *da'wa* or the call to Islam. On more than one occasion I heard him declare that his primary purpose as a scholar of Islam in America was to foster *da'wa* in the university educational system. Faruqi insisted that *da'wa* was not an attempt at proselytism or conversion, however, as much as what he defined as the mutual search for truth. Insofar as conversion may be the result of such an endeavor, he insisted, it means the conversion of both sides to the truth. It is logically impossible for either religion to have truth insofar as it differs from the truth proclaimed by the other. Therefore there must be one truth, and conversion to that truth is the aim of dialogue.[10] Al Faruqi, however, was no fan of deep theological engagement. His primary concern was for ethical rather than theological concerns, and he wanted to encourage both Muslims and Christians to follow the commandments of God. Dialogue for Faruqi was what he called a "dimension of the human consciousness . . . a category of the ethical sense,"[11] the only sort of interaction between humans that is really of value. Many of his Christian as well as his Muslim colleagues understood that Faruqi was deeply persuaded that the serious mutual pursuit of truth and the right behavior that it impels would in fact lead to the essence of what is to be found in the Qur'an. Real truth is Qur'anic truth, and thus the result of his serious interfaith engagement by definition is not pluralism at all but its opposite.[12]

Isma'il al Faruqi brooked little disagreement with his ideas, and his keen intellectual prowess made it difficult to survive long in debate with him. Both his methodology and his assumptions, however, were seriously challenged by friends and foes alike. His place as a forerunner of the interfaith dialogue experience in America is unrivaled, however, as he was among the first to seriously frame the challenge and pursue the goal of arriving at "truth" with vigor and commitment.

Pluralism as an Issue of Justice in Islam

One of the very interesting issues that has arisen as American Muslims address the question of pluralism and Islam is that of social justice. Some very articulate intellectuals are arguing that it is within the fabric of Islam itself that a serious critique needs to be levied. Acknowledging the inherently pluralistic nature of Islam, which they see affirmed by the texts and demonstrated throughout its history, they focus on ways in which Muslims today have fallen short of the ideal, as a result of which some members of the body of Islam are clearly not given full recognition. This critique has been most evident within the American context in the voices of women and representatives of minority racial-ethnic communities. If Islam truly affirms pluralism, they ask, why are these constituencies not being heard and taken into full consideration? Thus the discussion is not about the relationship between Islam and Christianity, or between Muslims and Christians in the United States, but rather about relationships within the Muslim community itself. Parallel discussions have been going on among Christians since the middle of the twentieth century, and the rich potential for dialogue lies in figuring out whether the analyses that work in one context are appropriate in the other.

An early and articulate spokespersons for the full inclusion of women in Islam, based on a close analysis of the Qur'an, is Amina Wadud of Virginia Commonwealth University. For many years she has argued strongly for the importance of women becoming directly involved in what she calls alternative exegesis of the Qur'an. When Muslims struggle with the question of women's equality in postmodern discourse, she argues, there is a huge gap because of the historical silencing of female voices, including the absence of those voices in scriptural interpretation. One way to close that gap is to employ what she calls the "new *ijtihad* approach," an alternative and women-inclusive mode of Qur'anic exegesis that will result in a continual, and radical, rethinking of the meaning of the sacred text and of the Sunnah (or way) of the Prophet. Nothing short of this will serve to explicate fully and accurately the vision of the Qur'an for the true relationships between men and women. Islamic pluralism, in effect, will be allowed to show its true self.[13]

Although Wadud is African American, the main focus of her ongoing work has been the rehabilitation of the Qur'anic interpretation of women and men rather than the status of Islamic racial minorities. Another African American Muslim searching for the realization of genuine pluralism within Islam is Gwendolyn Zohara Simmons of the University of Florida. Simmons critiques both the treatment of women in Islam and also what she sees as prejudice among Muslims themselves against people of color. Islam has failed, she concludes, to meet the challenges of genuine pluralism. "Frankly," she says, "I am tired of the contortions, the bending over backwards, and the justifications for the oppressive, repressive, and exclusionary treatment of women in majority Islamic societies as well as in minority Muslim communities in the U.S.A."[14] While Zohara Simmons is directly concerned about rehabilitating women's full roles in Islam, and like Wadud and others she argues for what she calls a gender-equitable interpretation of the Qur'an, she also suggests that prejudice based on race and skin color distinctions, along with those of gender and class, have never been absent from Muslim communities and continue to be present in contemporary America.

It is only fairly recently that African American Muslims like Zohara Simmons are starting to say publicly that despite the insistence of the Qur'an on egalitarianism, race, and color prejudice do exist in American Islam. One of the most articulate scholars to have addressed the exclusion of African Americans by members of the immigrant Muslim community is the University of Michigan's Sherman Jackson, although the issue of race is only one concern in his very energetic agenda. Jackson identifies what he calls "the problem of the false universal" as the major issue Muslims will have to face in the twenty-first century.[15] Specifically, he is calling attention to what he describes as the treachery of the noninclusion of black American Muslims in the configuration of an American Islam. The reality of 9/11 has made it crucial, he insists, that a reformed and pluralist Islam be honed for inclusion in American society. The danger comes when the universal is equated with the dominant, that is when primarily imported and traditional interpretations of Islam—he is particularly concerned about wholesale adoption of certain Middle Eastern worldviews—prevail to the exclusion of others. The great promise of Islamic tradition, he insists, is its ability to accommodate expressions of Islam that differ from and may even contradict each other. Remaining true to this heritage of Islamic pluralism and accommodation of difference that he sees as essential to the future of Islam in the United States, Jackson worries deeply that Western Muslims advocating reform offer an Islam that is pluralistic, tolerant, nonviolent, and egalitarian, but one that in fact is based on false universals.

Ultimately, such an interpretation fosters neither pluralism nor tolerance. Jackson makes the effective case that a truly pluralistic American Islam will be one that fosters what he calls, inspiringly, the concept of "the collective enterprises of good."[16]

As we see, therefore, "Islamic pluralism" can mean anything from democratic openness to racial equality to concern about the dominance of a particular imported Islamic ideology. Those who are dedicated to the struggle for genuine pluralism and equality within the body of Islam find an elegant spokesperson in the South African interpreter who now makes his home and teaches in the west, Farid Esack. His widely read *Qur'an, Liberation & Pluralism* is a courageous attempt to argue for the pluralism that he sees basic to the message of the Qur'an. The subtitle to the book, "An Islamic Perspective of Interreligious Solidarity against Oppression," reflects the fact that Esack writes out of his experience with struggles for liberation in South Africa. Hermeneutical responses to a situation of oppression-liberation, such as those presented in the South African context, quite naturally involve the quest for pluralism, albeit one that exacts a high price. "For those who eke out an existence on the margins of society," says Esack, "a pluralism of splendid and joyous intellectual neutrality is not an option."[17] True pluralism involves the liberation of all people in societies that are patriarchal, racially divided, and economically exploitative. Pluralism for Esack is thus both descriptive and prescriptive, and while his interpretation is based on a local struggle, Esack sees it as having universal implications.

Esack serves as a helpful bridge into a discussion of the arguments put forward as to whether the Qur'an itself is truly pluralistic. He cites a number of verses that he calls cornerstones of the Qur'an's acceptance of religious pluralism, lamenting the fact that traditional interpretation of scripture sometimes has been used to circumvent this obvious intention.[18] He identifies the doctrine of supercession as the culprit in the traditional refusal to acknowledge the validity of other religions for salvation.[19] Of the many important insights that Esack shares in this work on liberation, however, he is particularly incisive in insisting that the pluralism of the Qur'an is not a kind of liberal position in which coexistence means absolute equality. The Prophet and his community actively opposed beliefs that contravened the basic message of God's oneness. Speaking of his experience with apartheid in South Africa, Esack says that the struggle made clear the fact that Otherness takes many forms, some of which must be opposed. Thus while a theology of religious pluralism is linked to a theology of liberation, "the vague liberal embrace of all forms of otherness"[20] must be avoided. This assertion alone would make important grist for the mill of Christian-Muslim theological conversation.

Pluralism as a Qur'anic Vision

The interpreters we have looked at thus far have referred to certain verses of the Qur'an to support their respective arguments for an understanding of pluralism in Islam but, with the exception of Esack, they do not focus on the matter of Qur'anic perspectives on other religions. What follows, then, is a consideration of those who do address this question, either generally or specifically. Some affirmed their positions before 9/11 while others are clearly writing in response to that event and its aftermath.

The Islamic Roots of Democratic Pluralism, by Abdulaziz Sachedina of the University of Virginia, is seen as a classic in the discussion of pluralism in Islam and lays the groundwork for the commentary of a number of other scholars. The publication date is 2001, but it appeared before rather than after the attacks and the subsequent outcry for clarification about Islam. Sachedina is persuaded that within Islam itself lies the basis for democratic pluralism that will maintain the equality and dignity of all humanity. He argues both that the Qur'an provides "a prescription for coexistence among people of diverse faiths" and that Islam can serve as a model religion for furthering interpersonal justice within society.[21] If Islam were to realize its own principle of justice, forgiveness, and the forging of new social relationships, he says, the result would be a pluralistic and democratic Muslim global community.

Sachedina sets out an Islamic theology that fosters the original pluralism of the Qur'an by taking into account the fact that human life is constantly changing. He introduces the concept of *fitra,* which is understood to mean an individual's original state in response to revelatory guidance. In this natural state humanity is aware of good and evil, as well as the individual's relationship to the divine and to other people. In this sense, Sachedina views Islamic pluralism as the unity that binds all humanity in recognition of its natural predisposition toward monotheism. The Islamic ideal is a world community that shares a cross-cultural moral concern for egalitarianism. The author challenges Muslim thinkers and believers to pursue a discourse across cultures in which Islam, Christianity, and Judaism provide guidance. Himself an Ithna Ash'ari Shi'ite, Sachedina criticizes both Sunnis and Shi'ites for having hindered the progress of Islamic tradition: Sunnis for their exclusivist interpretations, Shi'ites for putting limitations on who qualifies to use human reason in interpreting the teachings of the Qur'an. Sachedina, then, emphasizes a theology based on the Qur'anic acknowledgement of people of other faiths and on the recognition that all humanity is created in the natural state of *islam.* It is this Islamic definition of the other as a dignified creature of God that provides the basis of a public rationale for religious pluralism. Sachedina sees this as the foundation of a preventive diplomacy that can serve to promote democracy, communication, and pluralism in the face of existing global violence.[22]

Reflecting elsewhere on the relationship of Islam to its sister Abrahamic faiths, Sachedina points to the efforts of some classical Muslim exegetes to separate their own salvation history from that of Christianity and Judaism.[23] Arguing for the unity of humankind at the level of universal moral-spiritual discourse, he insists that nothing in the Qur'an, either directly or indirectly, serves to abrogate previous scriptures. Perhaps, he ventures, conversations about abrogation of the two scriptures by the Qur'an may have taken their cue from Christian discussion about Christianity having superseded Judaism. In the colonial and postcolonial period Muslim exegetes to some extent have recaptured the pluralist thrust of the Qur'an. Here again he affirms the essential unity of the belief of the *ahl al-adyan al-ilahiya* (people of the divine religions) based on three factors: their *fitra* or innate disposition to believe in God, their continuous exposure to divine guidance through revelation, and their proclivity for doing good works.

Abdulaziz Sachedina has been a frequent participant in and contributor to interfaith dialogue sessions, especially Muslim-Christian, over the course of many years. He brings a sharp critical edge to the discussion and he encourages participants to work seriously with the sources of their traditions to better understand the scriptural grounds for interfaith engagement. In *The Islamic Roots* he argues that the Qur'an tacitly endorses what he calls "the salvific efficacy of the other religions of the Book."[24] A philosophy of "anti-pluralism," however, has characterized fundamentalist Muslims leading Islamic governments in modern nation-states.[25] Such leaders in turn often criticize the efforts of Muslims in the West to discourse on the subject of pluralism, accusing them of giving in to secular Western critique of Islam as inadequate to running a modern state. Sachedina defends himself by saying that his task has been to present a theology of interreligious relations in Islam that may depart from earlier interpretations, but not from the Qur'an itself. He argues that one way in which it is possible for religious people to work together for the common good without having to share religious doctrine is to articulate and proceed from each tradition's ethical imperative. Ethical discourse must be the major component of interfaith relations. "The challenge for Muslims today," he says, "as ever, is to tap the tradition of Koranic pluralism to develop a culture of restoration, of just intrareligious and interreligious relationships in a world of cultural and religious diversity."[26]

Responding to questions I put to him about his 1997 article "Islamic Theology of Christian-Muslim Relations,"[27] Sachedina drew more directly the implications of his position for interfaith dialogue. Dialogue presupposes what he calls the equality of two sides. No Christian or Muslim can sit in dialogue when in the depth of their hearts, because of a prejudicial attitude, they fail to accept the salvific efficacy of the other's religious tradition. Essential to dialogue is what he calls "internal purity of intention and mutual acceptance." Acknowledging that most Muslims today do consider Christians to be *kafirs,* he insists that for them it is the end of dialogue. When I asked if he considers one outcome of interfaith exchange to be the possibility of learning from the other so as to enhance one's own understanding of faith, he said that humans must first learn to discover that understanding each other is for mutual and reciprocal coexistence.

The depth of Sachedina's thought, as is true of Farid Esack, makes investigation of other contributors to the discussion on pluralism somewhat pale by comparison. We should nonetheless acknowledge again that both of those scholars made their respective cases before 9/11. Most other Muslim discussion about the question of pluralism has been carried out in the context of a post-9/11 defense of Islam for a questioning, and sometimes antagonistic, American audience. When UCLA Professor Khaled Abou El Fadl published *Authoritative and Authoritarian,* for example, in which he defended pluralism as a descriptor for the great, complex, and diverse civilization of Islam, the year was 1997. His argument was not about Islam and other religions, but about Islam itself, through which truth is accessible to all people regardless of race, class, or gender, and that every Muslim may potentially be the bearer of God's truth.[28] By the time he wrote *The Place of Tolerance in Islam* it was 2002, and the emphasis shifted from relationships within Islam to those between Muslims and others. "Is Islam tolerant of other religions?" he asked, and not surprisingly determined that the answer is yes. Abou El Fadl clearly writes in defense of an Islam that is to be distinguished from that propagated by exclusionary, intolerant Wahhabism. At the same time he is trying to answer the questions most on the minds of post 9/11 Americans about such things as killing in the name of Islam, *jihad,* treatment of Christian and Jewish citizens of Islamic states, and so-called Muslim intolerance.

Abou El Fadl also attempts to provide the context for Qur'anic verses that may in isolation appear exclusionary, stressing the importance of historical circumstances and of seeing an overarching moral construction of meaning to be more important than a literal reading of the text. The Qur'an, he says, both accepts and expects difference and diversity insofar as diversity is a primary purpose of creation. He defends Islamic civilization as both diverse and, on the whole, remarkably tolerant. Going somewhat farther than most of his coreligionists, Abou El Fadl says that while the Qur'an clearly claims absolute truth for Islam, "it does not completely exclude the possibility that there might be other paths to salvation," that the Qur'an recognizes the existence of a wide range of legitimate religious convictions and rulings, and that it is possible for non-Muslims to attain what he calls "the blessing of salvation."[29] Rather than press the theological ramifications of such potentially radical conclusions, however, he retreats into a discussion of the Qur'an's insistence that there is no compulsion in religion, that war is never holy, and that nonbelievers are not to be subordinated. It is, he insists, the responsibility of contemporary Muslim interpreters of the text to affirm its message of tolerance and openness to others.

The theme of justice in relation to tolerance and pluralism has been a recurrent one, as we have seen. It is strongly emphasized in the 2004 volume edited by Omid Safi of Colgate University entitled *Progressive Muslims*. The book has been received with excitement by many non-Muslims who see in it the beginnings of a hoped-for "renewal" of Islamic thought for the twenty-first century. For the most part it has engendered less enthusiasm on the part of Muslims themselves, however, and the actual "progressive Muslims" movement appears to be losing momentum. Nonetheless, it seems clear that the effort to affirm an Islam that is defined by justice, including gender justice, represents a hopeful early attempt to rethink the religion for a new age and time. In his introduction to the book, Safi sets the tone by insisting that pluralism is both the by-product and the presupposition of justice. Like Abou El Fadl, he is writing specifically in the post 9/11 period to offer an alternative to Wahhabism. "An important part of being a progressive Muslim," he says, "is the determination to hold Muslim societies accountable for justice and pluralism."[30] To be a pluralist Muslim one must think not only about the Qur'an and Sunnah, but about how to live on this planet in harmony with all other living creatures. It means, he insists, challenging and rejecting interpretations that he groups together as exclusivist, violent, and misogynist. We must open up a place for the many Muslims who aspire to justice and pluralism.

Safi explicitly challenges those who envision an Islam that is merely tolerant, arguing that the truly pluralistic society that Muslims must struggle to foster is one in which both differences and commonalities are engaged and honored.[31] Reminding us that we all have the same breath of God in our being (Qur'an 15:24, 38:72), he insists that the test of true pluralism is the openness to draw on what he calls our sources of wisdom and compassion, from wherever they come. He picks up a piece of the pluralism agenda proposed originally by Farid Esack in urging that Muslims might be helped to speak out against oppression in Islam by studying Christian liberation theology. Unlike Esack, he does not acknowledge that he has already engaged in such study himself.

Among the contributors to Safi's volume on progressive Muslims is Amir Hussain of California State University. Hussain addresses pluralism from the perspective of interfaith dialogue.[32] He offers a helpful addition to the conversation, even though it is longer on generalities than on creative contributions as to how to challenge some of the theological impasses that recur in Christian-Muslim encounters. Hussain, like some others, defends pluralism as an ideology based on certain verses of the Qur'an, though he does not say if he means by it the diverse contexts in which the text was revealed or an ideology of pluralism. He does acknowledge that the Qur'an, in some passages, is less than inclusive. In general, however, he interprets the text as pluralistic on the grounds that it "sets forth perennial principles of humane behavior."[33] One of the major challenges for Muslims as they engage in serious interfaith dialogue, he says, is the fact that the Qur'an really does seem to say different things in different places about the relationship between Muslims and members of non-Muslim communities. The challenge to dialogue is to come to terms with the full range of the Qur'anic message. Ultimately, of course, he admits that the litmus test is whether a dialogue partner is other than a monotheist, which must be the boundary of an Islamic religious pluralism. "Admittedly, there is a difference in dialogue and relationships with those other than Jews and Christians. As Islam is a strictly monotheistic religion, Muslims believe that the most grievous sin is polytheism."[34] Hussain, along with a number of other commentators, points to verses that affirm God's intention to create humanity to be divided into tribes and nations, as well as those that guarantee that there is no compulsion in religion. These verses mean that God was addressing all humanity and not just Muslims, he says, that diversity has a positive value and that people are encouraged to learn from their differences.

Successor at Temple University to the afore-mentioned Isma'il al Faruqi is Mahmoud Ayoub, acknowledged earlier as a life-long participant in Christian-Muslim (and also Jewish) dialogue and one of the most articulate spokespersons for broadening the Qur'anic vision in relation to the religions of the Book. Ayoub's youth in a Lebanon that was attempting a political balance between Muslim and Christian gave him a deep understanding of the two faiths that he has carried with him through a lifetime. While *da'wa* for Faruqi symbolized the call to the truth, for Ayoub it has consistently meant the call to God. Dialogue is never a competition, but working together for better mutual understanding and support of the distinctness of the religious experience of each participant in the conversation. " . . . Muslims must not seek to explain Christianity solely on the basis of what the Qur'an and subsequent Islamic tradition have said about it," Ayoub says, "but should seek to understand Christianity from its own sources and on its own terms. Similarly, Christians must not interpret Islam, especially

its sacred scripture, in accordance with their own understanding of the divine economy of salvation, however enlightened and universally attractive such
a divine scheme may be, but should take seriously the Islamic worldview and
its divine plan for the attainment of forgiveness, salvation and bliss in the
hereafter."[35]

Ayoub, who has often been called on to represent Islam to American
publics who remain mostly ignorant about the faith, is deeply committed to the
true Qur'anic understanding of Islam and makes no bones about his own
religious affiliation. Nonetheless, he was educated in Christian schools and
has an intimate understanding of the Bible and the Christian tradition. His
Qur'anic exegesis, at which he has spent much of his mature years, includes
many attempts to understand verses of the Qur'an in such a way that they
complement rather than contradict the message of the New Testament. While
he consistently denies the divinity of Christ, he is convinced that Islam has not
brought any understanding of God that differs from what is inherent in Christianity, and that the revealed word of God must be the common bond uniting
all people of faith. Like al Faruqi, he stresses the importance of ethics over
theology, although he describes it more as the opportunity to work together for
justice than the academic pursuit of an ethical consensus. Ayoub has written at
length about Qur'anic christology, what he calls the christology of the human
rather than the divine Jesus.[36] It is a shame, he reflects, that the Jesus who
could be a bridge of piety and spirituality between Islam and Christianity instead all too often has turned out to be a theological barrier.

One of the main benefits of dialogue for Ayoub is the possibility of developing and deepening friendships.[37] He fears that dialogue in the American
context has become "fashionable," sometimes with "touchy-feely" dimensions
that he and most Muslims want strongly to avoid, and is thus in danger of
losing its meaning. Dialogue as a concept, he says, is beginning to "wear out."
Recognizing that there are deep divisions in the Muslim community itself,
including those between Sunnis and Shi'ites, he urges more consistent intra-
faith dialogue, perhaps even before much creative interfaith or multifaith conversation can take place. In the best of worlds the dialogue should be between
or among people who have the skills and interests to delve deeply together
into scripture, history, and theology, Ayoub says, but he worries that such an
endeavor would be confined to a very few scholars and leave most participants from each community behind. In the end, both Muslims and Christians
engaged in the dialogue must make a basic decision either to allow the claim
to truth for the other or not. If the decision is not to allow such claims, he
is persuaded, then the dialogue is neither genuine nor does it have any point.

"God speaks many languages, and truth does not lie in what theologians have come up with. Truth lies in the *living religions.*"

Pluralism as a Theological Imperative

Mahmoud Ayoub is convinced that the Qur'an contains justification of the attitudes of both pluralism and exclusivism, depending on the context of the revelation. He himself stresses the former, and thus he regards the People of the Book (Jews and Christians) "as a large family of faith, speaking different languages, but worshipping the One God."[38] Human unity, according to the Qur'an, comes through our understanding of God's oneness, but nonetheless we do differ as a result of the diversity of our cultures, languages, races, and environments. Ayoub is persuaded that the message of the Qur'an is that diversity is acceptable, but conflict is not. He examines teachings and prayers coming from various of the world's great teachers and religions—Zoroaster, the Buddha, hymns to Varuna—who are not under the "protected" status of Christians and Jews, to whom he says the Qur'an guarantees reward on the last day. He does not automatically accord these non-Abrahamic faiths with the same status, but he does say that to the extent to which they have modeled the relationship of submission to and worship of the one God they are part of the stream of progressive revelation from which, as he puts it, only idolatry is excluded.[39]

Two other contemporary Muslim thinkers agree that the possibility of truth lies in religions that are past the boundaries of the People of the Book. The first is Mohamed Fathi Osman of the Institute for the Study of Islam in the Contemporary World in Los Angeles. Pluralism is one of the mainstays of Osman's ongoing messages about Islam in the West.[40] While the term pluralism initially referred to ethnic and religious differences, he says, it became extended to mean that because there is no single understanding of truth, many beliefs and communities must enjoy equal legitimacy. He finds this concept supported in Qur'an 49:13.[41] Pluralism in this sense must be the basis of equality for all participants and cooperation for the benefit of all. It is the positive affirmation of both particularity and diversity, based on constructive moral and practical relations. Osman is always careful to describe societies in which pluralism is inclusive of females as well as males, insisting the Qur'an provides no grounds for gender discrimination. He makes the interesting point that while pluralism can be presented as a rational ideology, "intellectual understanding . . . does not provide the same moral depth as spiritual conviction and religious commitment."[42]

Stressing the importance of dialogue among Muslims, Jews, and Christians, Osman also makes it clear, on the basis of the Qur'anic insistence that every human being has a spiritual compass and dignity granted by God (Qur'an 17:70), that the conversation should be extended to include Buddhists, Taoists, and members of other faiths. The diversity of humankind can be enriched when the particular specialties of individuals and groups are seen as complementing and enriching each other. What we need to do is to learn to interact with each other and to recognize that the differences with which we are born enrich us as humans. That said, and he makes the point more than once, the main focus of Osman's talk about pluralism remains within the Abrahamic family, reminding Muslims of the common ground shared by all People of the Book by virtue of their having been the recipients of the divine book of God. Unwilling to give up monotheism as an absolute, at the same time that he insists on an ultimately broader definition of pluralism, he argues that monotheists must stand together so that they can develop a monotheistic morality. This morality he defines first as that characterizing believers in the One God, and then he extends it to the general morality of all people everywhere.

While Osman, an Egyptian Sunni, proposes an ultimately more inclusive Qur'anic pluralism than most Muslims would accept, the Isma'ili scholar from Harvard Ali Asani seems to push the boundaries even farther. Asani, unlike Osman, clearly wrote his article entitled "On Pluralism, Intolerance, and the Qur'an" after the occurrence of 9/11.[43] Asani makes many of the same points echoed by others who want to affirm the pluralistic nature of Islam, giving examples of tolerance in the history of Islam, the Qur'an's affirmation of both universality and plurality, and the scriptural insistence that there is no compulsion in religion. His particular contribution, at least in terms of the writers considered here, is his move to expand the term "People of the Book" itself to include other religious groups such as those encountered by Muslims in the early days of the spread of Islam (he notes in particular the Zoroastrians in Iran and the Hindus and Buddhists in India). Not all Muslims would feel comfortable about stretching the concept of People of the Book in this way, he admits, but in Asani's understanding, "the fact remains that these types of interpretations were made possible by the pluralistic nature of the Qur'anic worldview."[44] Thus far there has not been a groundswell of agreement for Asani's breadth of understanding of what it means to belong to the category of People of the Book.

At least one long-standing extremely active participant in interfaith dialogue in America, however, has been willing to extend the discussion in a somewhat different direction when it comes to finding ways to encourage theological inclusion. Rather than an extended sort of pluralism, however, it might better be described as a suspension of dialogue on the everyday plane in favor of a philosophical understanding of truth that presumes knowledge on a more highly esoteric plane. Christians and Muslims who have been active in dialogue will not be surprised that my reference here is to the work and thought of Seyyed Hossein Nasr of American University, mentioned briefly in chapter three. Nasr has been a primary spokesperson for a better understanding of Islam and for Muslim-Christian dialogue in America since leaving his native Iran at the time of the Revolution in 1979. An Ithna Ash'ari Shi'ite, he is a highly prolific author who is trained in the Islamic sciences, philosophy, theology and esoteric Sufism. Like Farqui and Ayoub, he also is solidly grounded in Christian theology, philosophy, and ethics. Nasr calls himself a traditional Muslim, one who is quite persuaded that modernity has led people of faith, both Muslims and Christians, away from a realization of the role of the sacred in human lives. Nasr is uninterested in dialogue for the sake of mere conversation, and insists that in order for dialogue to have any chance of success the participants must be well trained in their own faith as well as familiar with the other. Himself a man of genuine theological and philosophical curiosity, he wants to engage with others who are serious about the pursuit of truth. That truth is not, as Faruqi would say, encapsulated in the ethical teachings of Islam, but is to be discovered by pursuing an epistemology in which a single reality, most basically the oneness of God, might be seen in several different ways, or from different perspectives.[45] Nasr thus reveals himself an advocate of the perennialist philosophy of such thinkers as Rene Guenon and Frithjof Schuon.

At a 1990 conference entitled "Christian-Muslim Encounter," held at Hartford Seminary in honor of Willem Bijlefeld, Nasr made what he called "Comments on a Few Theological Issues in the Islamic-Christian Dialogue."[46] On that occasion he identified the following concerns: the nature of God, finality, scripture, sacred language, sacred law, Christ, and modernism. To say that these are "a few" issues is understating the case—while they are only seven in number they provide the stuff for long-term and deeply challenging conversation. Then in 1998 in an article for *The Muslim World* journal (reprinted in 2000 in *Islam and Christian-Muslim Relations*) entitled "Islamic-Christian Dialogue: Problems and Obstacles to be Pondered and Overcome," [47] he again laid out the concerns that he considers fundamental both to serious theological exchange and to the common pursuit of a deeper understanding of the realm of the sacred in its fullest dimensions. He raised four major concerns, of which the first, entitled "theological issues," addresses many of the points he made in the 1990 presentation. The theological issues identified are Christian notions of incarnation and trinity, salvation, sacred law, and eschatology. His other "problems and obstacles" are freedom of worship, missionary activity, and differing attitudes toward modernism.

However, he says, the dialogue must take seriously the reality that the Qur'an rejects both the doctrine of the trinity and the incarnation. "Any emphasis upon a particular manifestation of the One in the direction of the many," he says, "is seen by Islam as a veil cast upon the plenary reality of *Divine Unity....*"[48] The key question for Nasr is that of the crucifixion. As part of his ongoing effort to move the dialogue from the superficial level of cordiality to the hard issues of theological difference, he says that the fact that the Qur'an does not accept the crucifixion of Jesus is "the one irreducible 'fact' separating Christianity and Islam."[49] The other doctrines that might appear to be irreconcilable, including the nature of Christ and even the concept of the trinity, Nasr believes can be interpreted from a metaphysical perspective in a way that can actually serve to bring differing views into harmony. In a novel interpretation, Nasr says that the apparently irreconcilable matter of the crucifixion is "a fact which in reality was placed there providentially to prevent a mingling of the two religions."[50] Nonetheless, he pursues his goal of seeking transcendent unity by continuing to press the issue. In my opinion, one of Seyyed Hossein Nasr's signal contributions to the theological exchange between Christians and Muslims, is his unwillingness to stop in front of "what seems to be an insurmountable obstacle"[51] and assume that we have reached an impasse beyond which there is no possibility of reconciliation. In several of his writings, one developed out of a dialogue at Harvard Divinity School with Roman Catholic theologian Hans Kung, he ventures to say that it may be possible to take a further step. That is, perhaps both views—that the crucifixion did take place and that the crucifixion did not take place—could be correct on one plane of understanding if one accepts the possibility that a single event might be seen and known in more than one way.

In a private conversation, I asked Seyyed Hossein Nasr if he thought it is important for Muslims and Christians together to discuss the question of who, ultimately, is saved. His answer was that each faith community, within its own confines, must clarify the matter first. Only after that should it be discussed in the context of interfaith dialogue. "In the long run," he said, "I believe that it is only members of the two communities who believe that salvation is NOT limited to their own faith who can carry on fruitful dialogue with each other."

Does the Qur'an Really Affirm Theological Pluralism?

There is probably little question that most Muslims would find themselves in agreement with the position of the Pakistani cleric who asked: "If you believe your religion to be true...then why would you think that religious pluralism is a good thing?" The authors cited in this review are not clerics but academics, and they are speaking not just to their own faith communities but to both the academy and a larger public audience. In one way or another they seem to insist on the inherent pluralism of Islam, defending the inclusion of this faith within pluralist American society in light of post-9/11 critiques of Islam as monovocal, violent, and exclusive. On a number of points they seem to be in general agreement:

1. The Prophet faced situations in which different religious communities had to be addressed.
2. Throughout history, Islamic societies existed in circumstances of pluralism, both internal and external.
3. The contemporary pluralist world in general, and American society in particular, must find ways in which to respect difference and foster cooperation (some of these interpreters write specifically to affirm the affinity of Islam and democracy).
4. All of these realities must be seen in light of the essentially pluralistic message of the Qur'an in which it is affirmed that God created *different* nations and tribes, that there is *no* compulsion in religion, and that only God is the ultimate knower of truth.

Pluralism, in the explicit understanding of many of these analysts, must include justice and equal treatment, as well as equal opportunity, for all.

The differences, if they are such, perhaps lie in the definition of "all." A few authors are clear that Islam so obviously reflects the truth of God that no other choice is possible. Pluralism for them seems to have a very tight definition, and sometimes seems more a philosophical imperative than a religious belief. Others insist that as the Qur'an affirms a continuing revelation to all People of the Book, pluralism means the acceptance of Jews and Christians as believers who can attain salvation. Among those who affirm this position, some defend the verses that seem to speak ill of Christians and especially of Jews on the basis of different contexts of revelation and of the overall pluralistic affirmations of the Qur'an. Still others admit that certain verses really are negative, and that dialogue has to come to terms with the apparently exclusive as well as obviously inclusive passages as honestly as possible. A very few are willing to say that the pluralism affirmed in the Qur'an is one that must find ways to relate to and accommodate those beyond the category of People of the Book (or, as in Asani's case, even to make the category itself more inclusive).

But therein lies the real problem. The essence of Islam is the understanding of monotheism. There is only one God, and those who believe otherwise are specifically accused in the Qur'an of having committed the sin of *shirk,* or association with God. Can full acceptance, or even the milder "tolerance," really be applied to the understanding of those who believe that God may have several persona, or even that there is ultimately no God at all? Most Muslims find such an idea virtually impossible to accept. Tightening the circle, can it be said that Christians, as People of the Book, are fully accepted under the umbrella of pluralism if they insist on the divinity of Jesus? The answer would seem to be no, but few of those who are arguing for Islamic pluralism choose to address that head-on. Including Christians in the category of monotheists affirms the original revelation to Jesus and his community, not later theological versions. Finally, then, for most Muslim theorists and theologians, pluralism can accommodate only the response of *islam*, submission that is the innate and natural recognition of the divine *one*.

Then what *does* one do with those Qur'anic verses that clearly and specifically affirm difference and promise that no person is under any religious compulsion? If a theological pluralism, such as that espoused by certain liberal Christians (recall Esack's warning about "the vague liberal embrace of all forms of otherness") simply is not possible in Islam, can one persuasively posit an Islamic way of understanding that affirms different religious cultures? The writers whose works are considered in this essay clearly believe that the answer is yes, both because current conditions mandate such understanding and because the Qur'an—at least in some verses—does seem to affirm it. The task has been engaged, but it is fair to conclude that it has certainly not been completed. Why would a Muslim think religious pluralism is a good thing? The Qur'an gives important clues, but not a definitive answer. There is little question that we will see even more attempts to frame a positive response to the question in the very near future.

8

New Directions in Dialogue

We began with the assumption that 9/11 made a definitive change in many arenas of American life, certainly in the ways in which Muslims and Christians are thinking about each other, entering into dialogue with one another, and in general coming to terms with how to live together as citizens of one country. Some five years later, it is clear that in the American public as a whole, tensions are continuing to rise as the world becomes more troubled and the war on terror ratchets up on a regular basis. New ways of doing business, so to speak, will need to characterize our attempts at dialogue. In this concluding chapter, we look at some of the new directions that may help Muslims and Christians share the difficult task of modeling to the world how engagement other than retaliation and aggression can succeed while warfare guarantees success for no one. Each of these new directions has already been mentioned briefly at point or another—here they are grouped together and elaborated.

Organizational Initiatives

One of the most encouraging changes in the field of Christian-Muslim relations is the notable increase in the ways that respective organizations are taking the initiative for promoting better understanding and fostering dialogues at the local and national levels. The National Council of Churches of Christ/USA began formal interfaith work in the 1970s, focused initially on building relationships with the Jewish and Muslim communities in America, and on basic education of Christians about Jews and Muslims. In 1986 the Governing Board of the NCCC/USA passed a resolution in which it called on churches and their members to pursue a better understanding of Islam, to encourage both conversation and cooperation, to defend the civil rights of Muslims, to "reject the religious and political demagoguery and manipulation manifest in the reporting of events related to the Middle East," and to challenge statements about Islam that reflect prejudice and stereotyping.[1] In 1992, the Christian-Muslim Relations offices of the NCCC were transferred from Hartford Seminary to New York City. At the same time a restructuring of the Council led to the clustering of interfaith activity, which had been compartmentalized into Christian-Jewish and Christian-Muslim committees, in an "Interfaith Relations Commission." Shanta Pramawardhana, a Methodist paster, formerly serving in Chicago, whose original home was Sri Lanka, is currently the Council's Associate General Secretary for Interfaith Relations. His work with the Commission follows that of Presbyterian Jay Rock, one of whose notable achievements was guiding the Commission through the development of a "policy statement" intended to reflect an interdenominational Protestant Christian theological stance on interfaith relations. The statement was completed in 1999 and entitled *Interfaith Relations and the Churches.*

Since 1992, a number of issues regarding Christian-Muslim relations have been on the agenda of the Commission:

1. Working to set up local conversations (sometimes referred to as "metropolitan bridges"), with the hope of developing regional and finally national dialogues. The national task of dialogue has often been frustrated because the Commission has found it difficult to identify national Muslim organizations (comparable to denominational structures) with whom to work in initiating conversations. Recently the situation has changed somewhat through the expressed interest of Muslim organizations such as the Islamic Society of North America (ICNA) and the Islamic Council of North America (ICNA) in a national Muslim-Christian dialogue.

2. Relating to the African American Muslim community. The Committee for some time planned a major dialogue among members of African American churches and members of the Ministry of Warith Deen Mohammed, but such a meeting has not yet occurred. (More recent thinking by the Commission favors including African American Muslims in multiethnic national Muslim-Christian dialogues.)

3. Along with Muslim leaders, establishing specific guidelines for Christian-Muslim dialogue.
4. Setting up a national consultation on Christian and Muslim understandings of law and human rights.
5. Working with Muslims to counter negative media images of Islam.

Under Shanta Pramawardhana's direction, the Commission on Interfaith Relations at the time of this writing is anticipating a Christian-Muslim dialogue, or perhaps set of dialogues, to be held at the national level to foster mutual understanding and develop relationships of trust in the North American interreligious context. Representatives of Protestant denominations such as the United Methodist Church, the United Church of Christ, the Presbyterian Church USA, and the Episcopal Church will work on this project along with various American Muslim organizations including ISNA, ICNA, W. D. Mohammed's Mosque Cares, the Fatullah Gulen Society, and the American Society for Muslim Advancement (a Sufi group). The purposes proposed for the dialogue are to provide a context for regular interaction; to identify and share issues of theological commonality and difference; to create educational resources that will promote or deepen interfaith dialogue and cooperation in local communities of Muslims and Christians; and to find ways in which Muslims and Christians united can respond appropriately and quickly to shared concerns of civil liberty, religious freedom, and violence affecting their respective communities. The project, well into its planning stages, is designed to begin sometime in 2006–2007.

Such cooperative ventures, of course, are not new. The efforts of theUnited States Council of Catholic Bishops in partnership with various Muslim groups have been described in detail earlier. As a result of these well-established sets of ongoing dialogues, Christians and Muslims were able to join together in response to the 9/11 attacks. On September 14, 2001, as a result of the cooperative efforts begun in these meetings, representatives of the USCCB, ISNA, ICNA, the American Muslim Council (AMC), the Muslim American Society, and various Islamic centers and Councils agreed upon and signed a declaration abhorring acts of violence and hate, affirming the essential nature of working for God's peace and justice, and committing themselves to "the many noble goals of interreligious cooperation."[2] Another offshoot of the regional dialogues has been the continuing efforts of the USCCB and the National Association of (Catholic) Diocesan Ecumenical Officers to offer various summer institutes and training sessions on Islam and Catholic-Muslim relations. Since 2004 the Associate Director of the Secretariat for Ecumenical and Interreligious Affairs at the USCCB has been Father Francis V. Tiso.

Many individual Protestant denominations have made formal statements moving toward a more tolerant and even appreciative stance *vis-à-vis* Islam. Some have formally established programs to help introduce Muslims from overseas to American churches and, in exchange, to help church members know more about Islam from a personal perspective. The Presbyterian Church U.S.A. has begun what they call the "Interfaith Listening Program" that offers opportunities for Presbyterians or other people of faith to meet and talk face-to-face with Muslims. As the brochure states, church partners in up to ten countries send two-person teams, each consisting of a Christian and a Muslim, "to visit congregations, presbyteries, colleges and local communities to share their experiences of the realities and challenges of Christian-Muslim relationships." The expressed hope is that teaming together will help Americans learn more about their colleagues from abroad and will help the visitors learn better how to work together for peace, justice and the healing of creation.[3]

The Common Global Ministries Board of the United Church of Christ and Christian Church (Disciples of Christ), convened by Peter Makari, has engaged in a similar project to bring Middle Eastern Christians and Muslims to the United States for a speaking tour. Working with the Near East Council of Churches in cooperation with the Arab Working Group for Christian Dialogue, the group has identified host locales in the United States. The stated purpose of the visits is to help provide information to counter the negative perceptions of the Middle East perpetrated on the American public by the press and other commentators. The first set of twelve visitors arrived in 2005 for a two-week/three-weekend visit, dividing into three groups of four religiously mixed teams to visit six major metropolitan areas (Atlanta, Chicago, Houston, New York/New Jersey, North Carolina, and Southern California) with a final group meeting in Washington, D.C. As their literature puts it, "The target . . . is a moderate—perhaps undecided—population open to dialogue and alternative viewpoints on theological, social, and political issues affecting the lives of Christians and Muslims in the Middle East. . . . Convincing the audiences that interfaith relationships have intrinsic value can be highly stimulating."[4]

National Muslim organizations do not make public statements about Christians in the same way that some Protestant denominations are describing different responses to Islam in their literature. Many of the Muslim groups, however, including both those that are specifically religious and those that are more political in nature, have as part of their general statements of purpose some indication of the importance of pursuing interfaith relations. The Islamic Society of North America, the largest Muslim religious organization, for example, includes among its goals "fostering good relations with other religious communities" as well as "interfaith and coalition building." The Muslim

American Society proposes "To present the message of Islam to Muslims and non-Muslims and promote better understanding between them." The Muslim Political Action Committee, pledges to "Build alliances with Muslim and non-Muslim groups," and the American Muslim Council "is dedicated to building interfaith and interethnic understanding."[5]

Among a growing number of cooperative Christian-Muslim ventures designed to promote dialogue and understanding in the United States, several are worthy of particular mention. One is THE ISLAM PROJECT, in which interfaith and community organizations partner with Muslim groups to focus attention on issues facing Muslims both in the United States and elsewhere in the world. Thus far ten cities have launched campaigns based on THE ISLAM PROJECT: Atlanta, Boston, Chicago, Cleveland, Dallas, Detroit, Los Angeles, San Francisco, Washington, D.C., and Wichita. National partners include the Center for Christian-Muslim Understanding (CMCU) in Washington, D.C., the Council on Islamic Education, the Freedom Forum, Hope in the Cities, ISNA, the National Conference of Community and Justice,[6] the North American Interfaith Institute (NAIN) and Harvard University's Pluralism Project. A facilitator's guide is provided giving instruction on how to plan an Islam Project with appropriate materials and questions, and offering the use of a prepared video entitled "Muslims and Muhammad." THE ISLAM PROJECT began in 2001 as an immediate response to the feelings of isolation and alienation that many American Muslims have experienced following American actions in Iraq and elsewhere overseas. In Los Angeles, for example, an organization called "Days of Dialogue" (a nonpartisan group designed to foster discussion among ethnic groups on issues of race, crime, and poverty) used THE ISLAM PROJECT to deepen a dialogue already underway. They worked with the local PBS station to air project video modules and promote discussion about American Islam. A "train the trainer" component helped leaders return to work with specific communities on dialogue and Christian-Muslim understanding.

Various efforts have sprung up across the United States in response to the violence being perpetuated in many places around the globe. One, for example, was a Muslim-Christian consultation on the danger of nuclear weapons from the perspective of the two faiths, held in May 2005 at the Rockefeller family mansion north of New York City. The conference was sponsored by the Islamic Society of North America, the Managing the Atom Project of the Kennedy School of Government, the Rockefeller Brothers Forum, and the Churches' Center for Theology and Public Policy. Attended by some 30 Muslim and Christian scholars, leaders and activists from the United States and abroad, as well as representatives of the four sponsoring organizations, the conference was designed to examine what guidance Islam and Christianity can give about the morality of the possession and use of nuclear weapons. Conversations included study of sacred scriptures and traditions from the two faiths as they apply specifically to the challenges presented by nuclear weapons.

With the backing of a growing number of Christian and Muslim organizations, tentative though in some cases it may be, dialogue in North America—especially if some major foundations were to be persuaded of the crucial importance of this endeavor—could be poised to take off in some very exciting directions.

Opening the Doors to Women

Over a century ago, a few Muslim thinkers began to realize that if Muslim societies were to keep up with the social, political, economic, and educational progress being evidenced in the West, they would have to use the languishing resources of half of their populations, namely women. Muslims and Christians are now beginning to realize that the same analysis may apply to efforts at mutual involvement. The dialogue on interfaith relations heretofore has occupied Muslim and Christian men considerably more than women. It is now essential, many people feel, to find ways not only to bring more women into the conversation but to tap their resources in helping find new ways to develop interfaith cooperation on concrete projects. (I recall a conversation several years ago with a Muslim woman from Ghana. When I asked if women were involved in Christian-Muslim dialogue she laughed. "Look at the men just sitting in the square," she said. "They can talk about such things all day and nothing happens. Meanwhile the Muslim and Christian women of the village figured out how to cooperate to bring running water directly to our homes.")

The question of female participation in the dialogue in America is complex. When the designated partners are specifically religious leaders such as priests and imams, as is the case with the Roman Catholic-Muslim conferences, it is primarily males who sit at the table. Other kinds of local dialogues are increasingly both initiated and populated by women, both Roman Catholic and Protestant, who have no problem holding their own in conversation with men. They are very glad when Muslim women are able to take part in these conversational circles, although in reality there are many reasons why it is often difficult for that to happen. Muslim women with whom I have talked give a variety of reasons for their lack of participation from their own perspective and experience. In their own words:

1. In general, women are less publicly visible in American Muslim communities than men. Therefore those Muslims and Christians who initiate and organize the dialogue don't know any women to invite.

2. Muslim men tend not do encourage the participation of women, so unless they are pushed they don't volunteer the names of women to dialogue organizers.

3. Women are interested in different issues than men. If Muslim women find that the conversation is basically about theological or doctrinal issues they assume they don't have anything to contribute and aren't generally very interested in such subjects anyway. (The same, of course, could be said for many Christian women and men.)

4. In traditional cultures, women often do not engage in open conversation with men outside of their families, let alone men of other religious traditions. Further, dialogues are almost always dominated by male authority figures, and Muslim women aren't comfortable speaking in such situations.

5. Many Muslim women simply prefer to listen rather than to talk (unless, of course, if they are talking in a group of all women), and are embarrassed when they are strongly encouraged by their Christian hosts to speak up and join the conversation.

6. "When I finally get up the courage to speak," said one recent immigrant, "I feel like my comments are seldom taken seriously and the conversation quickly returns to the men."

Several Muslim women have expressed their frustration that when women only are present at dialogues, Christians seem unable to resist focusing the conversation on questions about Islamic dress. When men are not around, the Christian women apparently feel that they have a green light to ask quite personal questions about why their colleagues are wearing certain kinds of clothing. Sometimes this can work as a great conversation starter, but some of the Muslim women with whom I spoke feel that despite their attempts to be neutral, non-Muslim women participants often find it hard to hide their opinion that anyone who chooses to wear the *hijab* is somehow backward or oppressed. Christians admit that this topic is fascinating to them, and some even say that it is hard for them to get on with other conversation until there has at least been some explanation from Muslim women about why they choose, if they do, to wear *hijab*.

Another Muslim expressed her annoyance that Christian women often insist on pushing a more "liberal" agenda; she reports that they seem to feel that women should be more open than men to moving forward on matters of gender equality, sexual openness, and the like. Muslims, she said, can be easily turned off by such expectations. When talking about women's concerns means discussing such things as women's roles in relation to men or sexual preferences, Muslim women may be uncomfortable and not feel these are appropriate topics for interfaith conversations. Often, women's groups have discovered that when talk turns to ways in which common problems with youth or elderly can be addressed, or in which a group of women can provide support for social and political causes, exciting progress can be made.

All of these responses need to be taken seriously by dialogue organizers, especially those women involved in the planning. However, change is certainly afoot in Muslim communities in America and so are Muslim women's attitudes toward many things, including the dialogue. Several concerns should be taken into consideration. First, women may come to be more open to various kinds of conversations if trust is established and they are not pushed to go beyond what they believe their religious tradition permits. Second, as Muslim men and women become more comfortable with each other's public presence, the conversation will flow more smoothly. Third, as non-Muslim women begin to learn more about their Muslims sisters they are developing the much-needed sensibilities to help them make the dialogue table feel open and welcoming to Muslim women as well as men.

In addition, several new things seem to be taking place regarding women's involvement in dialogue groups. One is that all-female interfaith gatherings are gaining in popularity with some Muslim women. Women are discovering that they have a lot to say to each other that is much more comfortably expressed when men aren't present. Muslim women seem to be especially interested in participating in sessions that involve women from the three Abrahamic religions (Islam, Christianity, and Judaism). Another new reality is that in some cases Muslim women are moving into leadership positions in ongoing interfaith forums involving both women and men. It also seems to be the case that African American women, most of whom who until recently have not been involved in many such sessions, are now beginning to get interested in women's interfaith dialogues.

Conversation between Christian and Muslim women is moving forward in several other interesting new directions. Some women have both the qualifications and the interest to engage in serious textual and theological study. For some time now, both immigrant and indigenous Muslims women have been undertaking what they understand to be *ijtihad*, individual interpretation of religious texts. They tend to see Islam as a dynamic evolving entity (often because of the initiative of women)[7] and to view themselves as having moved beyond the more static understanding of Islam held by many Muslims (especially males) who are currently involved in the dialogue. These conversations about *ijtihad* usually have much greater chance of providing the basis for a serious interfaith discussion if the group is all female. Given the obstacles in the way of being heard clearly in mixed sessions, many qualified Muslim women are not interested in fighting what they see as the same battles over and over again. In the words of one participant, they have already "moved on."

This can be exciting business for Christian women, some of whom have been fighting the same battles for new textual interpretations more inclusive of women for a few decades. Several years ago I hosted a conference at Hartford Seminary where female scholars of the Old Testament, the New Testament, and the Qur'an came together to talk about the methods that they use when they come to a "problematic" section of their holy scripture—one that has been translated by generations of men in ways that could be seen as disadvantageous to women. I asked them first to reflect together on what, for them, makes the text authoritative. Then they talked about their individual methodologies and how they approach the text in a way that is both critical and respectful. Finally they gave their own reasonable reinterpretations of how the problematic texts in question might be understood. Because these women were scholars of their scriptures, the conversation was at a rather sophisticated level. Similar exercises, however, can be carried out by women who do not necessarily have all the scholarly exegetical tools but for whom understanding scripture is of crucial importance.

Many women, both Muslim and Christian, are tired of endlessly discussing the same subjects and are using the dialogue as an opportunity to press agendas for serious action. Many are looking for new venues of discussion and cooperation in which to providing assistance to members of the broader community. Amina Wadud of Virginia Commonwealth University, long active in Muslim-Christian encounters, says that in her opinion traditional dialogue "isn't really going anywhere," and she is therefore moving more directly into an interfaith context in which she works for causes of justice and peace. Wadud is currently active in the World Conference on Religion and Peace (WCRP). Najeeba Syeed-Miller, Executive Director of the Western Center Foundation in Pasadena, California, uses the tools of mediation, facilitation, and reconciliation in her work on conflict intervention and resolution in California.[8] Syeed-Miller does dialogue in a different mode by working in an interfaith context with communities, courts, and schools to promote conflict resolution and help administrative agencies improve access to justice. Aminah Carroll, lone Muslim member of the Women's Interfaith Institute in the Berkshires, identifies gender prejudice and sexual abuse as common problems faced by women of all (or no) religions, and thinks that common cooperation could go far in helping solve such problems. "Inviting Muslim women to become a part of the solution to such socially ubiquitous problems is an act of inclusiveness that generous women of all faiths really ought to make," she says.

Riffat Hassan of the University of Louisville has taken the occasion of interfaith conversation as another forum for advocating the liberation of women from male dominance.[9] She claims the right of women to participate in inter- and intrareligious dialogue not passively, but by actively setting the agenda. Hassan has long believed in the necessity of continuing to carry on doctrinal discussions between Christians and Muslims.[10] Nonetheless, more recently she has turned her attention away from the traditional dialogical model. She is working actively for an end to the violation of women in her native Pakistan, and welcomes the participation of any Christian or other women who would like to join in an interfaith women's project for social justice.

Much discussion remains to be done by Muslim and Christian women, often with representatives of other faiths, and many women seem just to be waking up to the exciting possibilities of such interfaith conversations. For others who feel that they have done enough talking and are ready for action, there is a wide range of projects, both local and international, that may well serve to move the dialogue in some new and extremely engaging ways.

Youth and the Dialogue of Action

At first it seemed a natural. The interfaith group of which I have long been a member decided that it would be a good idea to bring Christian, Muslim, and other high school students to talk together, without adults present, about some of the things that have been happening in the world recently, and how they as youth think about these things. Kids love to talk with kids, we adults said to ourselves. All we need to do is to leave them alone and off they will go. We decided to make sure there was music available, since that seems to be an essential ingredient of teen interaction.

No, it didn't work that way. First we found that today's teens are so extremely busy that they didn't think they could fit one more thing into their schedules. The Christian kids we talked to said that it would be okay if some Muslims sat in on one of their meetings, but they weren't interested enough to be responsible for planning it. They definitely didn't think that getting Muslim and Christian teens together just to talk would work. The Muslims reported that members of their communities (a primarily African American and an ethnically mixed mosque) were not too enthusiastic about the project because they didn't want young people of different faiths mixing and getting too close to each other—especially if they were going to be listening to music, which some Muslims think is forbidden. Let's just leave the interfaith stuff to the adults, they decided.

The experience of our group, of course, does not necessarily reflect that of everyone trying to set up interfaith teen meetings. It does, suggest, that it isn't easy to do. Once in a while an unusual youth, Christian or Muslim, may enjoy being part of adult dialogue conversations, but it's rare. Generally it does not work to simply add them to the mix of adult participants already in place because young people's issues are different and they get easily discouraged when the agenda reverts to the interests of long-time dialogue partners. Muslims as well as members of other religious groups bemoan the teen years when their kids seem to drop out of any religious responsibilities that aren't forced on them. "Ahmed used to love to pray with his father in the mosque," said one mother, "but now his ears are on his portable and his eyes on the computer screen. I sometimes feel I need to call him on the phone to reach him!" Certainly the concerns that both Christian and Muslim parents have about their teenagers can be an interesting topic for the adults to pursue together, but it does not address the question of how to get the youth engaged with each other.

Muslims themselves, despite the misgivings they might have about letting their kids loose, so to speak, with Christian kids, really are acknowledging the importance of making serious attempts to involve their youth both in the internal activities of the community and in relationships with others in American society. The key to keeping kids active and interested in their churches and mosques, and perhaps even to bringing them together, seems to be involving them in a concrete action project. "Youth are not involved in the dialogue because they are concentrating on different things," Nihal Hassan, a young Muslim from Indianapolis, once wrote to me. "They are at an age when their personality is forming, and it would be very important to instill in them ideas of openness and understanding. But if they can be brought together to work on projects, that would be great." Yehya Hendi, chaplain at Georgetown University agrees. It is crucial to get the youth involved, he insists, but they aren't interested in theological issues or necessarily in talking about religion at all. In a statement made at a Board of Chaplaincy Directors meeting at Hartford Seminary in April 2003, Hendi said, "They [youth] are constantly changing in terms of their interests, backgrounds, and the things they are concerned about. The old issues don't do anymore."

As a young Muslim woman who has been working with interfaith youth projects commented to me in a personal conversation, "Kids are less interested in 'solid state' stuff than what is in flux. They need to be brought around to thinking that dialogue is cool by making it sound like something else. The terminology needs to be changed. They really are interested in issues like racism and sexism, and if you play it right they really are willing to do social action or social service activities." Before you try to get them into soup kitchens, though, you need to talk about what motivates them, and what religious values might come into play, she said. "Doing needs to be engaged with some kind of talking. It is mostly an advertisement to make talking more attractive."

One very successful interfaith venture with young people is Interfaith Youth Corps, an entrepreneurial, Chicago-based organization actively building a movement that, as its Web site advertises, encourages religious youth to work together to strengthen their identities, foster interreligious understanding and cooperate to serve the common good. As of this writing the Corps is looking to hire a Muslim Initiatives Coordinator to advance interfaith youth service learning work within the Muslim community in the United States.

In part because more colleges and universities are hiring Muslim chaplains, interfaith activity is starting to be on the agenda of a number of Christian and Muslim student associations. In the spring of 2006, Protestant chaplain Janet Cooper-Nelson and Muslim chaplain Ayesha Chaudhry engaged in a project to bring together young women of the two faiths at Brown University. They set up a series of workshops in which Christians and Muslims considered parallel materials from the Qur'an and the New Testament regarding women. The chaplains began by asking participants to jot down what they thought are the characteristics of "good women" in both traditions before discussing the texts themselves. The texts used were: (1) 1 Corinthians 11 and [Qur'an 24: 33 dealing with appropriate covering for men and women; (2) 1 Corinthians 14 and Qur'an 4: 34 looking at relationships between men and women; and (3) Galatians 3 and Qur'an 33: 35 considering similarity/equality between men and women. "We deliberately chose apparently contradictory verses from each text in order to present a complex view of gender in both traditions," said Chaplain Cooper-Nelson. At the end of each workshop participants were asked to return to the original questions to see if there were any changes. The workshops were followed by prayer and dinner. Both chaplains felt that the process was extremely engaging, and provided a unique opportunity for young Muslim and Christian women to talk together. They are planning to hold follow-up meetings.

What does seem to be the case, however, is that unless some special kind of program is set up for them, Christian and Muslim youth are generally more interested in programs that involve action rather than talk, and are multifaith rather than bilateral. Former MSA president Altaf Hussein talked with me about his activities with young representatives of a variety of faith traditions and the enthusiasm with which they engaged in such activities as building houses for Habitat for Humanity. "Youth want more community dialogue through interfaith engagement," says former ISNA president Muzammil Siddiqi. "They want activities and projects." Thus far the national Muslim Student Association does not have a task force that deals with interfaith issues. Such activities as do exist are classed under the Da'wah task force. At local chapter levels, however, there are some illustrations of Muslims and Christians working together for better understanding.

Like their adult counterparts, some Muslim students avoid interfaith activities for fear that they might get involved in things that are against their moral principles. They worry that if they make friends with non-Muslims they may be invited to go to parties where drugs or alcohol are present, for example, or where they may be expected to observe or join in sexual activities that they believe wrong or inappropriate. Still, it is inevitable that there is going to be more involvement of young Muslims, Christians, Jews, and others with each other. A growing number of college campuses have common kitchens for students who want to prepare their food in a kosher or *halal* [legally acceptable] way. When students are eating together, they will be talking together. As more colleges and universities insist on a high level of community involvement for their students, it is obvious that young men and women from different religious traditions will find themselves working together in shelters, food-banks, aid to the elderly, assistance for the physically challenged, and the like. Dialogue may come to have a very different kind of venue for young people than it traditionally has for their elders, and everyone can learn from the experiences of youth that are just now starting to be developed.

As an aside to this conversation about youth, it is interesting to note that the older generation, too, is clearly getting excited about interfaith understanding. The *Chicago Tribune* of March 30, 2005, reported that some 600 seniors, including some pastors, from Illinois, Indiana, and Wisconsin were participating in a daylong educational program called Building Bridges to Islam. Held at the Islamic Cultural Center of Northbrook, Illinois, the program was sponsored jointly by Elderhostel and the Chicago chapter of the Council for American-Islamic Relations (CAIR). This growing interest in Islam by American seniors is being evidenced in other cities where Elderhostel and Muslim groups are holding similar seminars. The first of these programs was developed in Santa Clara, California. The goal of the series is to offer Elderhostelers in cities across the country an opportunity to enhance their knowledge of Islam, as well as to interact with members of their local Muslim communities. It is obviously working, as seminars have now been held in cities such as Pittsburgh, Boston, Philadelphia, San Francisco, Los Angeles, Tampa, Miami, and Seattle, with more than 5,000 people enrolled.

I know of no instance in which a mixed group of Muslims and Christians, youth under twenty-one and seniors over sixty-five (nobody in between, please), has come together to talk about whatever topics they might find of common interest. But wouldn't that be an exciting idea? Especially if it were the young people who set the conversational table . . .

From Two to Three?

"So why is it that only Muslims and Christians have been invited to be part of this dialogue—how about the Jews?" is a question that both Christians and Muslims who are working on such planning need to consider. Without question there are growing efforts on the part of a number of people interested in interfaith communication, both those who are considering forming dialogue groups and those who have already established meetings, to emphasize the "Abrahamic" tie among the three religions of the Book. Therefore they feel that it is important to include Jews in what would they believe should become a three-way dialogue. Muslim-Jewish groups are being established in many areas of the country, sometimes with such determined nomenclature as "We Refuse to be Enemies."

The question isn't really is whether or not there should be "Abrahamic" dialogue groups—there are many in this country and they are doing very interesting things. The issue is whether already established Muslim-Christian dialogues should automatically be expanded to include Jews. As with most such questions, there are various points of view, suggested in the following:

1. The political situation in Israel-Palestine continues to be one of the most troubling in the world, and it is important for Americans to know more about what is going on. If a group of Americans, generally friendly toward one another and sharing each other's hospitality, the argument goes, cannot think creatively together about how to resolve the thorny issues of Jerusalem, settlements, and the like, how can we hope for peace among people who have shared so little mutual hospitality? The counter to this argument is that the issues are really political and not religious, despite the sanctity of Jerusalem for all three faiths. Christians coming for a religious dialogue and not wanting to take sides in an argument may well find themselves peripheral to the conversation as Muslims and Jews go back and forth in discussions about current political realities in Israel/Palestine. The stakes are terribly high, feelings become raw, and the trust absolutely necessary for a successful dialogue may never be established. Worse, hard won

trust can be lost. I personally have been part of several dialogues including Muslims, Jews, and Christians in which promises to avoid Middle East politics simply could not be kept and the groups had to dissolve in mutual disappointment and discouragement.

2. Some proponents of a three-way conversation say, of course correctly, that Christians and Jews have always seen themselves in some kind of theological relationship, and that Muslims understand that the revelation to Muhammad was a continuation of the monotheistic message that began with the prophets heralded in the Old Testament. We are one body of monotheistic faith, they argue, despite our theological differences, and we need to learn to talk with each other about those differences as well as what we have in common. That may well be true, is the response, but the fact is that Christians have not yet fully worked out what it means for Christianity to supercede Judaism, and Jews and Christians are still struggling together with the nature of their theological relationship. In the same way, Muslims really do consider that Islam fulfills and supercedes both Christianity and Judaism. Those who oppose the three way dialogue on theological grounds, then, say that it is up to each set of two traditions to work out its relationship fully with the other before bringing the three into conversation. All this is even truer, those who hold this position insist, if we consider the fact that most participants in interfaith dialogues are not sufficiently conversant with religious history and theology to be able to deal with such issues without specific guidance. Finally, they argue, most Christians have not fully come to terms with the guilt they feel about the Holocaust. That may cloud the attempts at dialogue between Christians and Jews, and even more so among the three faiths.

3. Thirdly, for some Christians and Muslims, it is a matter of local hospitality and generosity. How can we have a little group of Christian and Muslim folks talking about religious matters together and not include the local Rabbi and some members of his congregation? It just doesn't feel right, and doesn't do anything to help foster good relations in our city. The response to this argument is probably only agreement, and as a result three-way dialogues, and also those involving members of other religious groups present in a given area, are continuing to develop.

In addition to ongoing groups, many special projects are being undertaken to bring together Jews, Muslims and Christians across the country. On

October 30, 2005, for example, Iowa City was the site of an "October Surprise: A Call to Share Sacred Seasons Interfaith Walk, Oct. 30, 2005." The walk was sponsored by a group called Tent of Abraham, involving the Jewish organization Agudas Achim, the Newman Catholic Student Center, Gloria Dei Lutheran Church, First United Methodist Church, and the Iowa City mosque. At each center of worship a ten minute program of prayer and music in that community's tradition was held.[11] At Hartford Seminary each year two weeklong teaching seminars for youth and adults are offered, called "Building Abrahamic Partnerships." The goal of the seminars is to educate participants about the beliefs and practices of the three faiths, creating a safe environment in which relationships can be built across religious and communal boundaries.

A number of efforts are underway to support Jewish-Muslim cooperation among young people. For example, the nonprofit organization "Children of Abraham" invites young Jews and Muslims from around the world to be part of a new community, grounded in an understanding of the real circumstances that breed the unfamiliarity and suspicion characterizing the relationship between Islam and Judaism today. The programs offer participants the opportunity to explore interfaith relationships safely, through online discussion groups, social entrepreneurship, and photography. From March to May, 2005, participants entered Muslim and Jewish communities in their own towns to take photos of religious life as they viewed it from their own perspective. Photos were shared with over one hundred Muslim and Jewish participants from forty countries around the world via closed Web site, then discussed via message boards, chat-rooms, voice- and video-conferencing.[12] Other efforts are more localized, such as that by a Rabbi and an Imam from Wesleyan University in Connecticut who have collaborated on several Jewish-Muslim youth dialogue trips, including to Istanbul and to Israel/Palestine.

On the national scale, representatives of the three faith traditions undertook a major project during the 2004 presidential and congressional elections when they broached the issue of health insurance. "A broad coalition of groups that includes Christian, Jewish and Muslim communities hopes to move the plight of the medically uninsured to the top of the domestic agenda during this presidential and congressional election year," said *The New Orleans Times Picayune,* affirming that the group of about fifty clergy from the three faiths hoped take the fight for health coverage to their respective pulpits. The goal was to move the plight of the medically uninsured to the top of the domestic agenda.[13] Former Presidents Ford and Carter led the national effort, which was sponsored by a broad array of, sometimes competing, groups, including the United States Chamber of Commerce and the AFL-CIO, plus a number of Catholic, Protestant, Jewish, and Islamic groups.

No matter how the coalitions are built, there are solid reasons for con-tinuing dialogue efforts both among and between religious groups. This vol-ume has been dedicated specifically to an understanding of Christian-Muslim dialogue. Efforts at broadening the conversation, whether through talk or through action, can only help enhance the experience of all of those who take part.

Why Do We Want to Do It?

So why, after seeing how complicated all this dialogue business can get, do we want to continue to try to make it work? My own personal experiences have been mixed, some successful, some disappointingly short-lived. But I remain absolutely convinced that especially in these increasingly complex days we have no choice but to talk together and to work together. Most of my friends and colleagues who have engaged in the dialogue agree. Of the various reasons they have given for wanting to continue getting together, the following seem especially compelling:

Dialogue has it own way of facilitating an atmosphere of respect, trust, and finally genuine friendship. As groups discover together a purpose for continuing to meet and continuity is developed, participants begin to see each other as real people and not just representatives of one or another religion. Trust and the creation of genuinely safe space do not appear spontaneously. They may, in fact, take years to develop. Islamic Society of North America Executive Director Say-yid Saeed talks about the fact that their dialogues with Christians through the USCCB have been in existence for a long time has helped overcome some dif-ficult moments, as when the Church put forward the exclusive *Dominus Iesus* document discussed in chapter six. Once trust is established many good things can happen, from intimate dialogue to learning how to laugh together. When certain individuals from both communities have gained a reputation for being trustworthy in the dialogue it can go far in helping persuade others that the enterprise is worth the time and effort.

Dialogue sponsored by local churches can introduce Christians both to the reality of American pluralism and to the Muslims who are part of their own communities. In a number of different ways, churches are providing contexts in which the ex-periences of their parishioners are being enhanced through special programs on understanding Islam and talking personally with Muslims. One United Church of Christ congregation in Connecticut got so involved in the project that its pastor, Rev. Jamie Harrison, ended up receiving a Luce grant for the study of Christian theology in relation to Islam and writing a very helpful theological handbook for members of his denomination ("Pilgrims in a Multifaith World." Unpublished ms. Woodstock, Conn., 2003). In some cases, the overture to Muslims has led to a next step in which Christians and Muslims together have invited their Jewish neighbors to be part of the conversation.

Dialogue can go far in countering the negative images many Christians have about Islam and also that many Muslims have about Christian America. Countering anti-Muslim prejudice is an obvious hoped-for result of the dialogue and has been discussed often in this volume. Muslims are keenly aware of the negative impression that many Christians have of them and their faith, and many believe that trying to change that impression is one of the strong arguments in favor of their joining these face-to-face conversations. On the other side is the fact that Muslims may continue to harbor feelings of resentment about American foreign policies and fear about the excesses of American society and culture. It has been through the process of dialogue that many Muslims have come to realize and appreciate the openness to and appreciation of Islam and themselves as members of the Muslim community that is exhibited by many Christian participants. Imam Mohammad Ali Elahi of the Islamic House of Wisdom in Dearborn put it well when he said "Muslims see Christianity as a weapon in the hands of colonizers. Dialogue is a blessing and a source of great education, allowing Muslims get past the bitter memories of tragedies that have happened in the Middle East." As a result of dialogue encounters, increasing numbers of Christians are working together with Muslims to combat prejudice, misunderstanding and so-called disinformation in schools, the workplace, and other public arenas.

Dialogue helps participants to better understand their own religion and faith. For regular dialogue partners such an affirmation is a kind of truism. Christian missionary Phil Parshall expressed both his frustration at not persuading his Muslim friend of the truth of Christianity, and his deep appreciation of the faith of the latter who after many years of conversation professed himself not a convert but a better Muslim. "Because of . . . an interfaith retreat last summer," says Shahid Athar of the Indiana University School of Medicine. "I am now a better human and a better Muslim."[14] After some serious interfaith discussions in one of my recent classes a Christian student expressed his appreciation for the opportunity to reflect more seriously on his own faith. "To tell you the truth," he said, "I never thought much about the idea of the Trinity until I was forced to try to explain it to some Muslims. Now I think I'm beginning to see what it is all about." Imam Hamad Ahmad Chebli of the Islamic Society of Central New Jersey said that Imams are often called on to interact with American Christian culture and society and are ill-informed. Chebli comes to the dialogue because it makes him a better Imam.

Dialogue has joined Muslims with Christians and Jews in the struggle for social reform. Muslims are the first to admit that many times Christians and Jews have taken the lead in organizing interfaith collaboration in dealing with issues of civic concern. Moein Butt of the Islamic Society of Greater Butt expressed to me his regret that while the many mosques and Islamic centers in Houston are increasingly getting involved in community activities, Muslims are often very resistant to associating and working with them. But this situation is changing. Increasingly Muslims are expressing the need to play leadership roles themselves. "Other religious leaders may well be facing the same problems Muslims are," said Imam Talib Abdur-Rashid of the Muslim Alliance in North America at a meeting of national organization leaders at Georgetown University in June 2000. "Dialogue may help us understand that and work together on solutions." Muhammad Yunus of ICNA agreed, saying "We need to work hand in hand with brothers and sisters of other faiths in helping solve problems of American society." Some Muslims go so far as to see that the dialogue is primarily driven now by the social process and the recognition of the power of religious communities collaborating for social action. "We don't have the luxury or the time to spend talking theology," said Amir al-Islam to me in 2002. "We are committed to our faiths, but our faiths inform us that we have not thanked God and served God unless we serve the people. We must shift the way we look at each other and see if we can't work collaboratively."

The dialogue in America enjoys the particularly advantageous position of being at the mid-point of a long history of Christian-Muslim interaction. Here I borrow from Jay Rock, my Presbyterian friend and colleague in the interfaith work of the National Council of Churches. Rock notes that too often in today's conversations in the United States dialogue is carried out with what he calls "only a peripheral historical consciousness." Americans often have little awareness of the historical circumstances that have shaped them, he says, and certainly do not know much about the lives and histories that have shaped the consciousness of their dialogue partners. They may, therefore, also be relatively unaware of the importance of what we are able to create in terms of dialogue here today. "It is just here, in the midst of the unfolding of life of Christians and Muslims in the United States today," says Rock, where I find the most promise for Muslim-Christian relationship and conversation."[15]

Rock admits that we are living in troublesome days, but says that such times also offer the chance to work for new relationships in dialogue that have not been, and still are not, possible elsewhere. We are in the middle of our personal and communal life, the middle of a long flow of history in which Christians and Muslims have interacted for a long time, and in the middle of thinking through new contributions that this uniquely American context might have to make to the field of interfaith dialogue. Particularly as we move to a place in American history in which many Muslims no longer are newcomers but share with us a history of citizenship, we have the unusual opportunity to create a dialogue in which we really are, to use a much-quoted expression from Harvard scholar Wilfred Cantwell Smith, "talking together about us."[16]

And that seems to be the shape of things. The conditions are ripe, not to say urgent, and the players, at least many of them, are willing. It is my great hope that the next decade will see a flourishing not only of dialogue among Muslims and Christians but of many more ways in which we will learn to cooperate for our mutual enhancement as well as for the betterment of American society.

Notes

CHAPTER I

1. Some scholars have chosen to make the two words African American into one, as articulated by Sherman Jackson in his *Islam and the Black-american. Looking Toward the Third Resurrection* (New York: Oxford University Press, 2005).

2. Warith Deen Mohammed, whose movement will be described in detail in chapter three, has been a leader in establishing dialogs with Roman Catholic and other Christian groups.

3. This actually happened, recorded online on July 17, 2006. Plans included a 29,000 square foot facility including a mosque on a five-acre site.

4. The current Nation of Islam is estimated to be not larger than 50,000.

CHAPTER 2

1. R. W. Southern, *Western Views of Islam in the Middle Ages* (Cambridge: Harvard University Press, 1962), 3.

2. Mahmoud Ayoub, "Christian-Muslim Dialogue: Goals and Obstacles," *The Muslim World* 94/3 (July 2004): 315. See also Ayoub's "Roots of Muslim-Christian Conflict," *The Muslim World* (January 1987): 25–45.

3. Norman Daniel, *Islam and the West: The Making of an Image* (Edinburgh: University Press, 1960).

4. See Abdullah Saeed, "The Charge of Distortion of Jewish and Christian Scriptures," *The Muslim World* 92 (Fall 2002): 419–436.

5. See Mahmoud Ayoub, "Jesus the Son of God: A Study of the terms *Ibn* and *Walad* in the Qur'an and Tafsir Tradition," in Yvonne Y. Haddad

and Wadi Z. Haddad, eds., *Christian-Muslim Encounters* (Gainesville: University Press of Florida, 1995), 65–81.

6. Jane I. Smith, "Islam and Christendom. Historical, Cultural, and Religious Interaction from the Seventh to the Fifteenth Centuries" in John Esposito, ed., *The Oxford History of Islam* (New York: Oxford University Press, 1999), 305–345.

7. See Richard W. Bulliet, *The Case for Islamo-Christian Civilization* (New York: Columbia University Press, 2004), esp. 1–45.

8. A helpful and readable article on the religious complexities of Jerusalem is Karen Armstrong's "Jerusalem: the problems and responsibilities of sacred space," *Journal of Christian-Muslim Relations* 13/2 (2002): 189–196.

9. Jane I. Smith with David J. Zucker, "Jerusalem, The Sacred City: Perspectives from Judaism and Islam," *Journal of Ecumenical Studies* 32/2 (Spring 1995): 227–256.

10. Amin Maalouf, *The Crusades Through Arab Eyes* (New York: Schocken, 1984).

11. See, e.g., Jane I. Smith, "French Christian Narraives Concerning Muhammad and the Religion of Islam from the 15th to the 18th Centuries," *Islam and Christian-Muslim Relations* 16/4 (October 2005): 361–376.

12. Jan Slomp, "Calvin and the Turks," in Haddad and Haddad, *Christian-Muslim Encounters,* 126–142.

13. David Thomas, "The Bible in Early Muslim Anti-Christian Polemic," *Islam and Christian-Muslim Relations* 7/1 (1996): 29–38; Mark Swanson, "Beyond Prooftexting: Approaches to the Qur'an in Some Early Arabic Christian Apologies," *The Muslim World* 88 (July–October 1998): 297–319.

14. Mark Beaumont, *Christology in Dialogue with Muslims. A Critical Analysis of Christian Presentations of Christ for Muslims from the Ninth and Twentieth Centuries* (Oxford: Regnum, 2005).

15. See Wadi Haddad, "A Tenth-Century Speculative Theologian's Refutation of the Basic Doctrines of Christianity: al-Baqillani (d. 1013)," in Haddad and Haddad, *Christian-Muslim Encounters,* 82–94.

CHAPTER 3

1. Yvonne Y. Haddad and Jane I. Smith, *Mission to America: Five Sectarian Movements in the United States* (Gainesville: University Press of Florida, 1993), 49–78.

2. Differences between Sunnis, who make up nearly ninety per cent of the Muslim population of the world, and Shi'ites are mainly over questions of leadership. Shi'ites are waiting for the return of the hidden Imam who will lead the community to peace and justice. In the meantime the Ayatollahs are ruling in his stead.

3. See chapter seven for details.

4. Zahid Bukhari and Sulayman Nyang, eds. *Muslims' Place in the American Public Square* (Walnut Creek, CA: Altamira Press, 2004).

5. Haddad and Smith, *Mission to America,* 79–104.

6. Alex Haley, *The Authobiography of Malcom X* (New York: Random House, 1965, 1992), 6.

7. Many studies have been done on the Nation of Islam. Among the best are C. Eric Lincoln, *The Black Muslims in America* (Boston: Beacon, 1961); Robert Dannin,

Black Pilgrimage to Islam (New York: Oxford University Press, 2002); Aminah Beverly McCloud, *African American Islam* (London: Routledge, 1995); Martha F. Lee, *The Nation of Islam: An American Millenarian Movement* (Syracuse, N.Y.: Syracuse University Press, 1996).

8. http://www.themosquecares.com/; last accessed Sept. 25, 2006.

9. Whether or not a Muslim is "practicing" is a judgment call that I am unable to make. While poll-takers like to use such signifiers as wearing Islamic dress, attending the mosque regularly, or participating in the fast as measures of practice, there are many ways in which Americans Muslims may or may not associate themselves with activities generally considered among the duties and practices of Islam.

10. Harold Vogelaar, "Open Doors to Dialogue," *The Muslim World* 84/3 (2004): 403.

11. Gustavo Arellano, "Crusaders at the Gates. Avoiding Christian Proselytizers at the Islamic Society of Orange County," *Orange County Weekly,* Nov. 26–Dec. 2, 2004, 1.

12. Liyakat Takim, "Interfaith Dialogue in Post 9–11 America," *The Muslim World* 84/3 (July 2004): 348.

13. Marsha Snulligan Haney, "Theological Engagement in Interreligious Dialogue," *The Muslim World* 94/3 (July 2004).

14. Dan Harris, "A New Crusade? Evangelical Christians Rally Against Islam, Despite Bush Disavowal," ABC News, Dec. 16, 2004.

15. Jocelyne Cesari, *When Islam and Democracy Meet: Muslims in Europe and the United States* (New York: Palgrave Macmillan), 4.

16. Part of the "Faith Communities Today" Study Project of the Hartford Institute for Religious Research at Hartford Seminary. The survey sampled 631 mosques, of which 416 interviews were completed, with a 4 percent margin of error (see fact@hartsem.edu).

17. Walid Saif, "An Assessment of Christian-Muslim Dialogue," unpublished paper delivered at a Christian-Muslim Consultation sponsored by the World Council of Churches in Amersfoort, Netherlands, November 8, 2000.

18. See Yvonne Y. Haddad, Jane I. Smith and Kathleen Moore, *Muslim Women in America: The Challenge of Islamic Identity Today* (New York: Oxford University Press, 2006).

19. See Carol Anway, *Daughters of Another Faith* (Lee's Summit, Mo.: Yawna, 1996).

CHAPTER 4

1. Deedat, a South African, died in 1918, but his antagonistic commentaries about Christianity are still cited by some Muslims as authoritative.

2. Ahmad Sakr, *Da'wah Through Dialogue.* (Leicester: Foundation for Islamic Knowledge, 1999), 164.

3. It is interesting to note that the distinction made in current homiletic communication theory between proclamation and persuasion says that persuasion is one of several types of proclamation. The difference between the types, in a sense,

is the attitude toward the other. In persuasion, you are trying to convert or otherwise get the other to see and accept the superiority of your own way.

4. See Aminah McCloud, "Reflections on Dialogue," *The Muslim World* 94/3 (Summer 2004): 338–339.

5. Marsha Snulligan Haney, "Theological Engagement in Interreligious Dialogue," *The Muslim World* 94/3 (July 2004): 368.

6. "Toward a More Hopeful Future: Obstacles and Opportunities in Christian-Muslim Relations," *The Muslim World* 94.3 (July 2004): 383.

7. See "Muslims, Catholics Hold Dialogue on West Coast," *The Minaret* (April 2003): 8.

8. Recent literature on globalization suggests that there are different levels of recognition of the other in an encounter, from simple acknowledgement that the other exists, to an attempt to know the other on its own terms, to being personally transformed by the knowledge and relationship.

9. Neela Banerjee, "Proposal on Military Chaplains and Prayer Holds Up Bill," *The New York Times* (September 19, 2006): 1.

10. Salam al-Mariati, "Christian-Muslim Relations in North America: An Activist's Perspective," *The Muslim World* 94/3 (July 2004): 374.

CHAPTER 5

1. Samuel P. Huntington, "The Clash of Civilizations," *Foreign Affairs* 72 (Summer 1993): 22–50.

2. Fathi Osman, "The Christian-Muslim Dialogue Today. The Essence, the Contemporary Experience," unpublished paper presented at the Second Christian-Muslim Summit, Organized by the Community of St. Egidio of Italy, Barcelona, and Spain, October 5–7, 2004.

3. The conference does, however, hold annual meetings of "Seminarians Interacting," including Christian, Jewish, and Muslim students that have received excellent reviews from Muslim student participants.

4. Liyakat Takim, "Interfaith Dialogue in Post 9/11 America, *The Muslim World* 74/3 (2004): 350.

5. This view was expressed, for example, by Imam Fawaz Damra of the Islamic Center of Cleveland in an interview with the author in 2001.

6. Aminah McCloud, "Reflections on Dialogue." *The Muslim World* 94/3 (July 2004): 335–341.

7. June 10, 2000 MAPS regional seminar, Georgetown University, Washington D.C.

8. "Women in the Context of Change and Confrontation within Muslim Communities," in Virginia Mollenkott, ed., *Women of Faith in Dialogue* (New York: Crossroad, 1987), 96–109.

9. Mohammed Nimer, "Muslims in American Public Life," in Yvonne Haddad, ed., *Muslims in the West: From Sojourners to Citizens* (New York: Oxford University Press, 2002). In light of current conditions in Israel/Palestine, senior advisor to

MPAC Maher Hathout on May 25, 2001, sent a letter to the Jewish members of the dialogue saying that conversations will need to be suspended. "In times of hot situations. . . . We need to protect the dialog by slowing the speed until there is a better environment to optimize the process."

10. A. K. Ramanujan, "Where Mirrors are Windows," *History of Religions* 28/3 (1989): 187–216. See Jane I. Smith, "When Dialogue Goes Wrong," *Zions' Herald* 180/1 (January/February 2006): 34–35.

11. Marcia Hermansen, "Muslims in the Performative Mode: A Reflection on Muslim-Christian Dialogue," *The Muslim World,* 94/3 (July 2004): 305–312.

12. Ibid., 391–392.

CHAPTER 6

1. John Cobb, "The Meaning of Pluralism for Christian Self-Understanding," in Leroy S. Rouner, ed., *Religious Pluralism* (Notre Dame: University of Notre Dame Press, 1984), 214–215.

2. Samuel Marinus Zwemer, *Islam: A Challenge to Faith* (New York: Laymen's Missionary Movement, 1907); *Into All the World: The Great Commission: A Vindication and an Interpretation* (Grand Rapids, Mich.: Zondervan, 1943); *The Cross Above the Crescent: The Validity, Necessit,y and Urgency of Missions to Muslims* (Grand Rapids, Mich.: Zondervan, 1941). Zwemer is a forerunner of the general school of thought expressed by the Barthian thinking of Hendrick Kraemer, who in his book *The Christian Message in a Non-Christian World* (Grand Rapids, Mich: Zondervan, 1938) insisted that the only possible basis for a truth claim is God's revelation of the Way and the Life and the Truth in Jesus Christ. This truth must be made known throughout the world.

3. "Some Bases for a Christian Apologetic to Islam," *International Review of Missions* 54 (1965): 195. Marston Speight was head of the office of Christian-Muslim Relations of the National Council of Churches until its move to New York City in 1992.

4. The term evangelical has a number of technical meanings. I am using it here to refer to those persons and groups who espouse a conservative theological position, often including scriptural literalism.

5. David Roach, "WCC assembly demonstrates 'spirit of antichrist' prof says," *PB News,* Feb. 18, 2006. www.bpnews.net/asp.

6. Dudley Woodbury, "Contextualization among Muslims: Reusing Common Pillars," in Dean S. Gilliland, ed., *The Word among Us: Contextualizing Theology for Mission Today* (Dallas: Word, 1989), 282–308.

7. Mike Brislen, "A Model for a Muslim-Culture Church," in *Missiology* 24/3 (July 1996): 356.

8. See, e.g., Phil Parshall *Bridges to Islam. A Christian Perspective on Folk Islam* (Grand Rapids, Mich.: Baker Books, 1983); and idem, *Beyond the Mosque: Christians Within Muslim Community* (Grand Rapids, Mich.: Baker Books, 1985).

9. Phil Parshall, "Applied Spirituality in Ministry Among Muslims," in *Missiology* 11/4 (October 1983): 435–447.

10. Parshall, *Bridges,* 17–19.

11. Among the many theological schools in the United States that have programs in Islam and missions are such institutions as Gordon Conwell, Trinity Evangelical, Columbia Bible College, Wheaton Graduate School in Illinois, Dallas Theological Seminary, Moody Bible Institute, and, with different emphases, the Lutheran School of Theology at Chicago and Luther Seminary. Hartford Seminary in Connecticut has reverted from its earlier orientation toward training for the mission field in Muslim countries to a program of dialogue.

12. Tony Richie, "John Wesley and Mohammed: A Contemporary Inquire Concerning Islam," *Asbury Theological Journal* 58/2 (Fall 2003):79–99.

13. Ibid., 81.

14. Ibid., 92.

15. Tony Richie, "Neither Naïve nor Narrow: A Balanced Pentecostal Approach to Christian Theology of Religions," *Cyberjournal for Pentecostal Charismatic Research* 2/7 (2006):1–12.

16. Ibid., 7.

17. Alan Cooperman, "Evangelical Christians Reach Out to Muslims." *The Washington Post*, April 10, 2004, p. 3.

18. Uwe Siemon-Netto, "Faith: Evangelical-Muslim dialogue needed." *United Press International* 3/9/06; en.wikipedia.org/wiki/UPI.

19. Ibid.

20. Muhammad Shafiq and Mohammed Abu-Nimr, *Interfaith Dialogue: A Guide For Muslims* (in press).

21. See especially Kenneth Cragg, *Christ and the Faiths.* (Philadelphia: Westminster Press, 1986); idem, *Jesus and the Muslim: An Exploration* (London: George Allen & Unwin, 1985): and idem, *Muhammad and the Christian: A Question of Response* (London: Darton, Longman and Todd, 1984).

22. Paul Varo Martinson, *Islam: An Introduction for Christians* (Minneapolis: Augsburg, 1994).

23. Richard H. Drummond, "Toward Theological Understanding of Islam," in Leonard Swidler, ed., *Muslims in Dialogue: The Evolution of a Dialogue* (Lewiston, N.Y.: Edwin Mellen, 1992), 177–201.

24. For a thorough treatment of Christian attitudes toward Muhammad throughout history see David Kerr, " 'He Walked in the Path of the Prophets': Toward Christian Theological Recognition of the Prophethood of Muhammad," in Wadi Haddad and Yvonne Haddad, eds., *Christian-Muslim Encounters* (Gainesville: University Press of Florida, 1992), 426–446.

25. See especially Mark W. Thomsen, *The Word and the Way of the Cross: Christian Witness Among Muslim and Buddhist People* (Chicago: Division for Global Mission, Evangelical Lutheran Church in America, 1993).

26. Ibid., 106–108, 124–125.

27. See, e.g., John Hick, *God and the Universe of Faiths* (Oxford: Oneworld Publications, 1993), 120–132.

28. Ibid., 175.

29. In "Islam and Christian Monotheism," in *Islam in a World of Diverse Faiths,* ed. Dan Cohn-Sherbok (New York: St. Martin's Press, 1991), 1–17, Hick builds on his thesis of the "myth" of the trinity and the incarnation in Christian theology to suggest ways in which Muslims and Christians might come to some theological agreement.

30. See especially Wilfred Cantwell Smith, *Faith and Belief* (Princeton, N.J.: Princeton University Press, 1979); and idem, *Toward a World Theology* (London: Macmillan, 1981).

31. Wilfred Cantwell Smith, "The Christian in a Religiously Plural World," in John Hick and Brian Hebblethwaite, eds., *Christianity and Other Religions* (Philadelphia: Fortress, 1980), 105–106.

32. Wilfred Cantwell Smith, "Interpreting Religious Interrelations: An Historian's View of Christian and Muslim," in Richard W. Rousseau, ed., *Christianity and Islam: The Struggling Dialogue* (Scranton, Pa.: Ridge Row, 1985), 1–13.

33. Wilfred Cantwell Smith, "Is the Qur'an the Word of God?" in Will Oxtoby, ed., *Religious Diversity* (New York: Harper & Row, 1976), 39.

34. See, for example, John Cobb, *Can Christ Become Good News Again?* (St. Louis: Chalice, 1991).

35. John Cobb, *Beyond Dialogue* (Philadelphia: Fortress, 1982), ix.

36. John Cobb, "Global Theology in a Pluralistic Age," *Unitarian Universalist Christian* 43/1 (1988): 44.

37. John Borelli, "Christian-Muslim Relations in the United States: Reflections for the Future after Two Decades of Experience," *The Muslim World* 94/3 (July 2004): 321–333.

38. Pope John Paul II, "No Peace Without Justice, No Justice Without Forgiveness," *Origins* 31/28 (December 20, 2001).

39. Msgr. Michael L. Fitzgerald, M.Afr., "Christian-Muslim Dialogue. A Survey of Recent Developments," Pontifical Council for Interreligious Dialogue; www .catholic-hierarchy.org/diocese/dxird.html.

40. Paul F. Knitter, *No Other Name? A Critical Survey of Christian Attitudes Toward the World Religions* (Maryknoll, N.Y.: Orbis, 1985), 125.

41. See, among his many writings, Karl Rahner, *Foundations of Christian Faith: An Introduction to the Idea of Christianity* (New York: Crossroads, 1978).

42. See Paul F. Knitter, 70–74.

43. Hans Kung, *Christianity and the World Religions: Paths of Dialogue with Islam, Hinduism and Buddhism* (Garden City, N.Y.: Doubleday, 1986), 22.

44. Ibid., 24.

45. Ibid., 28.

46. Jacques Dupuis, *Christianity and the Religions: From Confrontation to Dialogue* (Maryknoll, N.Y.: Orbis, 2002).

47. Gavin D'Costa, *The Meeting of Religions and the Trinity* (Maryknoll, N.Y.: Orbis, 2000), 102–103.

48. Qamar-Ul Huda, "The 40th Anniversary of Vatican II: Examining *Dominus Iesus*, and Contemporary Issues for Inter-religious Dialogue between Muslims and Christians," *Islam and Christian-Muslim Relations* 15/3 (July 2004): 331.

49. Michael L. Fitzgerald and John Borelli, *Interfaith Dialogue: A Catholic View* (Maryknoll, N.Y.: Orbis, 2006).

50. Ibid., 41.

51. Walter Kaster, "Peace in the World, Dialogue among Christians and with Other Religions," September 27, 2002; http://www.vatican.va/roman_pontifical_councils.

52. Archbishop Alexander J. Brunett, "What Dialogue Means for Catholics and Muslims," first published in *Origins: CNS Documentary Service* 30/41 (March 29, 2001).

53. Fitzgerald and Borelli, *Interfaith Dialogue*, 67.

CHAPTER 7

1. Patricia Chang, "Muslim Visitors Question the American Way: Puzzled by Pluralism," *The Christian Century*, September 6, 2003, 8–9; available at http://www.religion-online.org/showarticle.asp?title=2894.

2. Will Herberg, *Protestant, Catholic, Jew: An Essay in American Religious Sociology*. Garden City, N.J.: Doubleday, 1955.

3. The analysis of contemporary American Muslim interpretations of pluralism in Islam are taken from my essay "Does Islam Encourage Pluralism? American Muslims Engage the Debate," written for the Woodrow Wilson International Center for Scholars conference, "The Influence of American Islamic Thinkers on Islamic Thought Abroad," May 11, 2005.

4. In English translations of the Qur'an the term is usually written with a capital I, Islam. As Arabic does not use capital letters, however, one might also render it *islam*, which could then lead to the translation "submission" suggesting that it is the act rather than the religion that pleases God.

5. Husein Kassim, *Legitimating Modernity in Islam: Muslim Modus Vivendi and Western Modernity* (Lewiston, Maine: Edwin Mellon, 2005), 138–146.

6. See, for example, Laith Kubba, "Recognizing Pluralism," *Journal of Democracy* 7 (April 1996), 86–89; available as "Islam and Liberal Democracy," http://muse.jhu.edu/journals/journal_of_democracy/v007/7.2kubba.html.

7. Sulayman Nyang, "Seeking the Religious Roots of Pluralism in the United States of America: An American Muslim Perspective," *Journal of Ecumenical Studies* 34 (1997): 402–417.

8. M.A. Muqtedar Khan, "Living on Borderlines: Beyond the Clash and Dialogue," in Zahid H. Bukhari et al., eds., *Muslims' Place in the American Public Square* (Walnut Creek, Calif.: Altamira), 2004, 90–93.

9. Isma'il al Faruqi, *Trialogue of the Abrahamic Faiths* (Alexandria, Va.: Al Sa'dawi, 1991). He described Judaism as the first and Christianity the second mo-

ment of Arab consciousness among religions of the book. The term *trialogue* has since been both adopted and criticized on the grounds that "dialogue" can include more than two parties.

10. Ismail al- Faruqi, *Islam and Other Faiths,* ed. Ataullah Siddiqui (Leicester: The Islamic Foundation, 1998), 241.

11. Ibid., 248.

12. "Thus, while allegedly offering a neutral foundation for Muslim-Christian relations," says Peter Ford, "based on mutual respect and on reason, what emerged in al-Faruqi's argument is that such a foundation is none other than Islam itself"; "Isma'il al-Faruqi on Muslim-Christian Dialogue: An Analysis from a Christian Perspective." *Islam and Christian-Muslim Relations* 4/2 (December 1993): 241.

13. Amina Wadud, "Alternative Qur'anic Interpretation and the Status of Women" in Gisela Webb, ed., *Windows of Faith: Muslim Women Scholar-Activists in North America* (Syracuse, N.Y.: Syracuse University Press, 2000), 3–21. Wadud's latest book is *Inside the Gender Jihad: Women's Reform in Islam* (London: Oneworld, 2006).

14. Gwendolyn Zohara Simmons, "Are We Up to the Challenge? The Need for a Radical Reordering of the Discourse on Women," in Omid Safi, ed., *Progressive Muslims. On Justice, Gender, and Pluralism* (Oxford: Oneworld, 2003), 235.

15. Sherman A. Jackson, "Islam(s) East and West: Pluralism between No-Frills and Designer Fundamentalism," in Mary L. Dudziak, ed., *September 11 in History* (Durham, N.C.: Duke University Press, 2003), 112–135.

16. Jackson, "Islam(s)," ibid., 132.

17. Farid Esack, *Qur'an, Liberation & Pluralism* (Oxford: Oneworld, 1997), 78.

18. See also Abdul Aziz Sachedina, *The Islamic Roots of Democratic Pluralism* (New York: Oxford University Press, 2001); and Khalid Abu El Fadl, *The Place of Tolerance in Islam* (Boston: Boston Review, 2002), who expresses similar regrets.

19. Supersessionism is the belief that Christianity is the fulfillment of biblical Judaism, and that Jews who deny that Jesus is the Messiah are no longer among the Chosen People.

20. Esack, *Qur'an, Liberation & Pluralism,* 179.

21. Sachedina, *The Islamic Roots of Democratic Pluralism,* 139.

22. Ibid., 11–14.

23. Sachedina, "Is Islamic Revelation an Abrogation of Judaeo-Christian Revelation?," in Hans Kung and Jurgen Moltman, eds., *Islam: A Challenge for Christianity* (Orbis, 1994), 94–102.

24. Ibid., 48.

25. For more information on this subject, see Yvonne Haddad, "Islamist Depictions of Christianity in the Twentieth Century," *Islam and Christian-Muslim Relations* 11/3 (October 2000): 75–94.

26. Ibid., 139.

27. *Islam and Christian-Muslim Relations* 8/1 (1997): 27–38.

28. Khaled Abou El Fadl, *The Authoritative and Authoritarian in Islamic Discourse: A Contemporary Case Study.* Riyadh: Dar Taiba, 1997, 16.

29. Abou El Fadl, *The Place of Tolerance in Islam* (Boston: Boston Review, 2002), 17. The volume, edited and with a preface by Joshua Cohen and Ian Lague, consists of an essay by Abou El Fadl and commentaries by Milton Viorst, Sohail H. Hashmi, Tariq Ali, Abid Ullah Jan, Stanley Kurtz, Amina Wadud, Akeel Bilgrami, Mashhood Rizvi, John L. Esposito, Qamar-ul Huda, and R. Scott Appleby, along with a final response by Abou El Fadl.

30. Omid Safi, *Progressive Muslims* (Oxford: Oneworld, 2004), 2.

31. Ibid., 24.

32. Amir Hussain, "Muslims, Pluralism and Interfaith Dialogue," in Safi, *Progressive Muslims*, 251–269.

33. Ibid., 258.

34. Ibid., 265.

35. Mahmous Ayoub, "Christian-Muslim Dialogue: Goals and Obstacles," *The Muslim World* 94/3 (July 2004): 316.

36. See, e.g., Mahmoud Ayoub, "The Miracle of Jesus: Reflections on the Divine Word," Macdonald Center Lecture, delivered at Hartford Seminary in December 1991.

37. This and the following are taken generally from years of interaction between the author and Ayoub, and specifically from a conversation held February 12, 2001.

38. Mahmoud Ayoub, "Islam and Christianity between Tolerance and Acceptance," *Islam and Christian-Muslim Relations* 2/2 (December 1991): 179.

39. Mahmoud Ayoub, "Islam and Pluralism," *Encounters* 332 (1997): 103–118.

40. See, for example, Mohamed Fathi Osman, *The Children of Adam: An Islamic Perspective on Pluralism* (Occasional Paper Series; Washington, D.C.: Center for Muslim-Christian Understanding, History and International Affairs, Edmund A. Walsh School of Foreign Service, Georgetown University, 1996); idem, "Monotheists and the 'Other': An Islamic Perspective in an Era of Religious Pluralism" in *Muslim World Journal* 88 (July–October 1998), 353–363.

41. "O mankind! We have created you male and female, and have made you nations and tribes that you may know one another...."

42. Osman, *The Children of Adam*, 45.

43. Ali Asani, "On Pluralism, Intolerance, and the Qur'an," *The American Scholar* 71/1 (Winter 2002), 52–60. A very similar piece is Ali Asani, "So That You May Know One Another: A Muslim American Reflects on Pluralism and Islam," *The Annals of the American Academy of Political and Social Science* 588 (2003): 40–51.

44. Ali Asani, "On Pluralism, 55.

45. Adnan Aslan, *Religious Pluralism in Christian and Islamic Philosophy* (New York: Curzon, 1998), 203–205.

46. Seyyed Hossein Nasr, "Comments on a Few Theological Issues in the Islamic-Christian Dialogue," published under that title in Yvonne Y. and Wadi Z. Haddad, eds., *Christian-Muslim Encounters* (Gainesville: University Press of Florida, 1995), 221–244.

47. Seyyed Hossein Nasr, "Islamic-Christian Dialogue: Problems and Obstacles to be Pondered and Overcome," *The Muslim World* 87/3–4 (July-October 1998): 218–237; repr., *Islam and Christian-Muslim Relations* 11/2 (July 2000): 213–227.

48. Seyyed Hossein Nasr, "Islamic View of Christianity," 128.

49. Seyyed Hossein Nasr, *Islamic Life and Thought,* 210.

50. Ibid., 210.

51. Nasr, "Comments on A Few Theological Issues," 464.

CHAPTER 8

1. Governing Board of the National Council of the Churches of Christ/USA, *Newsletter of the Office of Chrisitan-Muslim Relations* 34 (January 1987):4.

2. As found on the Web site of the United States Conference of Catholic Bishops. www.usccb.org/.

3. Presbyterian Church (USA) Interfaith Listening Program: http://www .pcusa.org/listening project/about.htm.

4. Communication from Peter Makari, January 18, 2005.

5. See Jocelyne Cesari, *When Islam and Democracy Meet: Muslims in Europe and the United States* (New York: Palgrave/Micmallan, 2004), 185–192.

6. Founded in 1927 as the National Conference for Christians and Jews, the title was changed in 1978 to the National Conference for Community and Justice (NCCJ). The new name reflects the breadth and depth of its mission, the growing diversity of the country, and the need to be more inclusive. An important initiative of the NCCJ has been its Seminarians Interacting Program, which brought young Jewish, Christian, and Muslim students together to visit their relative institutions for training religious leaders.

7. See, e.g., Hibba Abugideiri, "The Renewed Woman of American Islam: Shifting Lenses Toward 'Gender *Jihad?*' " *The Muslim World* 91/1–2 (Spring 2001): 1–18.

8. Syeed Miller presented a synopsis of her work at the "Muslims in America" conference, Cambridge, Mass., March 10, 2001. In an e-mail communication with the author June 11, 2001, she expressed her interest in continuing to work "in the area of interethnic dialogue."

9. She says, for example, that while Jews and Christians have been fighting sexism for a long time it is new for Muslim women who have been kept "in physical, mental and emotional bondage." Riffat Hassan, *"Women of Faith in Dialogue,"* ed. Virginia R. Mallenkott (New York: Crossroad, 1987), 97.

10. Riffat Hassan, unpublished lecture on Jesus and Mary in the Islamic tradition, at Hartford Seminary, December 1990.

11. See info@tentofabraham.org.

12. Codirectors are Ari Alexander, an American Jew who has worked with teens and university students on conflict resolution and cross-cultural dialogue, and Maria Ali-Adib, a Syrian Muslim living in London whose specialization is education reform.

13. Bruce Nolan, "Three Faiths Team Up on Health Insurance Issue." *New Orleans Times Picayune,* April 22, 2004, 1.

14. Shahid Athar, "Lessons from an Interfaith Retreat," *Indianapolis Star* (July 16, 2000): D3.

15. Jay Rock, "Christian-Muslim Relations in the Land of Selective History," *The Muslim World* 94/3 (July 2001): 19.

16. Wilfred Cantwell Smith, "Objectivity and the Humane Sciences," in W.G. Oxtoby, ed., *Religious Diversity: Essays by Wilfred Cantwell Smith* (New York: Harper & Row, 1976), 178.

Bibliography

Al Faruqi, Ismail. *Trialogue of the Abrahamic Faiths,* edited by Ataullah Siddiqui. Leicester: The Islamic Foundation, 1998. Herndon, Va.

———. *Islam and Other Faiths.* The Islamic Foundation.

Anway, Carol. *Daughters of Another Faith: Experiences of American Women Choosing Islam.* Lee's Summit, Mo.: Yawna, 1996.

Arinze, Cardinal Francis. *Christian-Muslim Relations in the Twenty-First Century.* Maryknoll, N.Y.: Orbis, 1989.

Armour, Rollin, Sr. *Islam, Christianity and the West: A Troubled History.* Maryknoll, N.Y.: Orbis, 2002.

Aslan, Adnan. *Religious Pluralism in Christian and Islamic Philosophy.* New York: Curzon, 1998.

Bagbi, Ihsan, et al. *The Mosque in America: A National Portrait.* Washington, D.C.: Council on American-Islamic Relations, 2001.

Beaumont, Mark. *Christology in Dialogue with Muslims. A Critical Analysis of Christian Presentations of Christ for Muslims from the Ninth and Twentieth Centuries.* Great Britain: Regnum, 2005.

Bill, James A. and John Alden Williams. *Roman Catholics and Shi'i Muslims: Prayer, Passion and Politics.* Chapel Hill: University of North Carolina Press, 2002.

Bormans, Maurice. *Guidelines for Dialogue between Christians and Muslims.* Pontifical Council for Interreligious Dialogue. New York: Paulist, 1981.

Brown, Stuart E., trans. *The Challenge of the Scriptures: The Bible and the Qur'an.* Muslim-Christian Research Group. Maryknoll, N.Y.: Orbis, 1989.

Bryant, M. Darrol and S.A. Ali, eds. *Muslim-Christian Dialogue.* St. Paul, Minn.: Paragon House, 1998.

Bukhari, Zahid and Sulayman Nyang, eds. *Muslims' Place in the American Public Square.* Walnut Creek, Calif.: Altamira, 2004.

Bulliet, Richard W. *The Case for Islamo-Christian Civilization.* New York: Columbia University Press, 2004.

Cesari, Jocelyne. *When Islam and Democracy Meet: Muslims in Europe and the United States.* New York: Palgrave Macmillan, 2004.

Cobb, John. *Beyond Dialogue.* Philadelphia: Fortress, 1982.

———. *Can Christ Become Goods News Again?* St. Louis: Chalice Press, 1991.

Cohn-Sherbok, Dan, ed. *Islam in a World of Diverse Faiths.* New York: St. Martin's Press, 1991.

Cragg, Kenneth. *Christ and the Faiths.* London: SPCK, 1986.

———. *Jesus and the Muslim: An Exploration.* London: George Allen & Unwin, 1985.

———. *Muhammad and the Christian: A Question of Response.* London: Darton, Longman & Todd, 1984.

Daniel, Norman. *Islam and the West: The Making of an Image.* Edinburgh: University Press, 1960.

Dannin, Robert. *Black Pilgrimage to Islam.* New York: Oxford University Press, 2002.

D'Costa, Gavin. *The Meeting of Religions and the Trinity.* Maryknoll, N.Y.: Orbis, 2000.

Dudziak, Mary L., ed. *September 11 in History*: Durham, N.C.: Duke University Press, 2003.

Dupuis, Jacques. *Christianity and the Religions: From Confrontation to Dialogue.* Maryknoll, N.Y.: Orbis, 2002.

El Fadl, Khalid Abu. *The Authoritative and Authoritarian in Islamic Discourse: A Contemporary Case Study.* Riyadh: Dar Taiba, 1997.

———. *The Place of Tolerance In Islam.* Boston: Boston Review, 2002.

Esack, Farid. *Qur'an, Liberation and Pluralism.* Oxford: Oneworld, 1997.

Esposito, John L., ed., *The Oxford History of Islam.* New York: Oxford University Press, 1999.

Fitzgerald, Michael L. and John Borelli, *Interfaith Dialogue: A Catholic View.* Maryknoll, N.Y.: Orbis, 2006.

Forward, Martin. *Interreligious Dialogue. A Short Introduction.* Oxford: OneWorld Publications, 2002.

Funk, Mary Margaret. *Islam Is . . . : An Experience of Dialogue and Devotion.* New York: Lantern Books, 2003.

Gilliland, Dean S., ed. *The Word among Us: Contextualizing Theology for Mission Today.* Dallas: Word, 1989.

Goddard, Hugh. *A History of Christian-Muslim Relations.* Chicago: New Amsterdam Books, 2000.

Haddad, ed., Yvonne. *Muslims in the West: From Sojourners to Citizens.* New York: Oxford University Press, 2002.

Haddad, Yvonne Y. and Wadi Z. Haddad, eds. *Christian-Muslim Encounters.* Gainesville: University Press of Florida, 1995.

Haddad, Yvonne Y. and Jane I. Smith. *Mission to America: Five Islamic Sectarian Communities in North America.* Gainesville: University Press of Florida, 1993.

Haddad, Yvonne Y. and Jane I. Smith, eds. *Muslim Communities in North America*. Albany: State University of New York Press, 1994.

———, eds. *Muslim Minorities in the West: Visible and Invisible*. Walnut Creek, Calif.: Altamira, 2002.

Haddad, Yvonne Y., Jane I. Smith, and Kathleen Moore. *Muslim Women in America: The Challenge of Islamic Identity Today*. New York: Oxford University Press, 2006.

Haley, Alex. *The Autobiography of Malcolm X*. New York: Random House, 1964.

Haney, Marsha Snulligan. *Islam and Protestant American Churches: The Challenges of Religious Pluralism*. Blue Ridge Summit, Pa.: Rowman and Littlefield, 1998.

Heim, Mark. *Salvations: Truth and Difference in Religion*. Maryknoll, N.Y.: Orbis, 1995.

Herberg, Will. *Protestant, Catholic, Jew: An Essay in American Religious Sociology*. Garden City, N.J.: Doubleday, 1955.

Hick, John. *God and the Universe of Faiths*. Oxford: Oneworld, 1993.

Hick, John and Brian Hebblethwaite, eds. *Christianity and Other Religions*. Philadelphia: Fortress, 1980.

Hussain, Amir. *Oil and Water: Two Faiths, One God*. Kelowna, BC: Copper House, 2006.

Ipgrave, Michael. *Scriptures in Dialogue. Christians and Muslims Studying the Bible and the Qur'an Together*. London: Church Publishing House, 2004.

———. *The Road Ahead: A Christian-Muslim Dialogue*. London: Church Publishing House, 2004.

Jackson, Sherman. *Islam and the Blackamerican: Looking Toward the Third Resurrection*. New York: Oxford University Press, 2005.

———. *On the Boundaries of Theological Tolerance in Islam*. New York: Oxford: University Press, 2002.

Kassim, Husein. *Legitimating Modernity in Islam: Muslim Modus Vivendi and Western Modernity*. Lewiston, Maine: Mellon, 2005.

Khalidi, Tarif. *The Muslim Jesus*. Cambridge: Harvard University Press, 2001.

Kimball, Charles. *Striving Together. A Way Forward in Christian-Muslim Relations*. Maryknoll, N.Y.: Orbis, 1991.

Knitter, Paul F. *No Other Name? A Critical Survey of Christian Attitudes Toward the World Religions*. Maryknoll, N.Y.: Orbis, 1985.

———. *Introducing Theologies of Religions*. Maryknoll, N.Y.: Orbis, 2002.

Kraemer, Hendrick. *The Christian Message in a Non-Christian World*. Grand Rapids, Mich.: Zonderman, 1956.

Kung, Hans. *Christianity and the World Religions: Paths of Dialogue with Islam, Hinduism, and Buddhism*. Garden City, N.Y.: Doubleday, 1986.

Kung, Hans and Jurgen Moltmann. *Islam: A Challenge for Christianity*. Maryknoll, N.Y.: Orbis, 1994.

Lee, Martha F. *The Nation of Islam: An American Millenarian Movement*. Syracuse, N.Y.: Syracuse University Press, 1996.

Lincoln, C. Eric. *The Black Muslims in America*. Boston: Beacon, 1961.

Maalouf, Amin. *The Crusades through Arab Eyes*. New York: Schocken, 1984.

Magonet, Jonathan. *Talking to the Other: Jewish Interfaith Dialogue with Christians and Muslims*. London: I. B. Tauris, 2003.

Martinson, Paul Varo. *Islam: An Introduction for Christians*. Minneapolis: Augsburg, 1997.

McCloud, Aminah Beverly. *African American Islam*. London: Routledge, 1995.

McDowell, Bruce A., and Anees Zaka, *Muslims and Christians at the Table: Promoting Biblical Understanding among North American Muslims*. Phillipsburg, N.J.: P&R Publishing, 1999.

Mollenkott, Virginia, ed. *Women of Faith in Dialogue*. New York: Crossroad, 1987.

Nasr, Seyyed Hossein. *Islamic Life and Thought*. Albany: State University of New York Press, 1981.

Osman, Fathi. *The Children of Abraham: An Islamic Perspective on Pluralism*. Occasional Paper Series. Washington D.C.: Center for Christian-Muslim Understanding, History and International Affairs, Edmund A. Walsh School of Foreign Service, Georgetown University, 1996.

Oxtoby, Will, ed. *Religious Diversity: Essays by Wilfred Cantwell Smith*. New York: Harper & Row, 1976.

Parshall, Phil. *Beyond the Mosque: Christians within Muslim Community*. Grand Rapids, Mich.: Baker, 1985.

———. *Bridges to Islam: A Christian Perspective on Folk Islam*. Grand Rapids, Mich.: Baker, 1983.

Posten, Larry A. with Carl F. Ellis, Jr., *The Changing Face of Islam in America: Understanding and Reaching Your Muslim Neighbor*. Camp Hill, Pa.: Horizon Books, 2000.

Pratt, Douglas. *The Challenge of Islam: Encounters in Interfaith Dialogue*. Aldershot, England: Ashgate, 2005.

Rahner, Karl. *Foundations of Christian Faith: An Introduction to the Idea of Christianity*. New York: Crossroads, 1978.

Rouner, ed., Leroy S. *Religious Pluralism*. Notre Dame: University of Notre Dame Press, 1984.

Rousseau, Richard W., ed. *Christianity and Islam: The Struggling Dialogue*. Scranton, Pa.: Ridge Row, 1985.

———. *Islam: The Struggling Dialogue*. Scranton, Pa.: Ridge Row, 1986.

Sachedina, Abdul Aziz. *The Islamic Roots of Democratic Pluralism*. New York: Oxford University Press, 2001.

Safi, Omid. *Progressive Muslims: On Justice, Gender, and Pluralism*. Oxford: Oneworld, 2003.

Sakr, Ahmad. *Da'wah through Dialogue*. Walnut, Calif.: Foundation for Islamic Knowledge, 1999.

Siddiqui, Ataullah. *Christian-Muslim Dialogue in the Twentieth Century*. Leicester: The Islamic Foundation, 1997.

Smith, Jane I. *Islam in America*. New York: Columbia University Press, 1999.

Smith, Wilfred Cantwell. *Faith and Belief*. Princeton, N.J.: Princeton University Press, 1979.

———. *Toward a World Theology*. London: Macmillan, 1981.

Smock, David R., ed. *Interfaith Dialogue and Peacebuilding*. Washington, D.C.: U.S. Institute of Peace Press, 2002.

Southern, R. W. *Western Views of Islam in the Middle Ages*. Cambridge: Harvard University Press, 1962, 1980.

Swidler, Leonard, ed. *Muslims in Dialogue. The Evolution of a Dialogue*. Lewiston, N.Y.: Mellen Press, 1992.

Thomsen, Mark W. *The Word and the Way of the Cross: Christian Witness among Muslim and Buddhist People*. Chicago: Division for Global Mission, Evangelical Lutheran Church in America, 1993.

Van Gorder, A. Christian. *No God but God: A Path to Muslim-Christian Dialogue on God's Nature*. Maryknoll, N.Y.: Orbis, 2003.

Wadud, Amina. *Qur'an and Women: Rereading the Sacred Text from a Woman's Perspective*. New York: Oxford University Press, 1999.

———. *Inside the Gender Jihad: Women's Reform in Islam*. London: Oneworld, 2006.

Van Nieuwkerk, Karin, ed. *Women Embracing Islam: Gender and Conversion in the West*. Austin: University of Texas Press, 2006.

Webb, Gisela. *Windows of Faith: Muslim Women Scholar-Activists in North America*. Syracuse, N.Y.: Syracuse University Press, 2000.

Zebiri, Kate. *Muslims and Christians Face to Face*. Oxford: One World, 1997.

Zwemer, Samuel Marinus. *Islam: A Challenge to Faith*. New York: Laymen's Missionary Movement, 1907.

———. *Into All the World: The Great Commission. A Vindication and an Interpretation*. Grand Rapids, Mich.: Zondervan, 1943.

———. *The Cross above the Crescent: The Validity, Necessity, and Urgency of Missions to Muslims*. Grand Rapids, Mich.: Zondervan, 1941.

Index